J. Howard Gore

Elements of Geodesy

J. Howard Gore

Elements of Geodesy

ISBN/EAN: 9783743343528

Manufactured in Europe, USA, Canada, Australia, Japa

Cover: Foto ©ninafisch / pixelio.de

Manufactured and distributed by brebook publishing software (www.brebook.com)

J. Howard Gore

Elements of Geodesy

ELEMENTS OF GEODESY.

BY

J. HOWARD GORE, B.S.,

Professor of Mathematics in The Columbian University; sometime Astronomer and Topographer U S. Geological Survey; Acting Assistant U. S. Coast and Geodetic Survey; Associate des Preussischen Geodätischen Institutes.

NEW YORK:

JOHN WILEY & SONS,

15 ASTOR PLACE.

1886.

PREFACE.

THE chief reason for making the following pages public is the desire to put into better shape the principles of Geodesy, and have accessible in a single book what heretofore has been scattered through many. The advanced student and practised observer will find nothing new in this work, and may, when accident throws it into their hands, lay it aside with feelings of disappointment. But it is hoped that the beginner will be enabled to get a clear insight into the subject, and feel grateful that the discoveries and writings of many have been so condensed or elaborated as to make the study of Geodesy pleasant. The plan pursued in the discussions that follow is to take up each division in its logical order, develop each formula step by step, and leave the results or conclusion in the shape that the majority of writers have considered the best. In the text only occasional acknowledgments have been inserted, though at the end of each chapter a list of books will be found to which reference has been frequently made. These lists are by no means complete, so far as the literature of the subject is concerned, but contain the titles of those books which were found the most helpful while engaged in self-instruction. The compilation of a complete Bibliography is now in hand, forming a part of a History of Geodesy, which will be finished in the course of a few years.

It is a pleasure to record the interest of Mr. Henry Gannett, Chief Geographer of the U. S. Geological Survey, which prompted him to read the manuscript and suggest important improvements.

I desire to acknowledge my obligations to my associate, Professor H. L. Hodgkins, A.M., for the interest he has shown in the work, and for his careful revision of the proof-sheets as they came from the press.

I also wish to express my indebtedness to my friend Miss Lizzie P. Brown for her suggestions, and for the elimination of errors that otherwise would have seriously blemished the work. It is hoped that errors do not remain in sufficient number or of such size as to impair the clearness or accuracy of the discussions that follow.

When page 102 was written, it was thought that a satisfactory formula could be procured for the computation referred to, but the increasing doubts regarding the coefficient of refraction have induced me to omit further consideration of the subject.

WASHINGTON, July, 1886.

GEODETIC OPERATIONS.

CHAPTER I.

AN HISTORIC SKETCH OF GEODETIC OPERATIONS.

ONE of the first problems that suggested itself for solution in the intellectual infancy of mankind was: "What is the earth, its size and shape?" The possibility of examining the constituency of the superficial strata answered with sufficient exactness, for the time being, the first part of the question. The natural conclusion deducible from daily experience and observation is: were the earth deprived of the irregularities produced by the valleys and mountains, its surface would be a plane. The exact date of the abandonment of this theory is unknown. Froriep refers to a Sanskrit manuscript containing the following sentence: "According to the Chaldeans, 4000 steps of a camel make a mile, $66\frac{2}{3}$ miles a degree, from which the circumference of the earth is 24,000 miles." Of the authenticated announcements of hypotheses, Pythagoras was the first to declare that the earth is spherical. This honor is sometimes assigned to Thales and Anaximander. Archimedes gave as an approximate value for the circumference 300,000 stadia. To Eratosthenes (B.C. 276) belongs the credit of making the initial step towards a determination of the circumference. He observed that at Syene, in Southern Egypt, an object on the day of summer solstice cast no shadow, while

1

at Alexandria the sun made an angle with the vertical equal to one fiftieth of a circumference. Considering that Alexandria was north of Syene, he reasoned that the entire circumference of the earth was 50 times the distance between those places, or 250,000 stadia; this he afterwards increased to 252,000 stadia. The neglect of the sun's diameter in the determination of declination, and the false supposition that Alexandria and Syene were on the same meridian, introduced considerable inaccuracies in his results, the exact amount of which, however, we cannot estimate owing to our ignorance as to the length of the stadium.

About two hundred years later Posidonius determined the amplitude of the arc between Rhodes and Alexandria from observations on the star Canopus at both places. At Rhodes he saw this star, when on the meridian, just visible above the horizon, and at Alexandria its altitude at the same time was $\frac{1}{48}$ of a great circle. From this he concluded that the circumference was 48 times the distance these places were apart, or 48 × 5000 stadia = 240,000 stadia. If we know the latitude of two points on the same meridian, the difference will be the amplitude of the arc passing through them, and the circumference will bear the same ratio to the length of the arc that its amplitude bears to four right angles.

Letronne has shown that the amplitude of the arc Posidonius used is only 5° = $\frac{1}{72}$ of a great circle, and Strabo gives 4000 stadia as the length of the arc, making the circumference 288,000 stadia.

Ptolemy in the second century gave 180,000 stadia for the circumference, but does not state his authority. Posch infers that it was taken from the Chaldean value, since Ptolemy gives a Chaldean mile equal to $7\frac{1}{2}$ stadia, and $7\frac{1}{2}$ times 24,000 = 180,000. In 827 an Arabian caliph imposed upon his astronomers the task of measuring an arc, and of deducing from it the length of the circumference of the earth.

Abulfeda in 1322 gave the following description of the method employed by them : There were two parties ; one starting from a fixed point measured a line due north with a rod, the other party going due south ; both continuing until the observed latitudes were found to differ by one degree from that of the starting-point. The first party found 56 miles and the second 56⅔ miles for a degree. The latter result was accepted, its equivalent being approximately 71 English miles.

This was a great improvement upon the methods of the Grecians, who estimated their distances by days' marches of so many stadia a day.

Fernel in 1525 made a measurement for the determination of the length of a degree by counting the number of revolutions made by a wheel of known circumference in going from Paris to Amiens. He applied a correction to reduce the broken line to a straight one, and the latitude observations were made with a 5-foot sector, giving for a degree 365,088 English feet. A few years later Father Riccioli made an arc-determination in Italy, but it was too short to be of any importance. The first attempt to determine the size of the earth by means of triangulation was by Willebrord Snellius in 1615. He measured a base-line with a chain between Leyden and Soeterwood, and connected it by means of triangles, 33 in number, so as to compute the distance from Alcmaar to Bergen-op-Zoom. This distance he reduced to its equivalent along a meridian, giving an arc of 1° 11′ 05″ amplitude, from which he found 55,074 toises for a degree (a toise being equal to 6.3946 English feet). Kästner has shown that the neglect of spherical excess in the reduction of these triangles causes an error of nearly a toise. In 1722 the measurements were repeated, using for the angle-determinations a sector of 5 feet radius ; this second reduction gave 57,033 toises for a degree. One can scarcely conceive of the amount of labor such an undertaking necessitated at a time when there were no logarithmic tables to lighten the work.

Norwood in 1635 measured with a chain the distance from London to York, obtaining for a degree 57,424 toises.

In the measurement of angles Snellius had sights attached to his sector, making a close reading impracticable.

While the telescope was made use of as early as 1608, no one had thought of putting it on an angle-reading instrument until Picard, in 1669, placed in the focus of a telescope spider-lines to mark the optical axis, which, according to some authorities, had already been done by Gascoigne in 1640. He measured a base-line nearly 7 miles long, and with a sector of 10 feet radius, to which was attached a telescope, the angles were carefully read, until Malvoisine and Amiens were connected by a chain of triangles. This gave an arc of 1° 22′ 58″, from which he computed 57,060 toises as the length of a degree. At this time the effect of aberration and nutation were unknown, which, if allowed for, would have shortened his arc by 3″. However, when his unit of linear measure was more accurately compared with the standard it was found to be too short, so that when Lacaille revised the work he obtained the identical result that Picard had previously announced.

The uncertainty of ascertaining the circumference of the earth from so short an arc was so keenly felt at this time that the extension of this arc both northward and southward was undertaken by the Cassini, father and son, Lahire, and Maraldi, carrying it from Paris to Dunkirk, and from Paris to Perpignan, the entire arc being about 8° 31′.

The published results of Picard's work were rendered famous by endorsing Newton's hypothesis of universal gravitation. Newton had attempted to prove this theory by comparing the force of gravity on a body at the moon's distance with the power required to keep her in her orbit. He used in his computations the diameter of the earth as somewhat less than 7000 miles. The result failed to show the analogy he had conceived; so he laid aside his theory, so brilliant in conception, so lacking in verification. But twenty years later, when Picard's length of a degree was made known, increasing the diameter of the earth by about a thousand miles, Newton was able to show that the deflection of the orbit of the moon from a straight line was equivalent to a fall of 16 feet in one minute, the same distance through which a body falls in one second at the surface of the earth. The distance fallen being as the square of the time, it followed that the force of gravity at the surface of the earth is 3600 times as great as the force which holds the moon in her orbit. This number is the square of 60, which therefore expresses the number of times the moon is more distant from the centre of the earth than we are. If with the rude means employed by Picard his errors had not eliminated one another, or if their extent had been discovered without knowing their compensating character, the undemonstrated law of gravitation would have remained as an hypothesis, celestial mechanics would have been without the mainspring of its existence, and we would now be groping in the darkness of an antecedent century.

Newton also maintained that, owing to the greater centrifugal force of the particles at the equator, a meridian section of the earth would be an oblate ellipse; that is, the equatorial axis would exceed the polar. If such were the case, the radius of curvature would increase in going from the equator towards the pole; and as the latitude is the angle formed by the normal with the polar axis, if the normal increases, the arc of a constant angle must become larger, therefore the oblate hypothesis requires for verification that the degrees increase in going from the equator towards either pole. Consequently the results of Cassini's long arc determination were awaited with impatience, until 1718, when the announcement was made that the northern degree was shorter than the southern; this pleased the French, as it gave them an opportunity to

again say that the country across the Channel was a "Naza-
reth from which no good thing could come." A degree of
the northern arc gave 56,960 toises, and of the southern
57,098 toises, from which it appeared that the earth was pro-
late.

Huygens in 1691 published his theory regarding centrifugal motion, describing experiments that proved that a rotat-
ing mass like the earth would have its greater axis perpendicular to the axis of rotation. Hence the terrestrial degrees
increase northward. It was a part of Newton's theory that as
the polar diameter is less than the equatorial, the force of
gravity must increase in going towards the pole, and therefore
a clock regulated by a pendulum would lose time when carried
towards the equator. When Richer returned in 1672 from the
Island of Cayenne, where he had been sent to make astronomic
observations, he found that his clock while at the island lost
two minutes a day when compared with its rate at Paris, and,
furthermore, the length of his pendulum beating seconds was
1¼ lines shorter than the Paris seconds pendulum, showing that
Cayenne was farther than Paris from the centre of the earth.
A portion of this difference in the lengths of the pendulums
was supposed to be due to increased counteracting effect of
centrifugal force nearer the equator, but Newton showed that
the discrepancy was too great for a spherical globe. Varin
and Des Hays had a similar experience with pendulums taken
to points almost under the equator.

Under the excitement occasioned by this sharp controversy, as
well as from a desire to know the truth, the French Academy
decided to submit the problem to a most crucial test by measuring one arc crossing the equator, and another within the
polar circle. Knowing the fierce criticism that would be
brought to bear upon every feature of the work, the partici-
pants determined to use the most refined instruments and
most approved methods. In May, 1735, an expedition consist-

ing of Godin, Bouguer, De la Condamine, and Ulloa set out for Peru. The base was selected near Quito at an elevation of nearly 8000 feet above sea-level. Its length was 7.6 miles as deduced from a duplicate measurement, made by two parties working in opposite directions. The measuring-rods were of wood, twenty feet in length, terminated at either end in copper tips to prevent wearing by attrition.

They were laid approximately horizontal, the deviation therefrom being estimated by a plummet swinging over a graduated arc. A comparison with a field standard was made each day, this standard being laid off from the toise taken from Paris, which afterwards became the legal unit in France, and is known as the Toise of Peru. The angles of the 33 triangles were measured on quadrants of 2 and 3 feet radius; these were so defective, however, that great care was necessary in determining the instrumental errors and applying them to each angle-determination. Twenty observations were made at different stations for ascertaining the azimuths.

The amplitude of the arc was found from simultaneous latitude-observations made at the terminal stations on the same star. Realizing that great uncertainties would arise from a faulty determination of the amplitude, the latitude-observations were made with sectors 12 and 8 feet radius, on the supposition that the larger the sector the more accurate would be the results. But the instability of the supports allowed such great flexure that they were almost wholly reconstructed on the field.

A southern base was measured as a check near Cotopaxi at an elevation of nearly 10,000 feet above sea-level. Its length, 6.4 miles, as measured, differed from the value computed from the northern base by only one toise, and the entire arc was but ten toises longer according to Condamine than found by Bouguer. The amplitude as deduced by Bouguer was 3° 7′ 1″, giving for the length of a degree reduced to sea-level 56,753 toises—the mean of the two computations just quoted. The field-work occupied two years, but the results were not published until the beginning of 1746.

Von Zach revised the calculations, finding the arc to be 71 toises shorter; and Delambre recomputed the latitudes, from which he found the amplitude increased by a little more than 2 seconds. According to the former, a degree would have at that latitude a length of 56,731 toises, while the latter would give 56,737 toises, a value indorsed by Arago.

The polar party, consisting of Maupertuis, Clairault, Camus, Le Monnier, Outhier, and Celsius, Professor of Astronomy at Upsal, reached its destinaton May 21, 1736. The river Tornea, flowing south, with mountains of greater or less elevation on each side, afforded in its valley a suitable location for the base, and the mountains, points for the triangle stations. The signals were built of trees stripped of their bark, in the shape of a hollow cone. The angles were measured with a quadrant of 2 feet radius provided with a micrometer, each angle being read by more than one person, the average of the means of the individual results being taken. Great care was exercised in centring the instrument and in checking the readings by observing additional angles whose sums or differences would give the angles wanted.

Latitude-observations were made by determining the difference of zenith distances of two stars with a sector consisting of a telescope 9 feet long, which formed the radius of an arc 5° 30′. This arc was divided into spaces of 7′ 30″, which were subdivided by a micrometer. From the observations corrected for aberration, nutation, and precession, the amplitude was found to be 57′ 26″.93 according to Outhier, 57′ 28″.75 according to Maupertuis, and 57′ 28″.5 as given by Celsius. The base was measured during the winter over the frozen snow and ice on the river Tornea, the terminal points only being on land. The measuring-bars were of wood, each 30 feet long, as determined by comparison with an iron toise carried from Paris. Daily comparisons were made by placing the rods between two iron nails, previously driven at a distance apart just equal to the length of one of the rods on the first day. It was found that they had not changed in length during the work.

There were two parties, each having four rods, which they placed end to end on the snow. In this manner the entire base was measured twice, both parties laying the same number of bars each day giving a daily check. The total difference in the two results was only 4 inches in a distance of 8.9 miles, a degree of accuracy that is quite *remarkable* when it is considered that the average temperature was 6 degrees F. below zero. From this arc a degree cut by the polar circle was ascertained to be 57,437 toises. While many precautions were taken, the disagreement in the astronomic reductions, and some instrumental errors that were afterwards discovered, caused some doubt as to the reliability of the work. If correct, a degree at this point would be 377 toises longer than a degree at Paris, a difference greater than the theorists had calculated, and more confirmatory of the oblate hypothesis than was wanted.

Cassini, De Thuri, and Lacaille revised the French arc previously measured by J. and D. Cassini, and, comparing the northern with the southern portion of the arc, they declared that the earth was oblate; this was announced in 1744. In 1743, Clairaut, reasoning that the earth, instead of being of uniform density, each particle being pressed down by all that is above, those near the centre must be denser than those nearer the surface. Starting with the hypothesis that the density is a function of the distance from the surface, he declared that the earth was oblate, but not to the extent that Newton had supposed.

Let us, in review, contemplate the condition of this problem at this period: Newton, in 1687, from a theoretic analysis, said the earth was oblate; this explained the behavior of Richer's clock in 1672. Huygens, in 1691, revolved a hollow metallic globe, and saw it protrude at the centre; hence, from analogy, he accepted the oblate hypothesis. Cassini's arc of 1718 declared the theorists wrong. The Lapland labors of Maupertuis, nineteen years later, negatived Cassini's conclusion. Clairaut, in 1743, endorsed Maupertuis, but failed to show so great an oblateness. In 1744, Lacaille, repeating the work of Cassini, changed the results until they conformed to theory; and hardly a year later came the fruit of the ten years' labor in Peru to assert that Newton, Huygens, and Clairaut were all right, in different degrees.

Lacaille, in 1750, went to the Cape of Good Hope to determine the moon's parallax, and while there he measured an arc of $1\frac{1}{4}$ degrees in south latitude 33° $18\frac{1}{2}'$, from which he deduced 57,037 toises as the length of a degree. The short time devoted to this work, and the inferior quality of his instruments, caused this determination to be lightly regarded. The next triangulation was executed by Boscovich in 1751-53, in latitude 43° N., where an arc of 2° gave 56,973 toises as the length of a degree. In 1768 Beccaria found 57,024 toises for a degree in latitude 44° 44′ N. Zach revised this work and found a difference of 15 toises in the length of the arc, and numerous errors in the angle-measurements. Also the proximity of the northern terminus of the arc to the mountains suggests that the unnoticed deflection of the plumb-line gave to the arc a wrong amplitude.

In connection with Liesganig, the indefatigable Boscovich measured an arc of 3°, giving for the northern portion in latitude 48° 43′, 57,086 toises for a degree, and for the southern part they found a degree to be 56,881 toises—a difference too great to give to the work much confidence.

The surveyors Mason and Dixon (1764-68), in locating the boundary-line between the properties of the Penn family and Lord Baltimore, a portion of which afterwards became the boundary-line between Pennsylvania and Maryland, saw that that part of the line separating Maryland from Delaware was located on low and level land, almost coinciding with a meridian. For this reason they concluded that it would be suitable for measuring the length of a degree. The Royal Society of London voted them money for the work. The whole distance was measured with wooden rods 20 feet in length; contact was carefully made with rods level, and thermometric readings made to correct for expansion. Latitude was ascertained from equal zenith-distance observations, and azimuth measured from a meridian mark determined from astronomic observations.

The amplitude of the arc was 1° 28′ 45″, and the length as measured gave for a degree 56,888 toises.

In 1783 the proposition was made on the part of the French geodesists to unite Paris and Greenwich by triangulation. General Roy was placed in charge of the operations on the English side of the Channel, and Count Cassini, Mechain, and Legendre attended to that part of the work that fell within France. In this work every precaution was taken to secure good results, and all refinements at that time devised were utilized. For the first time Ramsden's theodolite with a circle of 3 feet in diameter was employed in measuring the angles.

This circle was divided into 15-minute spaces, and was read at three points by micrometers rigidly connected with one another. The telescope had a focal length of three feet, and of sufficient power to render visible a church-tower at a distance of forty-eight miles across water. The history of this theodolite would form a large part of the history of the English triangulation. Sir Henry James, in speaking of it in 1863, said: "When it is considered that this instrument has been in use for the last seventy-five years, and that it has been placed upon many of our very highest mountains, on our most distant islands, and on the pinnacles of our loftiest churches, the perfection with which this instrument was made, and the care with which it has been preserved, is truly remarkable." Also Colonel Clarke, in 1880, remarks that it is as good as when it left the workshop.

The triangulation in England rested upon the Hounslow Heath base. The first measurement of this base was made in June, 1784, with a steel chain of 100 feet in length, giving for the length of the line, corrected for temperature, 27,408.22 feet. A second determination was made using wooden rods, terminating in bell-metal tips, the entire length being 20 feet 3 inches. In the course of the work it was noticed that the rods were affected by moisture so as to render the results, 27,406.26 feet, unreliable. At the suggestion of Colonel Calderwood, it was decided to measure the line with glass tubes. These were 20 feet long, supported in wooden cases 8 inches deep, and contact was made as in the slide-contact forms. In the reduction of the length of the base a carefully determined coefficient of expansion, .0000043, was employed, giving for the length of the base 27,404.0137 feet.

Another measurement made with a steel chain, using five thermometers for temperature-indications, gave a result differing from the last by only 2 inches. This length was the equivalent reduced to sea-level—a correction being applied for the first time in the history of geodesy.

In the French work nothing new was introduced except the repeating-circle. This was constructed on a principle pointed out by Tobias Mayer, Professor in the University of Göttingen, which was thought to eliminate errors of graduation that had at that time become a source of fear, owing to the imperfect means for graduating. By the method of repetition it was supposed that if a number of pointings be made with equal care, and the final reading be divided by the number of pointings, the error of graduation as affecting the angle so repeated would be likewise divided, and hence be too small to be appreciable. If all the parts of the instrument were rigid, and if the circle or telescope could be clamped in place without the one in its motion moving the other, the theory might be endorsed in practice. However, these conditions have never been definitely secured, nor is it likely that a clamp can be devised that will not give in its working a travelling motion. These obstacles did not present themselves with sufficient force to cause the French to abandon this form of angle-reading instruments until it had mutilated their labors covering a half-century.

Barrow, in 1790, measured an arc of 1° 8′ in East Indies, obtaining for a degree in latitude 23° 18″, 56,725 toises.

The year 1791 carries with it the honor of having witnessed the inception of the most majestic scheme ever devised for obtaining and fixing a standard unit of measure. Laplace and Lagrange, with the support of the principal mathematicians of that period in France, proposed to the Assembly of France that the standard linear unit should be a ten-millionth part of the earth's quadrant, to be called a metre; the length of this quadrant to be determined by the measurement of an arc of 9° 40′ 24″, of which nearly two thirds was north of the 45th parallel,—the northern terminus being Dunkirk, and the southern, Barcelona. Delambre was in charge of the work from Dunkirk to Rodez, and Mechain completed that portion extending from Rodez to Barcelona.

Two base-lines were measured, one at Melun, near Paris, and the other at Perpignan, each about seven and a quarter miles long. The measuring-bars were four in number, each composed of two strips of metal two toises in length, half an inch in width, and a twelfth of an inch in thickness. The two metal strips were supported on a stout beam of wood, the whole resting on iron tripods provided with levelling-screws.

One of the strips was made of platinum; the other, resting on this, was copper, shorter than the platinum by about 6 inches.

At one end they were firmly fastened together, but free to move throughout the remainder of their lengths; so that by means of a graduated scale on the free end of the copper and a vernier on the corresponding end of the platinum, the varying lengths owing to the different expansions of the two metals could be determined, and hence the temperature known. This was the invention of Borda, and is now known as the Borda scale, or metallic thermometer. The bars were compared indirectly with the toise of Peru by their maker, and No. 1 of this set afterwards became a standard of reference. The angles were measured with repeating-theodolites, and azimuth was determined at five principal stations by measuring the angle between another station and the sun, mornings and evenings. Latitudes were computed from zenith-distance observations at the termini and at three intermediate points. A commission was appointed to review all the calculations: they combined this arc with the Peruvian, deducing the length of a quadrant whose legalized fractional part is the present metre.

Nouet, while astronomer to the French expedition to Africa in 1798, measured a short arc, from which he found a degree to be 56,880 toises. The disagreement between the computed and observed azimuths obtained by Maupertuis—amounting to 34″ in the terminal line—caused considerable suspicion to attach to the entire work. The Stockholm Academy of Sciences decided to have the stations reoccupied, and consequently, in 1801, sent Svanberg, Palander, and two others to Lapland for that purpose. They did not recover all of the previously occupied stations, nor did they use the same terminal points, but deduced as an independent value for a degree 57,196 toises.

Major Lambton measured an arc of 1° 33′ 56″ in India in a mean latitude of 12° N. in 1802. After his death, in 1805, it was continued by Colonel Everest with such vigor that by 1825 an arc of 16° was completed.

The French gave the English an impetus to push forward

geodetic work by their co-operation in the connection already referred to, so that while in England a trigonometric survey was being prosecuted, the requisite care was bestowed upon it to make it of value in degree-determinations. From 1783 to 1800 this survey was under the direction of General Roy. Mudge continued the triangulation for two years, completing an arc of 2° 50', from which he found for the length of a degree in latitude 53°, 57,017 toises, and in 51°, 57,108 toises; therefore the degrees shorten towards the pole.

Mechain wished to carry his arc south of Barcelona to the Balearic Isles, but was prevented by his unfortunate death. However, the energetic mathematicians who made that period of the French history so brilliant would not allow such a feasible project to remain incomplete. So Biot and Arago spent two years, beginning in 1806, in extending the triangulation from Mt. Mongo, on the coast of Valencia, to Formentera, giving a complete arc of 12° 22' 13".44.

The latitude of Formentera was determined from nearly 4000 observations on α and β Ursæ Minoris, but owing to the fact that they were all made on stars on one side of the zenith, erroneous star-places would introduce serious errors in the resulting latitude, as demonstrated by Biot in 1825,[1] when he obtained for that station a latitude differing by 9" from the first. The length of a degree as published in 1821 was 57,027 toises in latitude 45° N. Bessel, using the corrected latitude of Formentera, found 56,964 toises; and in 1841 Puissant discovered another error which changed the degree's length to 57,032 toises. In the reduction of this work the principal of least squares was used for the first time in adjusting the triangulation in conformity with the geometric conditions, as will be explained in a future chapter.

The errors already referred to in the reduction of this work show the fallacy of accepting any determination of the earth's quadrant as an unvarying quantity from which a standard, if lost or destroyed, could be definitely restored with a length identical with the previous one. Even if the earth be perfectly fixed and stable in its size and shape, of which there is great doubt, and the ten-millionth part of a quadrant always the same, the uncertainties in obtaining the same value for this quadrant twice in succession outweigh the utility of the plan and the majesty of its conception. This is not intended as an argument against the decimal feature, or the readiness with which units of weight can be obtained from those of volume. In this respect the metric system is superior to all others now in use, and these advantages alone warrant its universal adoption, while the fixity of the standards preserved by the International Bureau of Weights and Measures is sufficiently certain to dispel all doubts as to the change of length of the metre, without feeling the necessity of frequently comparing it with a physical law or mass supposed to be immutable.

Prussia began geodetic work in 1802 with the measurement of a base-line near Seeburg by von Zach. This line was carefully measured and the end-points fixedly marked by inclosing in masonry iron cannons with the mouth upwards. In the mouth a brass cylinder was fastened by having lead run around it ; the cross-lines on the upper surface of the cylinders denoted the end of the line. The triangulation began in 1805, but was stopped by the war with France in 1806, although Gotha, the province in which the work was being prosecuted, remained neutral. After the battle of Jena the people of Gotha, fearing that the French would not regard their neutrality lasting, especially if they should be suspected of harboring concealed weapons, caused these cannons to be dug out and carefully hid, thus sacrificing some accurate work to allay a foolish fear.

Under Napoleon I. the importance of faithful maps for war purposes at least was keenly felt, and to secure men trained for the preparation of such maps the Ingénieur Corps was organized, also the École Polytechnique and the École Spéciale de Géodésie. The basis of an accurate cartographic survey must be a triangulation, and degree-measurements had such a strong hold upon the mathematicians that the advisability of giving to the triangulation the requisite accuracy to make it useful for such determinations was never questioned.

Switzerland and Italy were to join their work to that of France, to give an arc of parallel from the Atlantic Ocean to the Adriatic Sea. This was begun in 1811, and continued by one or more of the countries until its completion in 1832, giving an arc of 12° 59′ 4″. Owing to serious discrepancies between the observed and computed values, this work received but little credit. In one instance the difference in azimuth was 49″.55, and in longitude the difference between the geodetic and astronomic was 31″.29.

The French expedition to Lapland for the purpose of an arc-measurement incited the first astronomer of the St. Petersburg Academy, De l'Isle, to make a similar determination in Russia. In 1737 he measured a base-line on the ice between Kronstadt and Peterhof, and occupied several stations during that and the two following years. However, it came to an end very abruptly without leaving any definite results by which to remember it.

The first geodetic work in Russia that deserves the name was begun in 1817 under the patronage of Alexander I., with Colonel Tenner and Director Struve at the head. Tenner began in the province of Wilma and continued until 1827, by which time he had completed an arc of 4½°, using a base measured with an apparatus of his own devising, consisting of two parallel bars of iron firmly fastened together. The angles were read on a 16-inch repeating theodolite. Struve did not receive his instruments until 1821, but in the ten years following he finished an arc of 3½°.

There was now a gap of about 5½° between the Russian and

2

the Lapland arcs which it was desired to close up. In this work Struve was assisted by Argelander. They measured a check-base with Struve's apparatus, completing the entire task in 1844. In the mean time Tenner had added 3° 25′ to his arc. Just here it might be of interest to remark that Bessel had communicated to Tenner his discussion regarding the figure and size of the earth. This was appended to Tenner's manuscript record and placed in the care of the St. Petersburg Academy in 1834, three years before it was published by Bessel in the *Astronomische Nachrichten*, No. 333.

Permission was obtained from the Swedish authorities to continue this arc across Norway and Sweden. This also was placed under the direction of Struve, with the assistance of Selander and Hansteen. The former finished his share of the triangulation with a measured base in 1850. Hansteen completed the Norwegian portion, checking on a base of 1155 toises. The Russian parties, together with their co-laborers, by 1855 had completed a meridional arc of 25° 20′ 9″.29, extending from the Danube to the North Sea. Of this there were two great divisions—the Russian, with 8 bases and 224 principal triangles and 9 latitude-determinations; and the Scandinavian, with 2 bases, 33 principal triangles, and 4 astronomic stations. Prior to 1821 the principle of repetition was exclusively used on horizontal circles in its original form. Struve then decided that the periodic errors noticed when the simple method of repetition was employed could be partially eliminated by reversing the direction of rotation; but he soon abandoned this, and in 1822 began to measure angles a number of times on different parts of the circle.

The test of the accuracy of this work is in the difference in the lengths of junction-lines as computed from different bases. From an examination of ten of these differences, I have found that the average is 0.1718 toise, with 0.0179 as the minimum and 0.4764 for a maximum. The values found for a degree were: 57,092 toises in latitude 53″ 20′, 57,116 in 55° 34′, 57,121 in 56° 32, 56,956 in 57° 28′, and 57,125 in 59° 14′. The utility of this arc for degree-measurements is not proportionate to its immensity, because of the fewness of the astronomic determinations—only one in every two degrees of amplitude.

General von Müffling in 1818 connected the Observatory of Seeburg with Dunkirk, and determined the amplitude of the arc by measuring the difference in time between the stations two by two. This was done by recording in local time the exact instant at which a powder-flash set off at one station at a known local time was seen at the other. The amplitude of this arc, embracing 8 determinations of this kind in its chain, was 8° 21′ 18″.

Between 1818 and 1823 Colonel Bonne connected Brest with Strasburg, with a base near Plouescat. It is interesting to note that in this work angles were measured at night, using as a signal a light placed in the focus of a parabolic reflector. Differences of longitude were determined by powder-flashes.

Gauss began the trigonometric survey of Hanover in 1820, measuring an arc of 2° 57′, from which he found for a degree 57,126 toises in the same latitude in which Mudge in England obtained for a degree 57,016 toises, and Musschenbroeck, in Holland, 57,033 toises. It was while engaged upon this work that Gauss first used the heliotrope that has since borne his name.

Schumacher at the same time commenced the Danish triangulation with the advice and assistance of Struve. His arc of 1° 31′ 53″ gave for a degree 57,092 toises in latitude 54° 8′ 13″.

In 1821 Schwerd concluded from his measurement of the Speyer base that a short line most carefully measured would give as good results as a longer one on which the same time and labor would be expended. From his base of 859.44 M. he computed the length of Lämmle's base of 19,795.289 M., giving a difference of only 0.0697 M.

Colonel Everest was appointed to succeed Colonel Lambton in the direction of the great trigonometric survey of India in 1823. During the following seven years he measured three bases with the Colby apparatus as checks to the triangulation which he extended from 18° 3′ to 24° 7′. To Colonel Everest is due the credit of introducing greater care in all the linear and angular determinations. In the latter he employed the method of directions in greater number than did his predecessors.

In 1831 Bessel and Baeyer undertook a scheme of triangulation that was to unite the chains of France, Hanover, Denmark, Prussia, and Bavaria with that of Russia, and at the same time serve for degree-measurements. It was oblique, so that, by determining the direction and amplitude, degrees of longitude as well as latitude could be found. The base-line near Fuchsburg was measured with a slightly modified form of the Borda apparatus now known as Bessel's apparatus, of which there is now an exact copy in use in the *Landes Triangulation* of Prussia. The length of this base was 934.993 toises when reduced to sea-level. The ends were marked by a pier of masonry inclosing a granite block, in whose top was set a brass cylinder carrying cross-lines indicating the end of the base. Just above this was built a hollow brick column high enough for the theodolite support, with a larger square stone for a cap-stone. In the centre of this there was a cylinder coaxial with the one below, so that the instrument could be placed immediately over the termini of the base. The theodolites had 12- and 15-inch circles, read by verniers, and the angles were read by fixing the zeros coincident, and then turning to each signal in succession with verniers read and recorded for each. After completing the series, the signals were observed in inverse order, the means of the two readings giving a set of directions. The zero would then be shifted to another position, and all the signals sighted both in direct and inverted order, until a desired number of sets were secured. The method of reduction is given on page 99.

Two kinds of signals were used; one consisted of a hemisphere of polished copper placed with its axis vertically over the centre of the station. The sun shining on this gave to the observer a bright point, but not in a line joining the centres of the stations observing and observed upon; consequently a correction for phase, as explained on page 144 had to be applied. The other form consisted of a board about two feet square, painted white with a black vertical stripe ten inches wide down the centre. This board was attached to an axis made to coincide with the centre of the station, so as to permit the board to be turned in a direction perpendicular to the line of sight as different stations were being occupied.

The astronomic determinations were made at three stations with the greatest possible care; while the reduction of the triangulation was a monument to the methods devised by Gauss for treating all auxiliary angles as aids in finding the most probable corrections to be applied to those angles absolutely needed in the computation. The amplitude of the arc was $1° 30' 28''.97$. Using the two parts into which the arc was divided by Königsberg, the difference between the terminal points taken as a whole, and the sum of the two parts was only 0.973 toise, which is an evidence of the great accuracy attained in this work. The report of this triangulation was published in *Gradmessung in Ostpreussen, und ihre Verbindung mit Preussischen und Russischen Dreiecksketten*, Berlin, 1838; and while now nearly half a century has elapsed since its appearance, not only its influence is still felt, but the operations then for the first time described are now in use.

There is not a geodesist of the present time who is not indebted to this work for information as well as assistance, and

as long as exact science receives attention men will turn to
this fountain-head. My greatest inspiration comes from two
sources—both perhaps sentimental, but none the less effica-
cious. My copy of the above book was presented to Jacobi
by Bessel, as shown by the latter's superscription. This is before me in reality ; the other remains in memory as the cordial
greetings and encouragement of Baeyer, with whom I worked
in the Geodetic Institute.

From 1843 to 1861 Sir A. Waugh, who succeeded Sir George
Everest, added nearly 8000 miles to the Indian chains. After
him came General Walker's administration, and during the
following thirteen years he completed 5500 miles of triangle
chains, occupied 55 azimuth stations, and determined 89
latitudes.

In this work the triangle sides are from 15 to 60 miles in
length. In those cases where it was necessary to elevate the
instrument masonry towers were erected, some as high as 50
feet. Luminous signals were used—heliotropes by day, and
Argand lamps at night. The amplitude of the greatest Indian
arc is 23° 49' 23".54, but its exact value has been questioned,
owing to the uncertainties of the effect of local attractions in the
neighborhood of the Himalayas upon the latitudes and azimuths, as well as the negative attraction along the shore of the
Indian Ocean as pointed out by Archdeacon Pratt. When
the computed effects of these attractions are applied, there is
still a discrepancy.

A meridional arc of about 30° has been completed, but owing
to the impracticability of ascertaining the difference of longitudes its amplitude is not accepted as sufficiently accurate to
warrant its use in degree-determinations.

The purpose of this great trigonometric survey was to furnish a basis for topographic maps ; consequently the chains of
primary triangles are parallel at such a distance apart as to
allow the intervening country to be easily covered with

secondary triangles with the primaries for checks on each side of the chasm. There are 24 chains running north and south, and 7 east and west.

Between 1847 and 1851 the Russian chain was connected with the Austrian, having 12 sides in common; the greatest discrepancy being 0.101 toise, and the least 0.01 toise.

About the same time the junction of the Lombardy and Swiss chains showed a difference of 0.31 and 0.34 metre.

In 1848 the astronomer Maclear revised Lacaille's Good Hope arc, extending it to an amplitude of 3 degrees, from which he deduced for 1 degree, in latitude 35° 43', 56,932.5 toises. Comparing this with the French arc in approximately the same northern latitude, we find a difference of only 48 toises in a degree.

In 1831 Borden devised a base-apparatus with which he measured a base and began a triangulation over the State of Massachusetts, making the commencement of geodetic work in the United States. Borden read his angles with a 12-inch theodolite, using the method of repetition. Latitudes were determined from circumpolar altitude observations at 24 points.

Recently many of his stations have been re-occupied, introducing greater care in all features of the work and affording a check on Borden's results. Comparing the two sets of values for the geographical positions of the stations that are common, it appears that there is a systematic increase in the errors, being the greatest in the eastern part of the State, that being the furthest from the base-line. The average discrepancy in the linear determination is 1:11000, or somewhat less than 6 inches in a mile.

The United States Coast Survey, organized in 1807, had primarily for its object the survey of the coast, but this necessitated a carefully executed triangulation of long sides to check the short triangle sides whose terminal stations were sufficiently near one another for the coast topography and off-shore hydrography. It soon became apparent that but little, if any, additional care was needed to secure sufficient accuracy to make this trigonometric work a contribution to geodesy. By 1867 an arc of 3° 23′ was completed, extending from Farmington, Maine, to Nantucket, with two base-lines, seven latitude stations, and ten determinations of azimuth.

Summing the six arcs into which the whole naturally divides itself, it was found that a degree in latitude 43° and longitude 70° 20′ was 111,096 metres, or 57,000.5 toises.

By 1876 the Pamlico-Chesapeake arc of 4° 31′.5 was completed, embracing in its chain of triangles six bases and fourteen astronomic stations. The latitude of each of these stations was computed from the one nearest the middle of the arc, and the difference between this and the observed values, called station-error, attributed to local deflection. This in no case exceeded 3½ seconds; and in general it was in accord with a uniform law disclosed by the geology of the country over which the arc extends.

From an elaborate discussion of the sources of error in this arc, Mr. Schott concludes that the probable error in its length is not in excess of 3¼ metres. The length of a degree in latitude 37° 16′ and longitude 76° 08′ is 56,999.9 toises.

The triangulation is being continued southward, and in a very short time it is hoped that the entire possible arc of 22° will be reduced and the results announced. An arc of parallel is also under way, keeping close to the 39th.

Of this great arc of 49° about three fourths is completed. This is the longest arc that can anywhere be measured under the auspices of a single country. Consequently, considering the great advantage to be derived from perfect harmony of methods, it is no wonder that scientists in all parts of the world are anxiously awaiting the completion of this important work. Also, when done, it will be well done. The high stand-

ard of excellence introduced into this service at its beginning
makes the first results comparable with the most recent.

In 1857 Struve advocated the project of connecting the
triangulations of Russia, Prussia, Belgium, and England, giving
an arc of 69° along the 52d parallel. Bessel had already made
the Prussian-Russian connection, and in 1861 England and Belgium joined with tolerable success, finding in their common
lines discrepancies amounting to an inch in a mile.

The Prussian and Belgium chains are not yet satisfactorily
united; neither are the longitudes determined.

While a topographic map of Italy was begun in 1815, no
special interest was taken in geodesy until 1861, except in
rendering some slight assistance in that part of the French and
Austrian triangulation that overlapped. In this year Italy re-
sponded to the suggestion of Baeyer, adopted by the Prussian
Government, to form an association of the European powers to
measure a meridional and a parallel arc.

The Italian Commission was formed in 1865, and at once
elaborated plans for future work. It was decided to have six
chains of triangles, and for every twenty or twenty-five a carefully measured base ; also to connect Sicily with Africa ; direc-
tion-theodolites of 10- and 12-inch circles to be used. The base-
apparatus with which the first three bases were measured was
of the Bessel pattern. The base of Undine was measured with
the Austrian, and the next two with a Bessel equipped with
reading-microscopes for reading the divisions on the glass
wedges.

The numerous observatories are connected with the trigonometric stations, and one or two are to be erected in the meridian of the arc to determine its deflection.

The geodetic work in Spain began with the measurement of
the Madridejos base in 1858. The apparatus used in this work
was specially designed for it, and the precision introduced
into the measurement of the base, as well as in the depend-

ing triangulation, has given to the Spanish work great confidence.

This is especially fortunate, as it will form an important link in the chain extending from the north of Scotland into Africa, and in the oblique chain from Lapland to the same point. In addition to the central base first measured, three others were found necessary to check the system.

The general plan resembles that pursued in the India Survey in having parallel chains at such a distance from one another that the intervening country can be readily filled in with secondary triangles for the topographic purposes.

There are three of these meridional chains with amplitudes of about six, seven, and seven and a half degrees, and an arc of parallel of twelve degrees.

Likewise the Swedish coast-triangulation was begun in 1758 for the purpose of checking the coast-charts, and in 1812 another triangulation embracing fifty stations and five base-lines, measured with wooden rods, was started for a similar end. However, it was not until the announcement of Bessel's results that Sweden took an active interest in accurate work.

In 1839 the Alvaren base was measured with Bessel's apparatus, and again in the following year with the same bars, giving a difference of 0.0145 metre in the two results.

So far the work was purely cartographic, and it was the influence of Baeyer that caused a partial transformation in the methods, making them conformable to the system of the Permanent Commission for European Degree-measurements.

Three bases have been measured with a modified Struve apparatus, giving excellent results; in one instance the difference between the two measurements being only 0.0029 metre, and twenty-nine stations occupied, using Reichenbach and Repsold theodolites.

Under the auspices of this commission the following countries are prosecuting geodetic work: Austria, Bavaria, Belgium,

France, Hesse, Holland, Italy, Portugal, Prussia, Russia, Saxony, Spain, Switzerland, and Würtemberg.

LITERATURE OF THE HISTORY OF GEODESY.

Verhandlungen der allgemeinen Conferenz der Europäischen Gradmessung.

Roberts, Figure of the Earth, *Van Nostrand's Engineering Magazine*, vol. 32, pp. 228–242.

Comstock, Notes on European Surveys.

Baeyer, Ueber die Grösse und Figur der Erde.

Posch, Geschichte und System der Breitengradmessungen.

Merriman, Figure of the Earth.

Baily, Histoire de l'Astronomie.

Wolf, Geschichte der Vermessungen in der Schweiz.

Clarke, Geodesy.

Westphal, Basisapparate und Basismessungen.

Klein, Zweck und Aufgabe der Europäischen Gradmessung.

CHAPTER II.

INSTRUMENTS AND METHODS OF OBSERVATION.

THE perfection of an instrument is the result of corrected defects, and in the development of geodesy or degree-measurements improved methods were closely followed by better instruments. So that while discussing the progressive steps of one, the other cannot be wholly neglected.

For the uncultured peoples, distances can be given with sufficient accuracy as so many days' journey, and nothing but the necessity to carry on record some measured magnitude would call for a unit that could be readily attained. The first such unit of which there is any authentic information is the Chaldean mile, which was equal to 4000 steps of a camel; the next was the Olympian race-course, giving to the Greeks their unit— the stadium. The rods with which the Arabians measured the two degrees already mentioned—known as the black ell— have been lost, and not even their equivalent length known.

Fernel, in using the wagon-wheel for a measuring unit, found it quite constant in length and of a kind easily applied,—advantages that are appreciated to this day by topographers, who frequently measure meander lines by having a cyclometer attached to a wheel of a vehicle.

When Snellius devised the method of triangulation there were needed two forms of instruments—one for linear measurements, and another for angle-determinations. At this time angles were measured with a quadrant to which sights were attached; a rectangle with an alidade and sights pivoted to one of the longer sides, the other being divided into degrees; a square with the alidade in one corner and all four sides graduated; a compass with sights; a semicircle with alidade or compass at the centre. Also for navigators there was the astrolabe, an instrument devised by Hipparchus for measuring the altitude of the sun or a star.

Defects in graduation were early detected, and efforts to avoid them made by increasing the radius of the sector, the smallest used by the first astronomers being of 6 and 7 feet radius ; and it is said that a pupil of Tycho Brahe constructed a sector of 14 feet radius; while Humboldt says the Arabian astronomers occasionally employed quadrants of 180 feet radius. In the case of large circles, or parts of circles, the divisions that could be distinguished would be so numerous as to render the labor of dividing very great, and the intermediate approximation uncertain.

Nunez, a Portuguese, in 1542 devised a means of estimating a value smaller than the unit of division. He had about his quadrant several concentric circular arcs, each having one division less than the next outer, so that the difference between an outer and an inner division was one divided by the number of parts into which the outer was divided. This differs from our present vernier, first used by Petrus Vernierus in 1631, in which the auxiliary arc is short and is carried around with the zero-point.

A great impetus was given to applied mathematics by the construction of logarithmic tables according to the formulæ of Napier (1550–1617), and Briggs (1556–1630), especially in facilitating trigonometric computations, which had now become the basis of degree-measurements.

The first person to use an entire circle instead of a part was Roemer in 1672, who deserves our thanks for having invented the transit also. Auzout in 1666 made the first micrometer, and Picard was the first to apply it, and a telescope with cross-wires, to an angle-reading instrument. The results obtained with this instrument were so satisfactory that Cassini used it in his great triangulation begun eleven years later. The angles in Peru were measured with quadrants of 21, 24, 30 and 36 inches radius, each provided with one micrometer. These gave very fair results—the maximum error in closure of a triangle being 12 seconds, spherical excess not considered. This would give an error of one unit in 5000 in the length of a depending line—a value ten times better than any obtained during the preceding century.

With such close reading of angles the discrepancies between measured and computed lines were quite naturally attributed to the unit of measure, the method of its use, or its comparison with a standard. As early as the Peruvian work the uncertainty in the varying length of wooden rods because of dampness, and of metal rods on account of heat, was appreciated; and in the measurement of these bases an approximate average of 13° R. was assumed for the mean temperature. This happened to be the temperature at which the field standards had been compared with the copy before leaving Paris, hence the reason for legalizing this temperature for that at which the toise of Peru is a standard.

In 1752 Mayer announced the advantages to be derived from repeating angles, and a repeating-circle was constructed upon this principle by Borda in 1785, for the connection of the French and English work. The first dividing engine was made by Ramsden in 1763, and a second improved one in 1773, which did such good work that his circles soon became deservedly famous. In 1783 this maker furnished an instrument to the English party engaged upon the work just mentioned, this was the first to be called theodolite. It had a circle three feet in diameter, divided into ten-minute spaces, read by two reading micrometer microscopes. One turn of the micrometer-screw was equal to one minute, and the head was divided into sixty parts, so that a direct reading to a single second could be made, and to a decimal by approximation. It was also provided with a vertical circle of 10.5 inches diameter, read by two micrometers to three seconds. The success attained in the use of this instrument, giving a maximum error of closure of three seconds, was regarded as truly phenomenal.

Reichenbach began the manufacture of instruments, in Munich, in 1804, of such a high grade of workmanship that it was soon considered unnecessary to send to Paris or London in order to secure the best. He fortunately furnished Struve with a theodolite, putting a good instrument in the hands of one of the most skilful observers who has ever lived, which contributed no little to his reputation. His circles were almost wholly repeaters, a class of instruments exclusively used on the Continent, but not at all in England.

Littrow, at the Observatory of Vienna, was the first to abandon the method of repetition, in 1819; and Struve, in 1822, was the next to follow.

The inconvenience attending the use of large circles was very great, besides the irregularities produced from flexure on account of unequal distribution of supports. This led to the attempt to make a smaller circle with good graduation, and reading-microscopes. This end was achieved by Repsold, who made a ten-inch theodolite for Schumacher in 1839, with which it was definitely demonstrated that as good results could be secured with a ten or a twelve inch instrument as with a larger one, and with less expenditure of time and labor, not considering the difference in the first cost. So that now we find the effort heretofore spent in constructing enormous circles given to perfecting the graduation, and, while using the instrument, to protect the circle from sudden or unequal changes of temperature. Mr. Saegmuller's principle of bisection in dividing a circle keeps the errors of graduation within small limits, and the new dividing engines leave but little to be desired in the construction of theodolites.

Zonicles

In England and India eighteen-inch circles are now used in place of those of twice that size formerly employed. Struve had a thirteen-inch theodolite. In the U. S. Coast and Geodetic Survey the large instruments have given way to those of twelve inches. In Spain twelve- and fourteen-inch circles are found to be the best, while the excellent work of the U. S. Lake Survey was done with theodolites having circles of twenty and fourteen inches in diameter—the latter having the preference.

To describe the various forms of theodolites now in use would necessitate a number of illustrations, and in the end be tedious and unprofitable; the same general features being common to all, they only will be referred to. The end sought in the construction of theodolites is to get an instrument with parts sufficiently light to insure requisite stability, with circles large enough to allow close readings, with the telescopic axis concentric with the circle, a reliable means for subdividing the divisions on the circle, and a circle so graduated as to be free from errors, or to have them according to a law readily distinguished and easily allowed for. While every one concedes that the foregoing requisites are imperative, in respect to some there is a great difference of opinion as to when they are attained.

The illustration appended shows an eight- to twelve-inch theodolite of the form suggested by the experience of the skilled officers of the U. S. Coast and Geodetic Survey. In its construction hard metal is employed, and as few parts used as possible. The frame is made of hollow or ribbed pieces in that shape that gives the greatest strength for the material. The bearings are conical; clamps of a kind that avoid travelling motion; the circle is solid, and of a conical shape to prevent flexure. The focal distance is diminished so as to admit of reversal of telescope without removing it from its supports, and the optical power is increased to insure precision in bisecting a signal. They are made as nearly symmetrical as possible, and when there is no counterpoise provided, one of the proper weight is put in place. They are furnished with three foot-screws for levelling, resting in grooves converging towards the centre. Sometimes a circular level is set in the lowest part of the branching supports, and in other cases a single tubular level is made use of. The optical axis is marked by having in the principal focus spider-lines called a reticule, or a piece of very thin glass on which fine lines are etched. The arrangement of the lines is various, the forms depicted in the annexed cut being the ones most frequently found.

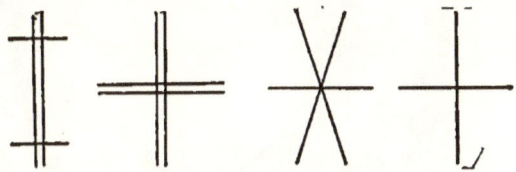

The instrument shown in Fig. 1 is one of directions in which the circle is shifted for new positions. With a repeater the only difference is the addition of a slow-motion screw to move the entire instrument in accordance with the method of repetition as explained on page 98.

The adjustments of a theodolite must be carefully attended to and frequently tested. They may be described in general as follow:

To Adjust the Levels.—When the tripod or stand is placed in a stable condition and the instrument mounted, bring it into a level position, as indicated by the level, by turning the foot-screws. Turn the instrument 180 degrees, correct any defect, —one half by means of the screws attached to the level, and the rest by the foot-screws. Place the instrument in its first position, repeat the corrections as before until no deviation is noticed when the circle is turned. If there is a second level, it is to be adjusted in the same manner.

3

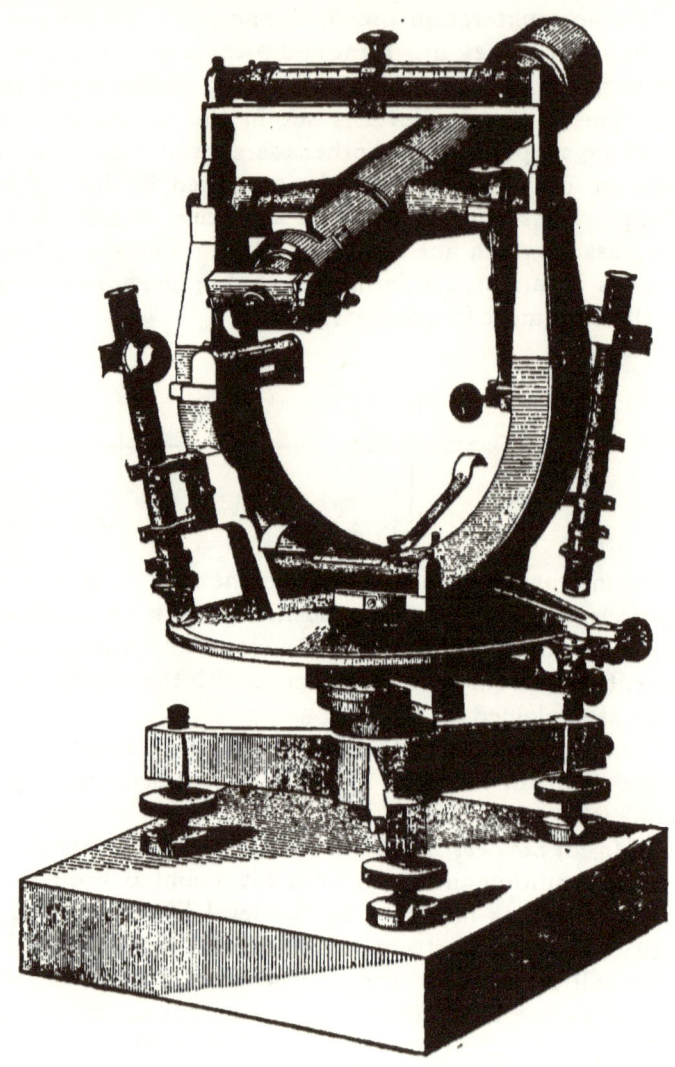

FIG. 1.

To Adjust the Spider-lines of the Telescope.—(1) Place the threads in the focus of the eye-piece, point to a suspended plumb-line when the air is still, and see if the vertical thread coincides with the plumb-line. If there is any deflection, loosen the four screws holding the diaphragm and move it gently till there is a coincidence, then tighten the screws and verify. (2) If the level is correct, place the circle in a horizontal position and sight to some clearly defined object; move the instrument sideways by means of the tangent screw and notice if the horizontal thread traverses the point throughout its entire length, if not, correct as in the above case.

To Adjust the Line of Collimation of the Telescope.—When the horizontal axis of the telescope can be reversed, point the instrument to some clearly defined object, then reverse the telescope and see if the pointing is good. If not, half the difference is to be corrected in the pointing and the other half by moving the entire diaphragm to the right or left, as the case may be. Continue this course until the pointing remains perfect after reversal. If the instrument does not admit of this reversal, it must be turned in its Y's; and if the reading is more or less than 180 degrees from the first reading, correct as before, until there is just 180 degrees between the readings before and after reversal.

The horizontality of the axis of the telescope is tested by placing on the axis a portable level that is in good adjustment. If a defect is apparent, it must be corrected entirely by raising or lowering the movable end.

After completing these adjustments, it is well to repeat the tests to see if any have been disturbed while the other adjustments were in progress. When large instruments with reading-microscopes are used, the corrections for runs and eccentricity must be determined. The former can be readily ascertained as follows: Turn the micrometer in the direction of the increasing numbers on its head till the movable crosswire bisects the first five-minute space ; call the reading *a*. Reverse the motion and continue to the preceding five-minute space ; call this *b*.　Suppose

$$a = 45° 40' + 4' 46''.4, \qquad b = 45° 40' + 4' 44''.2,$$
$$r = a - b = + 2''.2, \qquad m = \frac{(a + b)}{2} = 4' 45''.3.$$

Since the five-minute space contains 300 seconds, the correction to $a = r . a \div 300 = - 2''.1$; correction to $b = r(b - 300) \div 300 = + ''.11$; correction to $m = \frac{1}{2}(a + b - 300)r \div 300 = - 0''.88$.　The corrected reading is therefore,

$$45° 44' 45''.3 - .88 = 45° 44' 44''.42.$$

Occasionally the average error of runs is determined and a table computed from the formula just given for $a + b$ from 5

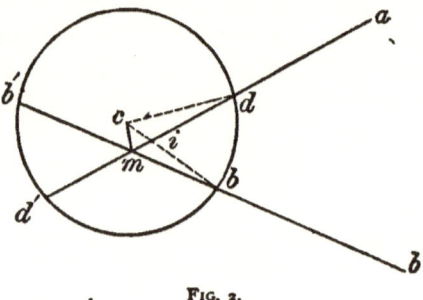

Fig. 2.

to 10 seconds.　But in very accurate work the correction for runs is made for each reading by recording the two micrometer-readings just mentioned for each pointing.　They are recorded as forward and backward, as seen on page 101.

The eccentricity is owing to the centre of the axis carrying the telescope not coinciding with the centre of the graduated circle.　As each point on the plate carrying the telescope must return to its former position after each complete revolution, there must be a point at which there is a maximum deflection as well as a point at which there is no deflection, and at the same time the intermediate positions have eccentric errors between these limits; therefore it is necessary to examine the whole circle. This can be done in connection with an examination of the two verniers. The difference in the reading of the two verniers may, however, be due to other causes: the constant angular distance between them may be more or less than 180 degrees, or it may be owing to errors of graduation, or errors of reading, or to the eccentricity referred to.

Let c be the centre of the limb,
m that of the telescope,
$\theta =$ angle *amb*,
$\theta' =$ angle *dcb*,
$E =$ the difference, or error,
$e = cm =$ the linear eccentricity,
$\omega = dcm$,
$r =$ radius of the circle,
$d = cdm$,
$b = cbm$,
$cim = \theta + b = \theta' + d$; therefore, $E = \theta - \theta' = d - b$.

As cm is never very large, we can put $mb = r$: in the triangle cdm, we have $\sin d = \dfrac{e}{r} \sin \omega$, and in the triangle bcm, we have

$$\sin b = \frac{e}{r} \sin bcm = \frac{e}{r} \sin (\omega - \theta').$$

Also, since d and b are small, we can write for sin b, $b \cdot \sin 1''$, and for sin d, $d \cdot \sin 1''$, so that we have,

$$E = d - b = \frac{e}{r \cdot \sin 1''}[\sin \omega - \sin (\omega - \theta')].$$

By expanding $\sin (\omega - \theta')$, and putting for the entire angles their values in terms of the half-angles, we find,

$$E = \frac{2e}{r \cdot \sin 1''}[\sin \tfrac{1}{2}\theta' \cdot \cos (\omega - \tfrac{1}{2}\theta')].$$

This expression is made up of two factors, and becomes o when either factor becomes o, as $e = 0$, or $\cos (\omega - \tfrac{1}{2}\theta') = 0$, that is, when $\omega - \tfrac{1}{2}\theta' = 90°$, or $\theta' = 2\omega - 180°$.

Therefore when the points are 180° apart the errors of eccentricity are eliminated. Likewise E is a maximum when $\cos (\omega - \tfrac{1}{2}\theta') = + 1$, that is, when $\omega - \tfrac{1}{2}\theta' = 0$, or $2\omega = \theta'$.

In accord with the principle that errors of eccentricity are avoided when the angle is read from two points 180° apart, circles are provided with two verniers that distance from each other. Instead of verniers, however, we may have two microscopes.

The practical difficulty of placing the zero-points just 180° apart makes it necessary to examine each circle to see what the angular distance between them is. This is best accomplished by setting one vernier, say A, on each 10° mark, and reading and recording vernier B. If a represent the amount by which the angular distance differs from 180°, and b the effect of eccentricity on this distance, we will have $B - A = 180° + a + b$, and when the verniers change places b will have a contrary effect, so that $B - A = 180° + a - b$; therefore if we take the mean of the differences $B - A$ for positions that are just 180° apart, we will have the angular distance unaffected by eccentricity. We so arrange our readings as to have on the same line those that are 180° apart. We also place under $B - A$ the first difference, and on the same line the second difference, the mean will be the average of the two, or $180° + a$, and the average of these means will be the mean distance between the verniers.

FIRST.		SECOND.		B − A.		
A.	B.	A.	B.	1st.	2d.	Mean.
0° 00′ 00″	180° 00′ 05″	180° 00′ 00″	0° 00′ 00″	+ 5″	0	+ 2″.5
10	10	190	05	+ 10	+ 5	+ 7 .5
20	05	200	00	+ 5	0	+ 2 .5
30	10	210	05	+ 10	+ 5	+ 7 .5
40	55	220	00	− 5	0	− 2 .5
50	00	230	05	0	+ 5	+ 2 .5
60	05	240	10	+ 5	+10	+ 7 .5
70	05	250	05	+ 5	+ 5	+ 5
80	10	260	00	+ 10	0	+ 5
90	05	270	10	+ 5	+10	+ 7 .5
100	00	280	55	0	− 5	− 2 .5
110	55.	290	00	− 5	0	− 2 .5
120	55	300	05	− 5	+ 5	0
130	05	310	05	+ 5	+ 5	+ 5
140	05	320	55	+ 5	− 5	0
150	05	330	00	+ 5	0	+ 2 .5
160	05	340	00	+ 5	0	+ 2 .5
170	05	350	05	+ 5	+ 5	+ 5

Therefore the angular distance = 180° + 3″.1. Mean = 3″.1.

Now, knowing the angular distance between the two verniers, the difference between it and the mean of $B − A$ will be the errors of eccentricity and graduation, or $b + g$.

Angle $dcA = m + A$, therefore $A = dcA − m$. If we call d the reading on the limb which is on the line of no eccentricity, that is on the line drawn through the centre of motion and centre of graduation, and n any angle read by the verniers, then $n − d$ will be the angle between the vernier and line of no eccentricity, or dcA. In the triangle Acm, sin Acm : sin A :: Am : cm, but sin Acm = sin dcA = sin $(n − d)$, and $Am = r$, nearly, making these substitutions:

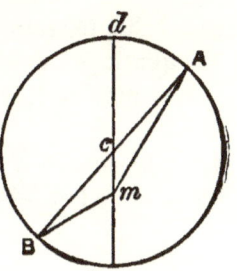

FIG. 3.

$$\sin (n - d) : \sin A :: r : e, \qquad \text{or} \qquad \sin A = \frac{e \cdot \sin (n-d)}{r}.$$

A being small, we can put for $\sin A$, $A \cdot \sin 1''$, and the angular value for e to radius r, $e \cdot \sin 1''$; then write for A in seconds, $A = e \cdot \sin (n - d)$, and for the two verniers, $b = 2e \cdot \sin (n - d)$. A reading b' at 180° from the former will have the same error, but with an opposite sign, $b' = -2e \cdot \sin (n - d)$. If we tabulate the differences between the mean in our first table and the various readings for $B - A$, placing on the same line those that differ by 180° from one another, they should be equal with opposite signs were it not for errors of graduation; let these differences be D and D', then $b + g = D$, and $b' + g = D'$,

$$\begin{array}{r}
2e \sin (n - d) + g = D \\
- 2e \sin (n - d) + g = D' \\
\hline
2g = D + D', \quad g = \tfrac{1}{2}(D + D').
\end{array}$$

Subtracting,

$$4e \sin (n - d) = D - D', \qquad 2e \sin (n - d) = \tfrac{1}{2}(D - D') = b,$$

or a value for b freed from errors of graduation. This will give 18 equations involving e and n.

Placing $\delta = \tfrac{1}{2}(D - D')$, we have ;

$$\delta_1 = 2e \sin (0° - d) = 2e(\sin 0° \cos d - \cos 0° \sin d) = -2e \sin d;$$
$$\delta_2 = 2e \sin (10° - d) = 2e(\sin 10° \cos d - 10° \sin d);$$

$$\vdots \qquad\qquad \vdots \qquad\qquad \vdots$$

$$\delta_{18} = 2e \sin (170° - d) = 2e(\sin 170° \cos d - \cos 170° \sin d).$$

Professor Hilgard's method for solving these equations with respect to $2e \cos d$ and $2e \sin d$, by least squares, is to multiply each equation through by $\cos n$, and sum the resulting equations; then each through by $\sin n$, and sum the results: this will give us two normal equations of this form; after factoring $2e \cos d$, and $- 2e \sin d$,

$$[\delta_1 \sin 0° + \delta_2 \sin 10° \ldots \delta_{18} \sin 170°]$$
$$= 2e \cos d [\sin^2 0° + \sin^2 10° \ldots \sin^2 170°]$$
$$- 2e \cos d [\sin 0° \cos 0° + \sin 10° \cos 10° + \ldots \sin 170° \cos 170°];$$
$$[\delta_1 \cos 0° + \delta_2 \cos 10° \ldots \delta_{18} \cos 170°]$$
$$= 2e \cos d [\cos 0° \sin 0° \ldots \cos 170° \sin 170°]$$
$$- 2e \sin d [\cos^2 0° + \cos^2 10° \ldots \cos^2 170°]$$

$\sin 0° \cos 0° = 0$, also for $\sin 10° \cos 10°$ we can put $\frac{1}{2}\sin 20°$ and so on with all the products of sines times cosines; and we find that this will give us pairs of angles that make up $360°$, whose sines are equal but with opposite algebraic signs, so the products reduce to zero. Again, we can arrange the second powers so that all angles above $90°$ can be written $90° + n$; $\sin^2 (90 + n) = \cos^2 n$, this added to $\sin^2 n = 1$, for example; $\sin^2 0° = 0$, $\sin^2 10° + \sin^2 100° = \sin^2 10° + \sin^2 (90° + 10°) = \sin^2 10° + \cos^2 10° = 1$.

This will give us half as many unities as we have terms less two for the pairs, and $\sin^2 90° = 1$ gives us $9 = \dfrac{N}{2}$. The normal equations will then reduce to

$$\Sigma(\delta \sin n) = Ne \cos d,$$
$$\Sigma(\delta \cos n) = - Ne \sin d;$$

by division, $\qquad \dfrac{\Sigma(\delta \cos n)}{\Sigma(\delta \sin n)} = - \tan d.$

n.	First $b+g$.	Second $b+g$.	$\dfrac{1\text{st} - 2\text{d}}{2} = \delta$.	sin *n*.	cos *n*.	δ sin *n*.	δ cos *n*.
0°	+ 2.1	− 2.9	+ 2.5	0.00	1.00	0″.00	+ 2″.50
10	+ 7.1	+ 2.1	+ 2.5	.17	.98	+ 0 .43	+ 2 .45
20	+ 2.1	− 2.9	+ 2.5	.34	.94	+ 0 .85	+ 2 .35
30	+ 7.1	+ 2.1	+ 2.5	.50	.87	+ 1 .25	+ 2 .17
40	− 7.9	− 2.9	− 2.5	.64	.76	− 1 .60	− 1 .90
50	− 2.9	+ 2.1	− 2.5	.76	.64	− 1 .90	− 1 .60
60	+ 2.1	+ 7.1	− 2.5	.87	.50	− 2 .17	− 1 .25
70	+ 2.1	+ 2.1	0	.94	.34	0 .00	0 .00
80	+ 7.1	− 2.9	+ 5.0	.98	.17	+ 4 .90	+ 0 .85
90	+ 2.1	+ 7.1	− 2.5	1.00	.00	− 2 .50	0 .00
100	− 2.9	− 2.9	+ 2.5	.98	− .17	+ 2 .45	− 0 .43
110	− 7.9	− 2.9	+ 2.5	.94	− .34	− 2 .35	+ 0 .85
120	− 7.9	+ 2.1	− 5.0	.87	− .50	− 4 .35	+ 2 .50
130	+ 2.1	+ 2.1	0	.76	− .64	0 .00	0 .00
140	+ 2.1	− 7.9	+ 5.0	.64	− .76	+ 3 .20	− 3 .80
150	+ 2.1	− 2.9	+ 2.5	.50	− .87	+ 1 .25	− 2 .17
160	+ 2.1	− 2.9	+ 2.5	.34	− .94	+ 0 .85	− 2 .35
170	+ 2.1	+ 2.1	0	.17	− .98	0 .00	0 .00
					$\Sigma(\delta \sin n) =$	+ 0 .31	
					$\Sigma(\delta \cos n) =$		+ 0 .17

$$\tan d = \frac{-\ 0.17}{0.31} = \tan 151° \ 15'\ 40'';$$

$$e = \frac{-\ 0.17}{18 \sin 151° \ 15'\ 40''} = -\ 0''.02.$$

The line of no eccentricity is that passing through 151° 15′ 40″; the sign of *e* being *minus*, we know that the centre of motion is in the opposite direction from the centre of graduation towards the reading *d*. In this case it is too small to be considered. To determine the error of graduation, we compute the values of $2e \sin (n - d) = b$; subtracting these results from those in the last table marked $b + g$ in the first column, we will have *g*. It is necessary to compute *b* for every 10° space, only up to 180°, since *b* has the same value for 180° $+ n$ that it has for *n*, with the opposite sign, then subtract these values from the second $b + g$.

n.	n − d.	2e sin (n − d).	n.	g.	n.	g.
0°	− 151°	+ 0.017	− 0°	+ 2″.083	180°	− 2.883
10	− 141	+ .025	10	+ 7 .075	190	+ 2.125
20	− 131	+ .030	20	+ 2 .070	200	− 2.870
30	− 121	+ .034	30	+ 7 .066	210	+ 2.134
40	− 111	+ .037	40	− 7 .937	220	− 2.863
50	− 101	+ .038	50	− 2 .938	230	+ 2.138
60	− 91	+ .040	60	+ 2 .060	240	+ 7.140
70	− 81	+ .038	70	+ 2 .062	250	+ 2.138
80	− 71	+ .037	80	+ 7 .063	260	− 2.863
90	− 61	+ .034	90	+ 2 .066	270	+ 7.134
100	− 51	+ .030	100	− 2 .930	280	− 7.870
110	− 41	+ .026	110	− 7 .926	290	− 2.874
120	− 31	+ .020	120	− 7 .920	300	+ 2.120
130	− 21	+ .014	130	+ 2 .086	310	+ 2.114
140	− 11	+ .007	140	+ 2 093	320	− 7 893
150	− 01	+ .000	150	+ 2 .100	330	− 2 900
160	+ 09	− .006	160	+ 2 .106	340	− 2.906
170	+ 19	− .013	170	+ 2 .113	350	+ 2.087

The sum of the squares of the 36 values for g give 714.7617, therefore the probable error in any one is $\sqrt{\dfrac{714.7617}{35}} = \pm 4''.6$; this divided by the square root of two gives the probable error of the reading of one vernier, owing to errors of graduation and accidental errors of reading $= \pm 3''.2$.

If an angle is the mean of five repetitions, the probable error of the average will be one fifth of $3''.2 = \pm 0''.64$.

If the effect of eccentricity be considerable, the correction to each angle should be computed by the equation $b = 2e \sin (n − d)$. The probable error in graduation and reading is used only in computing the probable error in a chain of triangles, as will be seen later. If the instrument has two reading-microscopes the procedure is essentially the same, but differs slightly when there are three. In this case every 5° or 10° space can be examined and the three microscopes read; as before, we shall call the reading of the zero-point n, and the microscopes A, B, and C.

	$n.$	$n + 120°.$	$n + 240°.$	
	0° 00′ 00″	+ 01″	+ 02″	
	120 00 01	00	− 01	
	240 00 02	− 04	00	
Sum	+ 03	− 03	+ 01	= + 1, average = + 0.3.
	− 02.6	+ 03.3	− 0.6	
One third	− 00.9	+ 01.1	− 0.2	

The first line gives the readings when the zero-point is n, the order of the microscopes is A, B, and C; in the next, zero is at $n + 120°$, and the order is C, A, and B; in the third, zero is at $n + 240°$, and the order is B, C, and A. The fourth line contains the sums, and the continuation the average; and by subtracting the sums from this average we have the fifth line containing three times the errors of trisection at this point.

Eccentricity is first determined: "Suppose α_n, β_n, and γ_n be the observed errors of trisection corresponding to n, $n + 120°$, and $n + 240°$, also $[\alpha_n \cos n]$, $[\beta_n \cos(n + 120°)]$, $[\alpha_n \sin n]$ ... etc., be the sums of all the $\alpha_n \cos n$, $\alpha_n \sin n$, etc., then d, the line of no eccentricity,

$$= - \frac{[\alpha_n \cos n] + [\beta_n \cos(n + 120°)] + [\gamma_n \cos(n + 240°)]}{[\alpha_n \sin n] + [\beta_n \sin(n + 120°)] + [\gamma_n \sin(n + 240°)]}$$

also e''

$$= - \frac{[\alpha_n \sin n] + [\beta_n \sin(n + 120°)] + [\gamma_n \sin(n + 240°)]}{\frac{1}{2}N \sin d}$$

where $N =$ number of trisections.

"The correction for eccentricity is $b = e \sin(n - d)$, then if α_n', β_n', $\gamma_n' =$ errors of trisections freed from errors of eccentricity, we will have :

$$\alpha_n' = \alpha_n - e \sin (n - d);$$
$$\beta_n' = \beta_n - e \sin (n + 120° - d);$$
$$\gamma_n' = \gamma_n - e \sin (n + 240° - d).$$

Knowing α_n', β_n', γ_n', the residuals are squared, and the probable error of graduation and reading found as in the preceding case."

Considering that the determination of latitude, longitude, and azimuth forms a part of practical astronomy, the only instruments that remain to be described are the base-apparatus and heliotrope. The former is referred to in the chapter on base-measuring, and the latter can be dismissed with a few words.

The first heliotrope was used by Gauss in 1820. It was somewhat complicated, consisting of a mirror attached to the objective end of a small telescope. This mirror had a narrow middle-section at right angles to the rest of it; this was intended to reflect light into the tube, while the remainder reflected the sun's rays upon the object towards which the telescope was pointed. Bessel devised a much simpler form that is still in use in Prussia. It has a small mirror, with two motions, fastened to one end of a narrow strip of board, while at the other end there is a short tube whose height above the board is the same as the axis of the mirror. In this tube cross-wires are stretched, and a shutter can be dropped over the end opposite the mirror. To use it, one fastens the screw that is attached to one end in a suitable support and then by means of a levelling screw at the other end, raises or lowers that end until the centre of the mirror, the cross-wires and the object towards which the light is to be reflected are in line. The mirror is then turned so that the shadow of the cross-wires falls upon their counterpart that is marked on the shutter when the light can be seen at the desired point. Perhaps the most convenient of all is the heliotrope that finds employment in the U. S. Coast and Geodetic Survey. It can be seen in Fig. 4. First of all, there is a low-power telescope provided with a screw for attachment to a tree or signal. On one end of the tube is a fixed ring of convenient diameter, say one and a half inches, while at the other end is a mirror of two inches in diameter, and at an intermediate point, nearer the mirror, is another ring of the same height and size as the other, but clamped to the tube, admitting of a motion around it.

To describe its use we will suppose it in adjustment. After having screwed it to a post, the telescope is turned until the cross-wires approximately coincide with the point to which the light is to be shown; then turn the mirror so that the shadow of the nearer ring exactly coincides with the other ring. Then as the earth revolving places the sun in a different relative position, it will be necessary to continually move the glass in order to keep the shadow of the back ring on the front one. If the sun is behind the heliotrope an additional mirror will be needed to throw the light upon the glass.

To effect the adjustment, it is necessary to have in the construction the centres of the rings and the mirror at the same distance from the optical axis of the telescope. Bisect some clearly defined point, then sight over the tops of the mirror and rings, turning the movable one until they are all in line with the object bisected by the telescope. Owing to the large diameter of the sun, a slight error in adjusting will not affect the successful use of this kind of heliotrope.

When the observed and observing stations are within twenty miles of one another, the light spot may be too large to be easily bisected; then it is best to place between the glass and rings a colored glass (orange is preferable), so as to reduce the light as seen to a mere spot. A code of signals can be adopted and messages exchanged between observer and heliotroper, such as "Correct your pointing," "Stop for the day," "Set on new station," "Too much light," "Not enough light," by cutting off the light with a hat or small screen ; a long stoppage standing for a dash, and a short one for a dot, when the words can be spelled out by the Morse code.

The maximum distance at which a heliotropic signal can be seen depends upon the condition of the atmosphere. Perhaps the greatest was on the "Davidson quadrilateral," where a light was seen at a station 192 miles away.

A very convenient form of heliotrope, especially for reconnoissance, is one invented by Steinheil, and known by his name. It differs from all others in having only one mirror and no

Fig. 4.

rings, making it so simple in use and adjustment as to form a valuable instrument. The glass has but one motion, but the frame has another at right angles to it.

As can be seen from the illustration, the entire instrument can be attached to an object by means of a wood screw, and clamped in any position by other screws. In the centre of the mirror the silvering is erased, making a small hole through which the light of the sun can pass; also in the centre of the frame carrying the mirror there is an opening fitted with a convex lens, and behind the lens is a white reflecting surface—usually chalk. To use the heliotrope, turn the glass so that the bright point caused by the sun shining through the hole coincides with the opening in the frame. This will give in the focus of the lens an image of the sun, which will be reflected back through the hole in the glass. Now, if the entire instrument be turned so as to bring this image upon the point at which the light is to be seen, the rays falling upon the mirror will be reflected in the same direction.

FIG. 5.

To see the fictitious sun, as the image is called, one must look through the hole from behind the glass, and as it is always small and quite indistinct, some practice will be needed to recognize it. This can best be acquired by turning the image upon the shaded side of a house, then it will be seen as a small full moon. The reflecting surface can be moved in or out by a screw from behind, and the only adjustment that is ever needed is to have this surface at that distance that gives the best image of the sun. After having placed the heliotrope in the correct position, it should be clamped, and then the only labor is simply to occasionally turn the glass so as to bring the bright spot into coincidence with the opening in the frame. In the Eastern States, through air by no means the clearest, a light from a Steinheil heliotrope has been observed upon at a distance of 55 miles.

They are made by Fauth of Washington.

CHAPTER III.

BASE-MEASUREMENTS.

As the foundation of every extended scheme of trigonometric surveys must be a linear unit, it is essential that the length of this base should be determined with the utmost degree of care.

But the labor and expense of measuring a base of favorable length are so great as to preclude repeated measurements. In order, therefore, to secure results at all comparable with the precision desired, an apparatus of great delicacy is needed. This becomes apparent when we consider that an apparatus of convenient length is repeated from one to two thousand times in the measurement of a base, and that even a small error in the length of the measuring unit will be multiplied so as to seriously affect the results.

And this error in a short line will be increased proportionally in the computed lengths of the long sides of the appended triangles. The figure and magnitude of the earth are determined from extended geodetic operations, and the elements so determined are conditionally used in the re-reduction of triangulation data, securing in this way a more probable expression for the shape of our planet.

From this it may be seen that all of our errors are of an accumulative character, and seriously affect the results unless fortuitously eliminated by a principle of compensation.

Since geodesy first received attention, the subject of most important consideration has been the construction of a base-apparatus that would secure good results without sacrificing

4

time and expense. The first form consisted of simple wooden
bars, resting on stakes previously levelled, and placed end to
end. When the configuration of the ground made it necessary
to make a vertical offset, it was done by means of a plumb-line.
Another form similar to this had a groove cut in the under
side to rest upon a rope drawn taut from two stakes of equal
elevation. In place of laying the rods on stakes or on a catenary
curve, it was once found convenient to place them on the ice, as
when Maupertuis measured the base in Lapland in 1736. This
line was measured twice, each time by a different party; the
difference between the two results was four inches. This was
close work in a measurement extending over a distance of 8.9
miles. The rods used in this case were thirty-two feet long,
made of fir and tipped with metal to prevent wearing by attrition. The Peru base measured at about the same time gave a
difference of less than three inches in the two measurements
in a distance of 7.6 miles. The wooden rods were found to
be affected by changes in the hydrometric conditions of the
atmosphere. This change was diminished by painting them.
Finally wood was abandoned as the material, and glass tubes
substituted. Of course with glass there was a continual change
in length due to expansion or contraction by thermal variations, that was not perceptible in the case of wood, but knowing the rate of expansion, the absolute length at any temperature can be theoretically computed. The temperature of each
tube during the entire measurement was ascertained by the
application of a standard thermometer, and the length of the
whole base was reduced to a temperature of 62° Fahr. The
difficulty of determining the temperature of the tubes was
considerable, since the thermometer reading gives the temperature of the mercury in the thermometer, or, at best, that of
the external air, which will always differ from the temperature
of the measuring-bar. In the case of a sudden change of temperature, the thermometer will respond more quickly than the

tubes, and its reading could not be taken as the reading of the tubes. This trouble suggested the construction of an apparatus that would serve to indicate change in temperature—as a metallic thermometer. On this principle, Borda made four rods for the special committee of the French Academy in 1792. The rods were made of two strips of metal—one of platinum, and the other of copper overlying the former. They were fastened together at one end, but free at the other and throughout the remaining length. The copper was shorter than the platinum by about six inches. It carried a graduated scale, moving by the side of a vernier attached to the platinum; the reading of the scale indicated the relative lengths of the two strips, and hence the length and temperature of the platinum. The strips rested upon a bar of wood—the entire apparatus being six French feet in length. Contact was made by a slide, the end of which was just six feet from the opposite end of the platinum strip when the zero-mark on the slide coincided with one on the end of the strip to which it was attached. The rods rested upon iron tripods with adjusting-screws for levelling, and the inclination was ascertained from a sector carrying a level. It is interesting to note that the length of the metre was first determined from the length of the quadrant computed from the base measured with this apparatus. Borda's compensating apparatus in some form has been used ever since it first came into notice. The principal varieties are: Colby, Bache-Wurdeman, Repsold, Struve, Bessel, Hossard, Borden, Porrò, Reichenbach, Baumann, Schumacher, Bruhns, Steinheil.

In these varieties—named after their inventors or improvers —the essential features sought for are:

1. The terminal points used as measuring-extremities must, during the operation, remain at an unvarying distance apart, or the variations therefrom must admit of easy and accurate determination.

2. The distance between these extremities must be compared with a standard unit to the utmost degree of accuracy, and the absolute length determined.

3. In its construction provision must be made to secure readiness in transportation, ease and rapidity in handling, stability of supports and accuracy in ascertaining exact contact and inclination.

The above conditions were secured in a great degree in the Bache-Wurdeman apparatus, as used in the U. S. Coast and Geodetic Survey since 1846. The description given by Lieutenant Hunt in 1854 will be found quite explicit. For the benefit of those who cannot consult the report which contains this description the following abstract is given: the apparatus sent to the field consists of two measuring-tubes exactly alike, each being packed for transportation in a wooden box; six trestles for supporting the tubes—three being fore trestles and three, rear trestles—each of which is packed in a three-sided wooden box; eight or more iron foot-plates on which to place the trestles, and a wooden frame is afterwards made to serve as a guide in laying down the foot-plates; a theodolite for making the alignment, and for occasionally referring the end of the tube to a stake driven in the ground for the purpose; a standard six-metre bar of iron in its wooden case, and a Saxton pyrometer for effecting a comparison.

The measuring-bar consists of two parts—a bar of iron and a bar of brass, each less than six metres in length.

These are supported parallel to each other; at one end are so firmly connected together by means of an end-block, in which each bar is mortised and strongly screwed, as to preserve at that point an unalterable relation. The brass bar, which has the largest cross-section, is sustained on rollers mounted in suspended stirrups; the iron bar rests on small rollers which are fastened to the iron bar, and run on the brass one. Supporting-screws through the sides of the stirrups are adjusted to sustain the bars in place, and also serve to rectify them. Thus, while the two bars are relatively fixed at one end, they are elsewhere free to move; and hence the entire expansion and contraction are manifested at one end. The difference in the length of the two bars is read on a scale attached to the iron bar by means of a vernier fastened to the brass bar. The scale is divided into half millimetres, of which the vernier indicates the fiftieth part, so that by means of a long-focus microscope the difference may be read to the hundredth part of a millimetre without opening the case. Since the compensation (described further on) can be made correct within its thirtieth part, it is evident that the true length of the compound bars may be known at any time from the scale-reading, with an uncertainty no greater than the thousandth part of a millimetre or a microm.

The medium of connection between the free ends of the two bars is the lever of compensation, which is joined to the lower or brass bar by a hinge-pin, around which it turns during changes of temperature. A steel plane on the end of the iron bar abuts against an agate knife-edge on the inner side of the lever of compensation. This lever terminates in a knife-edge, turned outward at such a distance from the centre-pin and the other knife-edge bearing, that the end edge will remain unmoved by equal changes of temperature in the two bars. The end edge presses against a steel face in a loop made in the sliding-rod. This rod slides in a frame fastened to the top of the iron bar, and passes through a spiral spring, which acts with a constant force to press the loop against the knife-edge. The outer end of the sliding-rod bears the limiting agate plane. Thus the end agate is not affected in position by the expansions of the brass and iron, acting as they do at proportional distances along the lever of compensation, measured from its sliding-end bearing. The rates of expansion for iron and brass . may safely be taken as uniform between the extreme expansions and contractions to which they are subject in practice, and the compensating adjustment once made is permanent.

The stirrups sustaining the rollers on which the brass bar runs are made fast to the main horizontal sheet of the iron supporting and stiffening work. This consists of a horizontal and a vertical plate of boiler-iron, joined along the middle line of the horizontal sheet by two angle-irons, all being permanently riveted. Circular openings are cut out from both plates to lighten them as much as practicable. A continuous iron tie-plate, turned up in a trough-form, connects the bottoms of all the stirrups. At the ends, stiffening braces connect the two plates.

We now pass from the compensating to the sector end of the tube, at which extremity are arranged the parts giving the readings, and for adjusting the contacts between successive tubes in measuring, thus making it the station of the principal observer. The sector-end terminates in a sliding-rod, which slides through two upright bars, and at its outer end bears a blunt agate knife-edge, horizontally arranged, which in measuring is brought to abut with a uniform pressure against the limiting agate plane of the compensating end of the previous tube. At its inner end, this sliding-rod rests against a cylindrical surface on the upright lever of contact, so mounted as at its bottom to turn around a hinge-pin. At top, this lever rests against a tongue, or drop-lever, descending from the middle of the level of contact, which is mounted on trunnions.* The sliding-rod, when forced against the side of the lever of contact, presses its top against the tongue of the level, and thus turns the level by overcoming a preponderance of weight given to its farther end, to insure the contact being always at a constant

---

* The device of the level of contact is supposed to be due to the elder Repsold, who applied it first to the comparing-apparatus used by Bessel, in constructing the Prussian standards of length. A duplicate of that comparator was procured for the Coast Survey, by F. R. Hassler, Superintendent, in 1842.

pressure between the agates, the same force being always required to bring the bubble to the
centre. The arrangement at the
two ends is shown in Fig. 6.

The sector is a solid metal
plate, mounted with its centre of
motion in the line of the sliding-
rod, and having its arc graduated
from a central zero to the limits
of ascending and descending
slopes on which the apparatus is
to be used. A .fixed vernier in
contact with the arc gives the
slope-readings. A long level and
bubble-scale are so attached and
adjusted to the face of the sector-
plate that the zeros of the level
and of the limb correspond to
the horizontal position of the
whole tube. If, then, on slopes,
the bubble be brought to the
middle by raising or lowering the
arc-end of the sector (a movement made by a tangent-screw,
whose milled head projects above
the tin case of the tube), the
vernier will give the slope at
which the tube is inclined, and
the sloping measure is readily
reduced to the horizontal by
means of a table prepared for
the purpose. The level of contact and the lever of contact,
with their appendages, are all mounted on the sector and par-
take of its motions. A knife-edge end of the sliding-rod presses

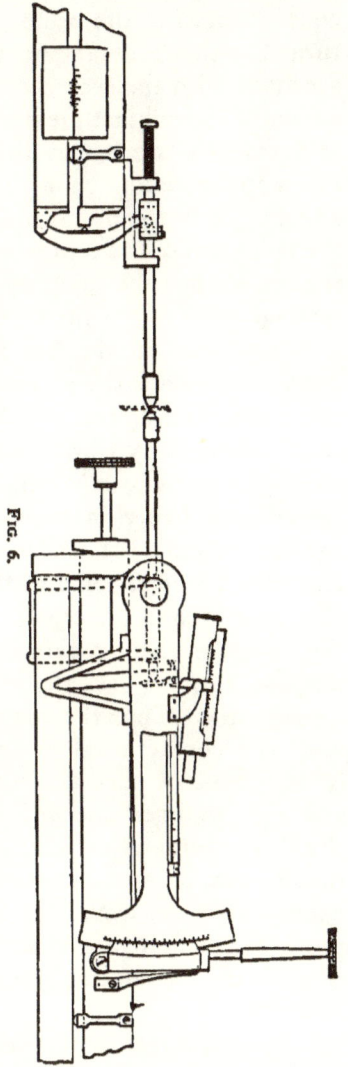

Fig. 6.

on the cylindrical face of the contact-lever, this cylinder being concentric with the sector, and the sector can therefore be turned without deranging the contact. In fact, the contacts are made with the sector-level horizontal, thus insuring the accuracy of the contact-pressure. The contact-lever is supported at bottom by two braces dropping down from the sector-plate, and a spring, acting on a pin in the lever, steadies it against an adjusting screw-end. A bracket from the sector-plate receives the trunnions of the contact-level. A small screw projects from the end of the tube to clamp or set the lever and level of contact against a pin in the sector for security in transportation.

What is called the fine motion, required for adjusting the contacts between the successive tubes, is produced by means of a compensating rod or tube, one end of which is attached to the truss-frame by a bracket over the rear trestle, and the other receives a screw terminating in a projecting milled head. This screw turns freely in a collar, bearing, by a projecting arm, against the cross-bar which joins the main brass and iron bars, and its nut is in the end of the compensation-rod. By turning the screw in one direction, the bars are pushed forward, and the opposite turning permits a spiral spring, arranged for the purpose, to push back the system of bars, which slides through its supports. Thus the contact is made by turning the screw until the contact-level is horizontal. The compensating-rod is composed of several concentric tubes, alternately of brass and iron, arranged one within the other, and fastened at opposite ends alternately. Thus, when a contact has been made by the fine-motion screw, changes of temperature will not produce derangement, as would be the case if this rod were not compensating. The arrangement permits the observer conveniently to work the fine-motion screw, and to observe its action on the contact-level.

The apparatus thus described is enclosed in a double tin tubular case, diaphragms being adapted for supporting and strengthening the whole. The air-chamber between the two cases, one and a half inches apart, is a great check on heat-variations. Three side-openings, with tin and glass doors in each tube, permit observations of the parts and of inserted thermometers. The ends are closed, only the sliding-rod ends projecting at each extremity, exposing the agates. Brass guard-tubes protect these, and for transportation tin conical caps are screwed on the tube-ends. The fine-motion screw, the sector-tangent screw, and the contact-lever-clamp screw project beyond the case. The tube is painted white, which, with the air-chamber and thorough compensation, effectually obviates all need of a screen from the sunshine, which has usually been deemed requisite.

The tube rests on a fore trestle and rear trestle, which are alike, except in the heads. Each trestle has three legs, composed of one iron cylinder moving in another by means of a rack, pinion, and crank, so as to raise or sink the head-plate. The levelling and finer adjustment are by means of a foot-screw in each leg, by working which a circular level on the connecting-frame is adjusted. A large axis-screw, resting on the connecting-frame, and rising into a tubular nut, is turned by bevelled pinions worked by a crank, and thus raises or lowers this tubular nut and the cap-piece which it supports at top. The axis-screw, the leg-racks, and the foot-screws give three vertical movements in the trestle, by which its capacity for slope-measurements is much amplified.

In the cap of the rear trestle, a lateral and a longitudinal motion are provided for, by means of two tablets arranged to slide, the upper one longitudinally on the lower one, and the lower laterally on the head-plate of the axis-screw tube. Long adjusting screw-handles extend to the observer's stand from these two plates and from the axis-screw, enabling him to raise or lower, to slide forward or back, to the right or the left, the rear end of the tube. The fore trestle is similar, except that its head is only arranged for a lateral movement, and a second observer makes its adjustments by a simple crank.

Four men can carry a tube, by levers passed through staples

in blocks strapped under the tubes. The principal observer and an assistant make the contacts and rectifications, the first assistant directs the forward tube, and another preserves the alignment with a theodolite. A careful recorder notes down the observations, and an intelligent aid places the trestles and foot-plates.

This scale referred to, known as Borda's scale, was introduced in Bessel's system, the only difference being that he used iron and zinc in the place of copper and platinum, and measured the interval with a glass wedge. In this the iron is the longer, and supports on its upper surface the zinc.

The zinc terminates at its free end in a horizontal knife-edge, and the iron bar very near this has attached to itself a piece of iron with a vertical knife-edge on each side in the direction of the length of the bar. The distance between the end of the zinc and this fixed point, changing with the varying temperature, is measured by means of a glass wedge, whose thickness varies from 0.07 of an inch to 0.17 of an inch, with 120 divis-

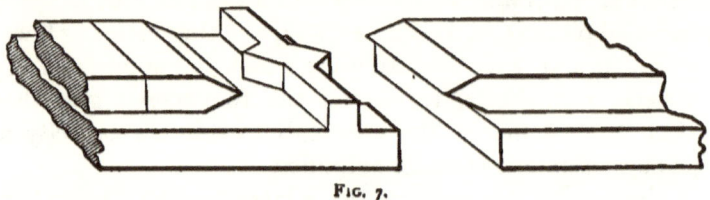

FIG. 7.

ions engraved on its face, the distance between its lines being 0.03 of an inch. The other vertical knife-edge, projecting slightly beyond the end of the bar, is brought, in measuring, very near the horizontal knife-edge in which the opposite end of the bar terminates, and the intervening distance measured with the same glass wedge. If the wedge in this case be carefully read and its thickness at each division accurately known, this method eliminates some of the uncertainties in the method of contact. A pair of Bessel bars, slightly modified, is now in use in the Prussian Landes-triangulation.

The annexed cut shows the arrangement of the knife-edges in the two ends of the Bessel bars.

The apparatus devised by Colby consists of a bar of brass and one of iron, fastened at their centres, but free to move the rest of their lengths. Each end of one of the bars is a fulcrum of a transverse lever attached to the same end of the other bar, the lever arms being proportional to the rates of expansion of the bars. In this way the microscopic dots on the free ends of the levers are theoretically at the same distance apart for all temperatures. As the terminal points were the dots on the lever arms, contact could not be made in measuring, so the interval between two bars was determined by a pair of fixed microscopes at a known distance apart.

In all forms of compensating-bars, the components having different rates of heating and cooling, their cross-sections should be inversely proportional to their specific heats, and should be so varnished as to secure equal radiation and absorption of heat. Struve's apparatus consists of four bars of wrought iron wrapped in many folds of cloth and raw cotton.

Contact is made by one end of a bar abutting against the the lower arm of a lever attached to the other, while the upper arm passes over a graduated arc on which a zero-point indicates the position of the lever for normal lengths. The temperature is ascertained from two thermometers whose bulbs lie within the bar.

From these descriptions it can be seen that the Bache apparatus was a combination of principles separately used before. It had Borda's scale, Colby's compensation-arm, and Struve's contact-lever; with this difference: the lever, instead of sweeping over a graduated arc, acted upon a pivoted level. The form used by Porro in Algiers consisted of a single pair of bars attached at their common centre and free to expand in both directions. Each end of one of the bars carried a zero-point, while the corresponding end of the other had a graduated scale like Borda's. In measuring, a micrometer microscope is placed on a strong tripod, with an adjustable head immediately over the initial point. The apparatus is then placed in position on another pair of trestles, completely free from the microscope-stands, and moved by slow-motion screws until it is in line and the zero-point in the axis of the microscope. The scale is then read by means of the micrometer; at the same time another similar microscope is being adjusted over the forward end and read. The bar is then carried forward, placed in position so that its rear end is under the second microscope, and the forward end ready for a third microscope previously aligned.

And so the work progresses until a stop is to be made; then the bar is removed and a point established under the forward end of the bar. Every precaution is taken to estimate flexure and to avoid uncertainties of collimation and unstable microscopes. In Ibañez's apparatus the component bars are copper and platinum, mounted upon a double T-iron truss. Flexure is determined by resting a long level on the bars at several points at equal distances apart. It differs from the preceding in having the bars exposed.

The Baumann apparatus, recently constructed for the Prussian Geodetic Institute, has platinum and iridium bars resting on an iron truss, with its entire length open to the free circulation of the air. Inclination is determined by a level of precision and flexure by a movable level.

There are six microscope stands, the same number of trestles for the bars, and thirty sets of heavy iron foot-plates.

The latter are put in position, and remain half a day before being used. For each microscope-stand there are two telescopes—one for aligning and one for reading the scales. Six skilled observers and about thirty laborers are needed in measuring. Only one base has been measured with this apparatus up to the present time—that of Berlin in 1884—but the results are not yet known.

The Repsold differs from the Baumann apparatus only in a few points, the chief being: the component bars are steel and zinc, and the two are suspended in a steel tube which is wrapped in thick felt. The small probable errors deduced by Ibañez and the officers of the Lake Survey in the results obtained with the metallic-thermometer principle appear to command its continuance in the construction of base-apparatuses. But in the Yolo base authenticated temperature changes were not always accompanied by corresponding indications of the Borda scale. In short, the behavior of the zinc component was so unsatisfactory that a new apparatus for the Coast and Geodetic Survey is under consideration, in which the scale-readings will be omitted, and either a partly compensated pair of bars or a single carefully protected bar of steel adopted instead, with daily comparisons with a field standard. For additional information on the various forms of base-apparatuses the authorities cited at the end of this chapter may be consulted.

It is interesting to note the results of various measurements under different auspices with the same or different forms of apparatuses. The following list gives the most important:

Name of base.	Measured by.	Apparatus.	Length.		Prob. error.
Dauphin Island..	U. S. C. and G. S........	Bache-W........	6.66	miles.	1 : 41000
Bodies Island....	"	"	6.75	"	1 : 425500
Edisto Island	"	"	6.66	"	1 : 418600
Key Biscayne....	"	"	3.6	"	1 : 454400
Cape Sable......	"	"	4	"	1 : 409600
Epping Plains....	"	"	5.4	"	1 : 551600
Peach Ridge.....	"	*Hasslen*...	5.8	"	1 : 561880
Fire Island	"	" ...	8.75	"	1 : 483980
Kent Island	"	Hassler......	5.5	"	1 : 22800
Beverloo	Nerenberg...........	Bessel...........	2300	metres.	1 : 16949
Ostend	"	"	2480	"	1 : 22222
Cape Comorin....	Eng. Trig. S	Colby	8912.5	feet.	1 : 667000
Keweenaw.....	U. S. Lake S.......	Bache-W	5.5	miles.	1 : 83310
Minnesota.......	"	"	3.8	"	1 : 530000
Chicago..........	"	Repsold	4.6	"	1 : 2089000
Sandusky...	"	"	3.8	"	1 : 1148600
Wingate	U. S. Geol. S	Slide-contact	4.1	"	1 : 54366
Yolo...	U. S. C. and G. S.......	Davidson......	17486.51	metres.	1 : 700000
Aarberg	Ibañez and Hirsch......	Ibañez.....	2400.07	"	1 : 6000000
Weinfelden	Hirsch.......	"	2440.29	"	1 : 3500000
Joederen.........	Haffner and Overgaard.	Swedish Acad'y..	3318.55	"	1 : 2090000
Ilidze	Kalmer and Lehrl.....	Austrian.........	4061.34	"	1 : 3700000
Speyer..........	Schwerd	Schwerd	859.44	"	1 : 715000
Foggia...........	Italian Government.	Bessel...........	2016.569	toises.	1 : 1333065
Naples...	" "	"	340.224	"	1 : 963784
Axevalla	Stecksen........... ...	Wrede	1357.033	"	1 : 1577945

Perhaps a better idea can be obtained of the accuracy of base-measurements when we give a comparison of the measured length of a line with its length as computed from another base. A few such comparisons are here given:

Epping measured...................... .... 8715.942 metres.
Computed from Massachusetts base........ 8715.865 "
    "   "   Fire Island base.......... 8715.900 "
Massachusetts base measured.... .... 17326.376 "
Computed from Epping base............. 17326.528 "
    "   "   Fire Island.............. 17326.445 "

Combining the errors of preliminary measurements with the computed error in the triangulation, the appended results are obtained:

Probable error in junction-line.	Due to base.	To triangulat'n	Both.
From Epping base....	0.17 metre.	0.76 metre.	0.78 metre.
" Massachusetts base............	0.20 "	0.32 "	0.37 "
" Fire Island base	0.39 "	0.66 "	0.77 "

Considering the distance apart of these bases, it is safe to say that if the errors are constant the maximum error in the length of any line of the triangulation is not more than 0.22 of an inch to the statute mile. The above are the results of measurements by the Bache-Wurdeman apparatus, angles measured with a thirty-inch repeating-theodolite, and the triangulation computed by Mr. Schott. Simply with the purpose of comparing the results obtained by different apparatus, I make an extract from the report of the U. S. Lake Survey:

Chicago base measured................ log. in feet 4.3917929
    "   "   computed from Fond du Lac "   "   4.3918010
            Difference = 0.14 metre.
    Distance from Chicago to Fond du Lac, 150 miles.

Olney base measured................ log. in feet 4.3349231
"   "   computed from Chicago..... "   " 4.3349231
Difference = 0.06 metre.
Distance from Chicago to Olney, 200 miles.

The Madridejos base, measured by General Ibañez with his improved Porro apparatus, was divided into five segments; the central one was about 1.75 miles long. This one was measured twice, and used as a base in computing the length of each of the other segments. The relation between the measured and computed values may be seen in the following table:

Segment.	Measured (metres).	Computed (metres).	Difference (metres).
1	3077.459	3077.462	− 0.003
2	2216.397	2216.399	− 0.002
3	2766.604	2766.604	
4	2723.425	2723.422	+ 0.003
5	3879.000	3879.002	− 0.002
Total........	14662.885	14662.889	− 0.004

The Wingate base, measured with a slide-contact apparatus, was divided into three segments; the middle one was measured twice to see if a discrepancy sufficiently great to warrant a re-measurement existed. The two results were in sufficient accord to admit of the acceptance of the entire measurement as correct. However, each segment was used as a base for the computation of the other segments.
The length of the line was:

With measured first and computed 2d and 3d... 6724.5309 m.
"   second   "   1st and 3d... 6723.7132 "
"   third   "   1st and 2d... 6723.8248 "
Measured value of the whole line........ 6724.0844 "

Giving these values equal weight, the length may be written 6724.0383 ± 0.12 metres.

Colonel Everest, with the Colby apparatus, measured in India three bases, and joined them in the scheme of triangulation, measuring the angles with a thirty-six-inch theodolite.

	Dehra Dun.	Damargida.
Measured length in feet...........	39183.87	41578.54
Computed " "	39183.27	41578.18

Only instructions of the most general kind can be given for the mechanical part of measuring. The details vary with each form of apparatus. The location of the base is a matter of prime importance, and must be considered in connection with the purpose for which the base is needed. If for verification, it should be suitably situated for connection with the chain of triangles it is intended to check.

If it is intended to serve as an initial base, a favorable condition for immediate expansion should be sought. As the base will usually be from three to seven miles long, the points suitable for the first triangle-stations should be somewhat farther than that apart, permitting a gradual increase in the lengths of the sides. The best initial figure is undoubtedly a quadrilateral of which the base is a diagonal, giving an expansion from either side, or from the other diagonal.

If this be impracticable, the base must be a side of a complete figure. Of course the termini must be intervisible, and at the same time visible from every point of the line. If the ground is irregular, having slopes exceeding three degrees in inclination, it must be graded to within that limit, with a width of about twelve feet. The method of alignment varies with the views of the person in charge.

A good plan is to select a point approximately at the middle of the line. Place a theodolite there, and direct the telescope to the temporary signal at one end and read the angle to the other end; if it differs from 180°, move the instrument in the proper direction until the angle is just 180°. Assistants are then sent towards each end, and, from signals from the person at the instrument, secure points in line: these should be placed about a quarter of a mile apart. Considerable experience has shown that the best form of aligning signal is a piece of timber of suitable size, 2x4 inches or 4 inches square, driven in the ground and sawed off a few inches above the surface. In the top of this, bore a hole at the central point for the insertion of an iron pin, twice as long as the hole is deep. Take a corresponding piece of timber six or eight feet long and make a similar hole in its end. It can then be adjusted to the stake in the ground, and made stable by two braces, after being made perpendicular by means of a plumb line or a small theodolite. The advantage of this form of signal is that it can be removed when the measuring reaches this point, and be replaced for a future measurement without going to the trouble of making a second alignment. A plan of aligning differing from this is to have the instrument carefully adjusted and placed three or four hundred yards from the end. Direct the telescope to the temporary signal at that point, turn it in its Y's, or 180° in azimuth, and fix a point directly in line. Then place the instrument over the point so selected and locate another point in advance, and so on till the opposite end is reached. This will only be possible when one terminus has been decided upon and the general direction of the line. Each terminus of the base is marked by a heavy pier of masonry of secure foundation with upper surface eighteen inches or two feet below the surface of the ground. In the centre of the large stone forming a part of the top of the pier a hole is drilled; in this, with its upper face even with the top of the stone, is placed, and secured by having poured around it molten lead, a copper bolt or a piece of platinum wire.

5

On the upper end of this bolt or wire a needle-hole may be drilled, or a pair of microscopic lines drawn, whose intersection marks the end of the base. Immediately above this should be placed a surface-mark to which the position of the theodolite can be referred in the triangulation; also a set of witnesses consisting of four stones projecting above ground, so placed that the diagonals intersect above the under-ground mark.

When both ends are marked in this way before measuring, the distance from the end of the last bar to the terminal mark, already fixed, is measured on a steel scale horizontally placed.

The only advantage possessed by this method is, that both monuments have an opportunity to settle before the distance between them is determined. It is believed, however, that greater inaccuracies will result from the uncertainty in this scale and its use than from the irregular settling of the pier placed after the measurement is finished. Before beginning the accurate measurement it is advisable to make a preliminary measurement with a steel tape or wire, marking every hundred lengths of the apparatus to be used. This will serve as a check upon the record as the final work advances; and if the line is to be divided into segments it will show where the intermediate monuments are to be erected. When these intermediate stations are occupied the angle between the ends and the other points should be measured with great care, so that, if the line be found to be a broken one, the exact distance between the termini in a straight line can be computed. If the required distance cannot be obtained without crossing a ravine or marsh, the feasible parts can be measured, and the other portion computed by triangulation.

The form of record will of course vary with the kind of apparatus used, but too much care cannot be taken in keeping the record. The principal data needed in the reduction may be stated as follow:

1. The time—showing the time at which each bar was placed in position in order to form some idea of the average speed attained in the work.

2. The whole number of the bar. When a preliminary measurement has been made as suggested, the hundredth bar should end near the stake previously driven ; if not, a remeasurement must be made from the last authentic point. This should be at the end of the even-hundred bar, and perhaps more frequently, especially if the day should be windy, endangering the stability of the bars, or if the ground should be boggy or springy. The simple method for placing this point is to set a transit or theodolite at right angles to the line and at a distance of twenty-five or thirty feet from it. After levelling, fix the cross-wires of the instrument upon the end of the bar; then, pointing the telescope to the ground, direct the driving of a stake in a line with this and with the aligning telescope. The height of the telescope should be half the height of the bar, so that the focus need not be changed.

Then in the top of this stake a copper tack is driven, and on its upper face are drawn two lines coinciding with the vertical threads of the two instruments. If they are in good adjustment the intersection of these lines will mark the end of the bar. A record must always be made when a stub is thus placed. It is also advisable to place a stub under the instrument used for this horizontal cut-off, so that if it should be necessary to begin work at this point the instrument would occupy the same position that it occupied before, eliminating by this means the error that would arise from not having the transit at right angles to the line.

Probably a more accurate method is to have a metal frame one inch wide and two inches long with screw holes admitting of attachment to a stake. This frame has sliding inside of it another that can be moved by a milled-head screw, with a set screw to hold it in place. On the upper surface of this frame is a small dot or hole. When the approximate position of the end is determined by a plummet, a stake is driven in the ground until only an inch or so remains above the surface: to this· is attached the outer frame ; then, with the theodolite previously set upon the end of the measuring-bar, direct the movement of the inner frame until the hole or dot is bisected by the cross-wires, when the frame is clamped in place and verified. When microscopes are used, the dot can be brought under the micrometer-wire that marked the position of the zero-point on the bar.

3. The designation of the bar as A, B, or 1, 2, etc., so that it may be known how many times each bar was used. Since the two are never of the same length, the distance obtained by each bar must be separately computed and the two values added to get the entire length of the line.

4. Inclination. When going up-hill the inclination is recorded plus, and minus when going down. However, as the correction for inclination is always subtracted, the sign is of small consequence.

5. Columns for the sector-error and the corrected values for the inclination. Before beginning work each day the rods should be placed on their tripods and be made perfectly horizontal by raising one of them. To determine this, set up a carefully adjusted theodolite at such a distance that both ends of the bar can be seen. Set the thread on one end of the bar, revolve the instrument in azimuth, and see if the thread be on the other end: when such is the case, bring the bubble of the sector in the middle of the tube and see what the scale-reading is; if zero, then there is no error. This test should be applied at the beginning and close of each day's work, and the average error added to or subtracted from the reading of inclination for that day. With secondary apparatus this is unnecessary, as the positive and negative readings will be about equal, so that the number of readings that are recorded too

great will be corrected by those that are too small by the same quantity.

6. Temperature. The thermometers should be read about every ten bars, and in the Borda rods the scales more frequently. When the temperature gets above 90° Fahr., it is advisable to stop work, especially if the bars are not compensated, as the adopted coefficients of expansion at that temperature are unreliable.

The Repsold apparatus, as used on the Lake Survey, and the Davidson, with which the Yolo base was measured, were protected during measuring by a canopy made of sail-cloth mounted on wheels, so as to move along as the work advanced.

In all kinds of apparatus it is advisable to measure when the bars indicate a rising temperature, and also during the time required for them to fall through the same amount.

7. A column for corrections for inclination, computed from a formula to be given.

8. A column for remarks, explaining delays, stoppages, the placing of stubs, etc.

GENERAL PRECAUTIONS TO BE TAKEN WHILE MEASURING.

The rear end of the bar must be directly over the marking on the initial monument.

The inclination must never be so great as to endanger a slipping of the bars forward or backward.

The trestles should be so firmly set that there can be no unequal settling after the bar has been placed on them.

A bar should not be allowed to remain more than a minute in the trestles, lest its weight should change their position.

When a stoppage is made to allow the aligning-instrument to advance, a transit should be set up, as already described, and its cross-wires firmly clamped on the end of the bar; then, before resuming work, the position of the bar can be restored if from any cause it has changed.

When the end has been transferred to a temporary mark, as

when a stop is made for night or dinner, in resuming work it is best to place the bar that the work closed with in the same position it had before stopping; then the new day's work goes on as though there had been no break. If this plan is not adopted, either in the transferrence to the ground or from it, the end sighted will be more than the standard length from the other end, being held out by the spiral spring that keeps the agate beyond its proper distance, rendering it necessary to record an index-error for every transferrence; whereas in the plan suggested there can be no danger of omitting to record this index-error, nor of recording an erroneous value.

This precaution refers to that species of apparatus which consists of a *pair* of bars, one abutting against the other, and not where only one bar is used, as in the Repsold, Baumann, and others.

The alignment must be made with precision, for all errors of this kind are of the same character and do not cancel one another.

Before beginning actual work the party should measure a short distance several times, by way of practice, until the disagreement between two measures is made very small.

COMPUTATION OF RESULTS.

In order to know the horizontal distance between the two ends of the base it is necessary to know the number of times the measuring-unit was used, and its exact length each time that it was employed. To this must be added index-errors, and the amount by which the last bar fell short of the terminus. Also, there are to be subtracted the quantities that were needed to reduce each length to its horizontal projection, and those negative errors that could not be obviated.

A carefully kept record will show how often the bars were used; but to ascertain their length is a more difficult problem, depending upon: (*a*), a knowledge of the exact length of the adopted standard; (*b*), a known relation between the measuring-bar and the standard at a certain temperature; (*c*), a knowledge of the temperature of the bars each time used, and the coefficients of expansion.

The Committee Metre is the standard of linear measures now in use, and with a certified copy of this, all our units are compared. This comparison can be described only in outline. We have two firmly built pillars at a convenient distance apart for the bars that are to be compared. On one is an abutting-surface, and on the other is a comparator. In general, this comparator consists of a pin held out by a spiral spring but capable of being withdrawn by a micrometer-screw. This pin works a lever on whose longer arm is a point that is to be brought into coincidence with a fixed zero-mark. Between these two pillars is a carriage rigidly constructed but completely isolated from them. On this carriage are placed the standard and the bar that is to be compared. The former is placed between the abutting-surface and the micrometer-pin, the screw is turned until the zero-marks coincide, and the turns and division recorded.

The carriage is then moved along until the bar is brought into place and the micrometer is again read. The difference in the readings will correspond to the difference in lengths in terms of micrometer turns and divisions—the value of a turn and a division being found by measuring with the screw the length of a standard centimetre. In very accurate comparisons the bars are immersed in glycerine, which can be readily kept at the same temperature for a long time.

The temperature is ascertained from three thermometers— one at each end, and one at the middle. Also, to eliminate accidental errors, a number of readings are made with the bars reversed, turned over, taken in different order, and at different temperatures. The average difference will be the difference in the lengths of the standard and the bar at the average temperature, supposing that the coefficients of expansion remain constant. Then knowing the temperature at which the standard is correct and its coefficient of expansion, its true length can readily be computed for this average temperature. To this, add the average difference just referred to and we have the exact length of our bar at this mean temperature. To illustrate: let M be the standard, A the bar under comparison, μ the difference in microns, which is obtained by multiplying the turns and divisions of the micrometer by the previously ascertained value of one turn.

Temp.	$A - M.$
° F.	$\mu.$
57.58	$+$ 7.5
52.60	$+$ 7.5
55.29	$+$ 9.8
55.16 $= t_0$	$+$ 8.27

Therefore, $A = M + 8.27\mu$ at 55°.16. Suppose e be the coefficient of expansion for M, and T the temperature at which M is correct, then we have $A = M + e(55°.16 - T) + 8.27\mu$.

To determine e we must have the pillars of the comparator at a fixed distance apart, and then measure this distance with a bar at different temperatures. In order to insure the bar being at the same temperature, it is best to place it in glycerine previously heated, and leave it there for half an hour. Let D be the difference between the constant distance and the distance as observed at various temperatures, t_0 the average, and t the observed temperatures.

$t.$	$D.$	$t - t_0.$	$D - D_0.$
° F.	$\mu.$		
99.08	441.5	$+$ 28.13e =	178.9
83.68	342.9	12.73e =	80.3
72.08	268.2	1.07e =	5.6
57.58	175.9	$-$ 13.37e = $-$	86.7
42.39	084.5	$-$ 28.56e = $-$	178.1
70.95 $= t_0$	262.6 $= D_0$		

Forming the normal equations by multiplying each equation by the coefficient of e in that equation, and taking the sum of the resulting equations, we get $1948.92e = 12,306.4\mu$, or $e = 6.315\ \mu$. Substituting this value of e, we have for A, $A = M + 6.315\mu(55°.16 - T) + 8.27\mu$. There is a probable error in this determination which can be carried through the future computations.

The way in which the temperature-observations are utilized depends upon the accuracy desired; ordinarily the average temperature of each bar in a segment is employed. So that if we have n lengths of a four-metre bar with the above coefficient of expansion, a length equal to A at 55°.16, and the average temperature t in that segment, we shall have the distance $= n[A + 4 \times 0.000\ 006315\mu(t - 55°.16)]$. When greater accuracy is required, the length of each bar can be computed in the same manner, and the aggregate length obtained by summation.

When a Borda scale or metallic thermometer is used, it is necessary to know how much in thermometric scale a division is equal to. The scale is usually divided into millimetres, and read by a vernier or microscope to 0.01 mm.

Temp.	$t - t_0$.	Scale $= S$.	dS.
° F.	°		
109.41	$+$ 31.79	8.60	$+$ 0.92
94.11	$+$ 16.49	8.17	$+$ 0.49
79.21	$+$ 1.59	7.74	$+$ 0.06
61.16	$-$ 16.46	7.16	$-$ 0.52
44.22	$-$ 33.40	6.72	$-$ 0.96
77.62 $= t_0$		7.68 $= S_0$	

By letting x be the quantity representing the differential expansion of the component bars, and as it varies with the temperature, we may take the values of $t - t_0$ as the coefficients of x and solve by least squares. The normal equation will give $2671.54x = 78.05d$, or $x = 0.02922d = 29.22\mu$.

That is, a change of one degree Fahr. is represented by 0.029 division, or the smallest value that can be estimated on the vernier, $0.01d = \frac{1}{3}°F$.; consequently the scale-readings can be readily converted into degrees of temperature and the reduction for length made as in the preceding case, or the change in length may be found directly in terms of scale-readings. If we have a four-metre bar with the coefficient of expansion just found, $0.01d = \dfrac{4 \times 6.315}{2.92}\mu = 8.64\mu$.

Then if S_0 be the scale-reading at which M is a standard, and S any other reading during the measurement or the average, $A = M + 8.64\mu(S - S_0)$, and the entire line

$$= n[M + 8.64\mu(S - S_0)].$$

Correction for inclination: if R represent the length of a bar, h its horizontal projection, and θ the angle of inclination, it is apparent that $h = R.\cos\theta$, then d the correction $= R - h$ $= R - R.\cos\theta = R(1 - \cos\theta) = 2R.\sin^2\frac{1}{2}\theta$. As θ is small $\sin^2\frac{1}{2}\theta = \frac{1}{4}\sin^2\theta$ (nearly), so we may write

$$d = \frac{R\sin^2\theta}{2} = \frac{\sin^2 1'}{2}R\theta^2; \qquad \log\frac{\sin^2 1'}{2} = 2.626422.$$

Having determined by comparison the average length of the bars, a table should be computed for each, giving the values for d for each fractional part to which the sector can be read, and within the limits observed. Then from this table corrections for inclination can be taken and inserted in the record-book. If there are any index-errors, as stated might occur in the transferrence of the end to the ground, they must be added to the computed length.

Probable error. This may be derived—

1. By measuring the base a number of times, then deducing

the probable error in accordance with the principle of least squares.

2. By dividing the line into segments and computing the other segments from each one as a base by triangulation.

3. By checking one base from another in the chain of triangulation, and determining the probable error in the second from that of the first and of the measurement of the angles in the triangulation.

4. From all known sources of error in measurement.

The fourth method is the only one that needs expansion at this point. The principal sources of error in measurement are:

1. In determining the length of the bar.
2. Backward pressure.
3. Error of alignment.
4. In transferring end to the ground.
5. In the determination of inclination.
6. Personal errors of the observers.

These are determined as follows: the first is obtained from repeated comparisons with the standard, and is made up of two parts—uncertainty in the expansion of the bars, and accidental errors in comparing. Of these the former is found from the residuals in the series of determinations of the coefficients of expansion. Calling this r_1', we have for the entire n bars $n.r_1'$. Likewise the error from comparison is found in a similar manner from the series of comparisons, if we designate this r_2', the entire error $r_2 = n.r_2'$.

The error of contact depends upon the force with which the agate is held out beyond its proper position. When a bar is in its right place, and the next bar brought into contact with it, the pressure necessary to bring it to its place forces the rear bar backward; and when the rear bar is taken away the forward bar, being relieved of this pressure, moves back by the same amount. Consequently the total backward movement is double the effect of pressure. This must be determined by experiment in various positions of the bar. As every bar except the first and last are doubly affected, these each being changed only once by this pressure, the total correction will be twice the displacement multiplied by one less than the number of bars. Usually this is too small to be considered, and applies to those bars only that are used in pairs—one bearing in contact against the other.

By (3) is not meant the uncertainty of having the line as a whole straight, but in placing the bar exactly in that line. The aligning instrument is placed in front at distances varying from 50 to 900 feet, and the alignment is effected by bringing the agate of the bars into coincidence with the vertical thread of the telescope; or when the bars are provided with a vertical rod immediately over their centres, this is sighted to. It is apparent that the bisection of this may not be perfect; and, in fact, when the light falls unequally upon the object sighted to, the illuminated spot is bisected, which may be altogether to one side of the centre.

However, the error of bisection cannot be greater than the radius of the agate or aligning-rod, and its effect upon the true length of the line will depend upon the distance to the transit. The nearer the transit, the less is the likelihood of making an erroneous bisection. By placing a scale directly under the agate, and having the person at the transit direct the moving of the bar until he considers it in line, make a note of the scale-reading, and after a number of trials the average variations may be taken as the error most likely to be committed at that distance. Suppose it was found that the errors were a for the maximum, and b for the minimum distances, the angular variations might be written: a times one second divided by the length of the bar, call this m, and similarly for b, which we will call n. The correction for this deviation will be the difference between the length of the bar and the vertical projection for this angular deviation. As already shown, this is equal to $\dfrac{R \cdot \sin^2 m}{2}$, and $\dfrac{R \cdot \sin^2 n}{2}$.

Only the first and last few bars of each segment will need to have this total lateral correction applied; for the remaining bars it will be sufficient to take the average of m and n, in the formulæ just given. As the total correction from this cause will never amount to a tenth of an inch, it is usually omitted, and its probable error is never considered.

The error from the fourth source is determined from experiment, as in the preceding case. Suppose it is 0.082 mm.; as there is a double transfer, the entire error will be 0.082 $\sqrt{2}$ mm. $= 0.11$ mm., and the total for n bars will be 0.11 $\sqrt{n} \cdot$ mm. $= r_4$.

The fifth source of error is quite apparent. The sector that shows the inclination usually reads to single minutes, sometimes to ten seconds. As it is impracticable to obtain more than one reading for each inclination, there is an uncertainty as to its correctness. This will vary with the skill of the observer and the character of the sector used. The probable error of a single determination should be ascertained as follows: place the bar firmly in its trestles and make several readings of the scale when the bubble of the level is in the same position. From a number of such scale-readings the probable error is deduced in the usual manner.

To determine the effect of this error on the computed corrections for horizontal projections, the average observed inclination must be approximated. Suppose this to be $2°$, the probable error of inclination $30''$, and the length of the bar R. It has already been shown that the correction for inclination $d = R(1 - \cos \theta)$. As θ in this case is taken as $2°$, an approximate value for the change in d by a mistake of $30''$ in θ can be computed by getting d' when $\theta = \theta \pm 30''$; $d' = R[1 - \cos(\theta + 30'')]$, and the probable error in any one determination will be the difference between d and d' or r_4', $r_4 = e\sqrt{n}$ where $n = $ the number of bars and $e = d - d'$.

To recapitulate: those errors that are known to exist and the direction of whose effect is unmistakably determined can be applied in the reduction of the length of the base, while those that are merely probable must be used simply in obtaining the probable error of the measurement as a whole. The value for the length of the base must be diminished by the amount of backward pressure, errors of alignment, and errors of inclination; but the remaining errors having a double sign must be regarded as probable; if individually they be represented by r_1, r_2, r_3, ... r_n, and the total error by R, we will have

$$R = \sqrt{r_1^2 + r_2^2 \ldots r_n^2} = \sqrt{\Sigma[r^2]}.$$

As the sides of the triangulation are at different elevations and the base and check-base not on the same plane, it is necessary to know their lengths at some common-datum plane. This by common consent is the half-tide level of the ocean.

bg, height above half-tide $= h$;

ae, the half-correction for reduction $= \dfrac{c}{2}$;

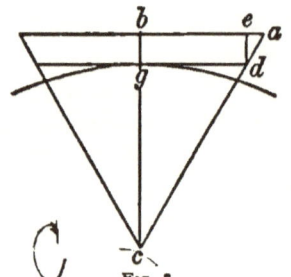

FIG. 8.

$ae : ed :: ab : bc$;

$$ae = \frac{ed \cdot ab}{bc} = h \cdot \frac{ab}{cg + bg};$$

$$2ae = c = h \cdot \frac{2ab}{cg + bg} = h \cdot \frac{B}{cg + bg};$$

bg is so small in comparison with cg that it may be omitted, and we write;

$$c = \frac{h \cdot B}{\text{radius of curvature}} = B\left(\frac{h}{R} - \frac{h^2}{R^2}\right), \text{ where } R = \text{radius of}$$

curvature at the mean latitude of the base.

From the corrected value for the length of the base c is to be subtracted. If the elevation of the base was found by different methods, or from different bench-marks, an uncertainty may arise in the value of h, giving a probable error for c.

REFERENCES.

U. S. Coast and Geodetic Survey Reports as follows: 1854, pp. 103–108; '57, pp. 302–305; '62, pp. 248–255; '64, pp. 120–144; '73, pp. 123–136; '80, pp. 341–344; '81, pp. 357–358; '82, pp. 139–149; also pp. 107–138; '83, pp. 273–288.

Clarke, Geodesy, pp. 146–173.

Report of U. S. Lake Survey, pp. 48–306.

Zachariae, Die Geodätische Hauptpunkte, pp. 79–110.

Jordan, Handbuch der Vermessungskunde, vol. ii. pp. 73–113.

Expériences Faites avec l'Appareil à Mesurer les Bases.

Compte Rendu des Opérations de la Commission pour étalonner les Règles employés à la Mesure des Bases Géodésiques Belges.

Westphal, Basisapparate und Basismessungen.

Gradmessung in Ostpreussen, pp. 1–58.

CHAPTER IV.

FIELD-WORK OF THE TRIANGULATION.

SUPPOSING that a base has been carefully measured, or the distance between two stations previously occupied accurately known, the next thing to be done is to lay out a scheme of triangles covering the desired territory. Their arrangement into figures depends upon:

1. The special purpose of the work.

2. The character of the country over which the system is to be extended.

If the object is to measure arcs of a meridian or of a parallel, for the purpose of determining the figure of the earth, great care should be exercised in selecting triangles that are approximately equilateral; for if in the computation a very long side is to be computed from a short one, an error in the latter will be greatly magnified in the former. If the purpose is simply to meet the wants of the topographer, the stations should be selected with special reference to his needs and without regard to the character of the figures thus formed. In an open prairie where signals have to be erected without any assistance from natural eminences, their arrangement may be made in strict accord with theoretical preference.

The plainest system of the composition of triangles into figures is a single string of equilateral triangles which possess the advantages of speed and economy of time and labor. Hexagonal figures are preferred by some, but the general preference is for quadrilaterals with both pairs of diagonal points intervisible. This system covers great area and insures the greatest accuracy.

Equilateral triangles will furnish nine conditions.

Hexagons, with one side in common, twenty-one conditions.

Quadrilaterals, twenty-eight conditions, covering the same area (approximately).

Signals.—After deciding upon the positions of the stations, the next subject for consideration is the kind of signals to be used. In short sights, the best form is either a pole just large enough to be seen, or a heliotrope fixed on a stand or a tripod carefully adjusted to the centre of the station. As the helio-tropers are usually persons with but little experience, range-poles should be previously set, enabling them to point their instruments with some degree of precision.

(For a description of the heliotrope, its adjustments, and use, see page 45.)

Owing to the fact that there are so many days during which it is impossible to use the heliotrope, and also the additional trouble that frequently when the sun is shining the air is so disturbed that the object sighted is too unsteady to bisect with any certainty, the effort is constantly being made to devise some form of night signal to take the place of day signals.

The great obstacle to the successful solution of this problem has been the dimness or expense of the lights that have been tried, such as oil-lamps, magnesium, or electric lights. In June, 1879, Superintendent Patterson of the U. S. Coast and Geo-detic Survey directed Assistant Boutelle to make an exhaustive series of observations with the various methods of night signals, with a view to determine the most effective method to be used in triangulation.

The special points to be considered were :

1. Simplicity and cheapness.

2. Adaptability to the intelligence of the men usually em-ployed as heliotropers.

3. Ease of transportation to heights.

6

4. Penetration, with least diffraction and most precision of definition.

5. The best hours for observation.

6. Lateral and vertical refraction, and the extent to which the rays are affected by the character of the country over which they pass.

An accurate account of the various experiments made by Captain Boutelle are given in Appendix 8 of the C. and G. S. Report for 1880. I shall take the liberty of quoting his conclusions; they are:

"The experience of the past season enables me to state with some precision the cost of the magnesium light, so much superior to every other yet tried.

"The success in two instances of burning the light by a time-table established that method as perfectly practicable.

"It reduces the time of burning it to twenty minutes per hour, or to eighty minutes for four hours' observation. With a delivery of ribbon of fifteen inches per minute, the cost will be two dollars per night for each light used. The average number of primary stations observed upon at any one station is six, of which three would require the magnesium light, making the expense six dollars per night. The nights when observation would be practicable and the lights burned may be taken as averaging three in a week, or seven at each station.

"Apart from the first cost of apparatus, we should therefore have as the additional outlay for night observation for a primary triangulation:

" 1. Additional pay of six heliotropers.............. $3.00
" 2.   "   cost of burning three magnesium lights
                 every other night................ 3.00
" 3.   "   cost of kerosene-oil for three lamps... 0.20
" 4.   "   cost per day for supplies, etc........ 0.80
                                                      _____
   " Whole additional daily cost.... .... $7.00

" To offset this additional party expense there will be :

" 1. The shortening of time required in occupation of each station by the addition of four hours of observing each clear day after sunset. The average time of observation each day being two hours, this time will be tripled on each clear day and night.

" 2. Necessity for encamping at many stations may be avoided, where now the probabilities of a long detention and the lack of any decent quarters within a reasonable distance require the transportation and use of equipage.

"The conclusions to which the experiments and results have led me may be generally summed up as follows :

" 1. That night observations are a little more accurate than those by day, but the difference is slight so far.

" 2. That the cost of apparatus is less than that of good heliotropes.

" 3. That the apparatus can be manipulated by the same class of men as those whom we employ as heliotropers.

" 4. That the average time of observing in clear weather may be more than doubled by observing at night, and thus the time of occupation of a station proportionally shortened. Hazy weather, when heliotropes cannot show, may be utilized at night.

" 5. That reflector-lamps, or optical collimators, burning coal-oil, may be used to advantage on lines of 43.5 miles and under. But for longer lines the magnesium lights will be best and cheapest, as being the most certain.

" 6. That for the present we should keep up both classes of observation, both by day and night ; and that the observers in charge of the various triangulations should be informed of the progress already made, and encouraged to improve on the methods and materials thus far employed in night observations."

At this time many of the parties in charge of triangulation-work, under the auspices of the Coast Survey, make night observations. The wisdom of this plan is duly appreciated by all who have observed in the Eastern or Middle States.

It might be safely said that more time is spent in waiting for suitable weather than in reading the angles, and any means for diminishing this waste will be gladly adopted, especially by those who have had their patience taxed by having to wait day after day for the haze to pass by.

For short sights or for secondary triangulation a reflecting-surface, such as a tin cone, will be sufficient. Still better is a contrivance made of tin, in the shape of the children's toy, that is made to revolve by a current of air, and fixed on an axis in the top of a pole or tree. If it is of the proper shape, in turning it will catch the sun's rays at the right angle to send a reflection to the desired point, except when the sun is on the opposite side from the observer. In lines still shorter a simple pole, supported by a tripod, or a straight tree will answer. Care must be taken, however, to have the pole or tree no larger than is necessary to render it visible, as large bodies are difficult to bisect. A diameter of 6 inches will subtend an angle of one second at a distance of 20 miles; for 40 miles, 12.3 inches; and at 60 miles, 18.5 inches. Sights have been made upon a tree 12 inches in diameter at a distance of 55 miles.

Much time can be gained and accuracy secured by making the observations at the most favorable time. For instance, if a pole is to be sighted, the proper time is in the morning when looking towards the east, and in the evening when looking westward. If a reflecting object is used, the opposite rule to the above must be followed.

It is frequently necessary to elevate the instrument and observer in order to obtain a longer length of line, or to overcome some impediment. Fig. 9 will give an idea of the form that has been found most convenient. When it is to be constructed on a hill or mountain, it will be found advisable to cut the

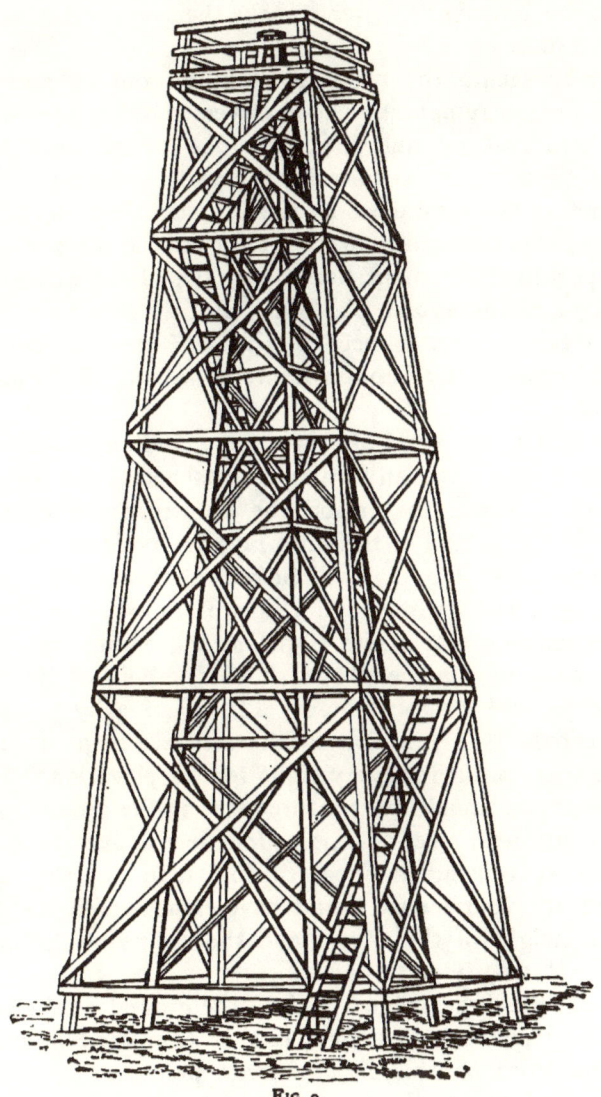

FIG. 9.

timbers at the bottom, in order to save the transportation of useless materials.

In order to secure the requisite stability, and to prevent shaking of the instrument by the observers moving around, it is necessary to have a double structure—one for the theodolite, and one to support the platform for the party observing. For a low structure the form used by the Prussian Geodetic Institute will be found sufficiently firm.   It is a vertical piece of timber to support the instrument, braced by a tripod, the whole surrounded by a quadrangular platform.   But when a height of more than twenty feet is needed, the kind devised by Mr. Cutts, and improved by Captain Boutelle, will be found more satisfactory.

I have worked on several of this pattern, and can vouch for their rigidity; and when an awning is attached to the legs of the scaffold to shade the tripod, the unfortunate results of "twist" from the action of the sun's rays are avoided.

From a glance at Fig. 9 it will be seen that the signal consists of two parts—a tripod and a square scaffold.   It is the average experience that a safe signal, strong enough to withstand the heaviest winds we have, should be built of timbers 6 by 8 inches, with diagonal braces 2 by 2 and 3 by 3.   The size of the base is a function of the altitude, a good ratio being one foot radius for every eight feet of elevation.   The legs of the tripod should be set three feet in the ground, and would, if continued, meet at a point four feet above the platform.   So that for a signal whose scaffold is to be eighty feet above the station-surface we would have eighty-seven feet for the vertical height of the tripod, and the radius of the base would be $\frac{87}{8} + 0.67$ ft. $= 11.54$ ft.

To lay out the base, drive a stub in the ground at the central point, and with a radius equal to that computed describe a circle ; mark off on this circumference points with a chord equal to the radius, and the alternate points will be the places for the feet of the tripod.   With a level, or an instrument that can be used as a level, the bottom of the holes for the tripod can be placed on the same plane, by marking on a rod a distance that is equal to the height of the axis of the instrument and three feet more, then the holes are to be dug until this mark coincides with the cross-wires of the telescope when the rod is in each hole.

The tripod, being the highest and the innermost structure, should be raised first. The plans adopted for this differ with different persons; some frame two legs with their bracing, raise them with a derrick, guy their tops, raise the third and brace it to the other two. A platform is built on the top of this on which the derrick is placed, another section is then lifted into place as before, the derrick again moved up until the top is reached. Then the blocks are attached to the top of the tripod, which is well guyed, and the sides of the scaffold raised as a whole or in sections.

If the station is wooded, one or two large trees may be left standing and the blocks attached to their tops for raising the timbers. Signals ninety-four feet high have had their sides as a whole put in place, held there with guys until the opposite pair was raised and the whole braced together. This can also be done in the case of the tripod, by laying the single piece down with its foot near its resting-place, and the pair lying in the same direction framed together; then with ropes rigged to a tree left standing, or to a derrick, the pair is raised until it stands at the right inclination, and held in place with ropes until the single piece is brought into position. To keep the feet from slipping, an inclined trench can be made towards the hole, or they can be tied to trees or a stake firmly driven into the ground. I have put up tripods in a way still different. By framing one pair, and attaching between their tops the top of the third by means of a strong bolt, the whole stretched out on the ground in the shape of a letter "Y," with the feet of the pair fastened near their final resting-place. The apex is lifted and propped as high as possible, then a rope is passed through between the legs of the pair and attached to the leg of the single one near its lower end. It will be seen that as this leg is drawn towards the other two the apex is hoisted up.

I have erected a high signal in this way by hitching a yoke of oxen to the single leg and hauling it towards the other two. If a tree should be in a suitable place, a rope passing through a block, attached as high up as possible in the tree, will be of great service in hoisting the apex.

A good winch will be of great use, and plenty of rope will be needed, and marline for lashing. If all the timbers are cut and holes bored ready for the bolts, the labor of erection will be of short duration. Captain Boutelle's tables, enabling one to cut the timbers for a signal for any height, are inserted here:

DIMENSIONS IN FEET.

	Tripod.				Scaffold.			
Vertical height of floor above station point.	Vert. length.	Slant length.	Three feet below station-point.		Vert. length.	Slant length.	Three feet below station-point.	
			Rad.+0.67	Side of eq. triangle.			One half diagonal.	Side of square.
32	39	39.31	5.54	9.60	38	38.52	14.33	20.26
48	55	55.43	7.54	13.06	54	54.75	17.00	24.04
64	71	71.55	9.54	16.52	70	70.97	19.66	27.80
80	87	87.68	11.54	19.99	86	87.19	22.32	31.57
96	103	103.80	13.54	23.45	102	103.41	25.00	35.35

DIMENSIONS OF TRIPOD.

Slant dist. from top.	Vert. dist. from top = L.	R = radius. $=\frac{L}{8}+0.667.$	Length of hor. brace = 1.732R.	Length of diagonal braces.	Size of braces.
Feet.		Feet.	Feet.	Feet.	Inches.
0	0.00	0.667			
5	4.96	1.287	2.229		
8	7.94	1.659	2.873		
13	12.90	2.279	3.947	6.02	3 by 2
20	19.85	3.148	5.452	8.39	3 by 2
29	28.78	4.264	7.385	11.00	3 by 2
40	39.69	5.628	9.748	13.87	3 by 2
53	52.59	7.240	12.540	17.05	3 by 3
68	67.48	9.102	15.765	20.55	3 by 3
85	84.35	11.212	19.420	24.40	3 by 3
103.80	103.00	13.542	23.455	25.00	3 by 3

	Vertical length from top.	Slant length along outside edge.	Slant length along centre post.	Half diag. from station-point to outside edge.	Horizontal braces side of square.	Size of horizontal braces.	Diagonal braces.	Size of diagonal braces.
	Feet.	*Feet.*	*Feet.*	*Feet.*	*Feet.*	*Inches.*	*Feet.*	*Inches.*
	3	3.05	....	8.49	12.00	3 by 4	.....	.....
	19	19.27	....	11.15	15.77	3 by 4	21.27	3 by 3
	35	35.49	....	13 82	19.54	3 by 4	23.90	3 by 3
	51	51.71	....	16.49	23.32	4 by 4	26.81	3 by 3
	67	67.93	67.50	19.15	27.08	4 by 4	29.91	3 by 4
	83	84.15	83.60	21.82	30.86	4 by 4	21.66	3 by 4
Ground........	99	100.38	99.70	24.50	34.65	.....	*22.23	3 by 4
Bottom of holes	102	103.42	102.72	25.00	35.36	.....	.....	.....

* One foot from ground.

The floor of the scaffold should be twelve feet square, giving room for a tent large enough for the observers to move around in, and sufficient space outside to pass around while fastening the tent to the railing.

A good shape for an observing tent is hexagonal, four and a half feet across, and six and a half high, one side opening for its entire length for exit and entrance, and the other sides having a flap that opens from the top to a little below the height of the instrument. This will keep out the sun, and also, by opening only that part that is needed, the tendency of the wind to cool the sides of the circle unequally can be diminished. A corner post will be needed at each vertex, and the top can be supported by a rafter running from each corner of the platform meeting over the centre. To determine the size of the base of the scaffold, we find the ratio of the half diagonal to the vertical height and add to this the half diagonal of the top. One foot in six has been found to give stability to the signal, so that for a scaffold 80 feet high with 3 feet in the ground, we have for the half diagonal of the base $\frac{83}{6}$ + the half diagonal of the top = 23 feet, and the side of the square 27.6 feet. The slope can be found by trigonometry, tan. of slope = vertical height divided by half the difference of the upper and lower diagonals. It is well to brace the signal by wire guys running from each length of timber in the scaffold legs.

Probably the highest signal ever erected was built by Assistant Colonna of the U. S. Coast and Geodetic Survey in California.

A large red-wood tree was cut off 100 feet from the ground and a twofold signal built,—a platform fastened to this high stump, and a quadripod from the ground for the support of the instrument. The total height was 135 feet. The observers were hoisted up in a chair attached to a rope passing through a fixed pulley at the top, and hauled by a winch on the ground.

When the country is approximately level, the curvature of the earth will obstruct a long line of sight, unless the instrument be elevated or a high signal erected. When we know the distance within a mile or two between the points on which it is desired to establish stations, the problem is to find how high the signals or scaffolds must be in order to be intervisible. Also, when two suitable points of known altitudes are chosen, with an intervening hill of known elevation, the problem is to find how high one must build to see over it.

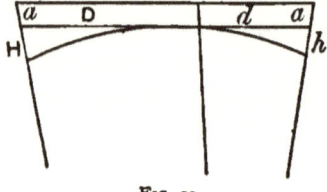

FIG. 10.

Let h = height in feet;
d = distance of visibility to horizon in feet;
R = average radius of curvature in feet,
$\log R = 7.6209807.$

The distance d being a tangent, it is a mean proportional between the secant and the external segment, that is, $h : d :: d : h + 2R$, but h is so small compared with $2R$ that it can be omitted, and we have $h = 0.6672d^2$. This is to be increased by its 0.07th part for terrestrial refraction, making $h = 0.7139d^2$,

or $d = \dfrac{\sqrt{h}}{0.845}.$

If we wish to know how far above the horizon the line of sight passes from two points of known elevation, we find the distance to the point of tangency.

Let $D =$ the whole distance ;
 $d =$ the shorter distance ;
 $a =$ the height above the tangent ;
 $m =$ the coefficient of d^2 in the above expression.

$$h - a = md^2, \qquad H - a = m(D - d)^2 = mD^2 - 2mDd + md^2;$$

by subtraction

$$H - h = mD^2 - 2mDd, \qquad \text{or} \qquad 2mDd = mD^2 - (H - h);$$

therefore, $$d = \frac{mD^2 - (H - h)}{2mD}.$$

This gives the distance from the lower point to the point of tangency ; then the height at which this tangent strikes either station can be found by the above formula, $h = 0.7139d^2$, or $a = h - 0.714d^2$.

If there is an intervening hill, we first compute the point of tangency of the line from the higher station ; then, how high up the intervening hill this tangent strikes. To this add the amount by which the lower hill exceeds this tangent plane : if this be more than the height of the intervening hill, it can be seen over ; if less, the difference will show how much must be added to the height of the terminal stations.

If the intermediate hill be so heavily timbered as to render it impracticable to have it cleared, the height of the trees must be added to the elevation of the hill ; and at all times it is best that the line of sight should pass several feet above all intermediate points. The following table gives the difference between the true and apparent level in feet at varying distances:

GEODETIC OPERATIONS.

Distance, miles.	Difference in feet for—			Distance, miles.	Difference in feet for—		
	Curvature.	Refraction.	Curvature and Refraction.		Curvature.	Refraction.	Curvature and Refraction.
1	0.7	0.1	0.6	34	771.3	108.0	663.3
2	2.7	0.4	2.3	35	817.4	114.4	703.0
3	6.0	0.8	5.2	36	864.8	121.1	743.7
4	10.7	1.5	9.2	37	913.5	127.9	785.6
5	16.7	2.3	14.4	38	963.5	134.9	828.6
6	24.0	3.4	20.6	39	1014.9	142.1	872.8
7	32.7	4.6	28.1	40	1067.6	149.5	918.1
8	42.7	6.0	36.7	41	1121.7	157.0	964.7
9	54.0	7.6	46.4	42	1177.0	164.8	1012.2
10	66.7	9.3	57.4	43	1233.7	172.7	1061 0
11	80.7	11.3	69.4	44	1291.8	180.8	1111.0
12	96.1	13.4	82.7	45	1351.2	189.2	1162.0
13	112.8	15.8	97.0	46	1411.9	197.7	1214.2
14	130.8	18.3	112.5	47	1474.0	206.3	1267.7
15	150.1	21.0	129.1	48	1537.3	215.2	1322 1
16	170.8	23.9	146.9	49	1602.0	224.3	1377.7
17	192.8	27.0	165.8	50	1668.1	233.5	1434.6
18	216.2	30.3	185.9	51	1735.5	243.0	1492.5
19	240.9	33.7	207.2	52	1804.2	252.6	1551.6
20	266.9	37.4	229.5	53	1874.3	262.4	1611.9
21	294.3	41.2	253.1	54	1945.7	272.4	1673.3
22	322.9	45.2	277.7	55	2018.4	282.6	1735.8
23	353.0	49.4	303 6	56	2092.5	292.9	1799.6
24	384.3	53.8	330.5	57	2167.9	303.5	1864.4
25	417.0	58.4	358.6	58	2244.6	314.2	1930.4
26	451.1	63.1	388.0	59	2322.7	325.2	1997.5
27	486.4	68.1	418.3	60	2402.1	336.3	2065.8
28	523.1	73.2	449.9	61	2482.8	347.6	2135.2
29	561.2	78.6	482.6	62	2564.9	359.1	2205.8
30	600.5	84.1	516.4	63	2648.3	370.8	2277.5
31	641.2	89.8	551.4	64	2733.0	382.6	2350.4
32	683.3	95.7	587.6	65	2819.1	394.7	2424.4
33	726.6	101.7	624.9	66	2906.5	406.9	2499.6

The following example will illustrate its use: Suppose we have a line of 14 miles from A to B, and at B it is convenient to build a signal 21 feet high. By looking in the table in the fourth column, we find that the line of sight will strike the horizon at 6 miles, leaving 8 miles to be overcome at A. Opposite 8 in the first column we find 36.7 feet in the fourth, therefore at A we will have to build 37 feet to see B.

To illustrate the second problem:

Let h' = height of higher station = 1220 feet;

        h = height of intervening hill = 330 feet;

      h'' = height of lower station = 700 feet;

      d = distance from h to h'' = 24 miles;

     d' = distance from h to h' = 40 miles;

$d + d'$ = distance from h' to h'' = 64 miles.

700 feet strikes the horizon at 34.9 miles, 64 − 34.9 = 29.1 miles from that point to the other station. By looking in the table at 29.1 miles, the tangent strikes the other station at 486 feet, 1220 − 486 = 774 feet, the distance the top is above the tangent, and 29.1 − 24 = 5.1 miles that the point of tangency is from the intervening hill, and hence strikes it at 15 feet. Now, if we conceive a line to be drawn from the top of the higher to the top of the lower, we will have with the tangent a right-angle triangle in which the elevations at the higher and intervening hills above the tangent are proportional to their distances from the lower; or, 24 : 64 :: x : 774, x = 290.6; that is, this sight-line strikes the intervening hill at 290 feet above the tangent, and the tangent strikes it at 15 feet, or the sight-line hits the intervening hill at 305.6; as this is 330 − 305.6 = 24.4 feet below the top, the two stations are not intervisible.

The lower station being the nearer the intervening hill, it would be the one to build on. To determine the height of the necessary signal, we have the following proportion:

$$40 : 64 :: 24.4 : x, \quad \text{or} \quad x = 38.4 \text{ feet.}$$

In determining the altitude of stations, or intervening hills, an aneroid barometer will give a result sufficiently accurate. If the barometer is graduated to inches and decimals, the following table, giving heights corresponding to readings of barometer and thermometer, will be useful in estimating the height:

Ba-rom-eter.	Mean of Observed Temperatures, Fahrenheit.						
	32°.	42°.	52°.	62°.	72°.	82°.	92°.
30.0							
29.9	87.5	89.4	91.4	93.3	95.3	97.2	99.2
29.8	175.3	179.2	183.1	187.0	190.9	194.8	198.7
29.7	263.4	269.3	275.1	280.9	286.8	292.7	298.5
29.6	351.8	359.6	367.4	375.2	383.0	390.9	398.7
29.5	440.5	450.3	460.0	469.8	479.6	489.4	499.2
29.4	529.5	541.3	553.0	564.7	576.5	588.2	600.1
29.3	618.8	632.6	646.3	659.9	673.7	687.4	701.3
29.2	708.4	724.2	739.9	755.4	771.3	787.0	802.8
29.1	798.3	816.1	833.8	851.3	869.2	886.9	904.7
29.0	888.5	908.2	927.9	947.6	967.4	987.2	1007.0
28.9	979.0	1000.7	1022.4	1044.2	1065.9	1087.8	1109.6
28.8	1069.9	1093.5	1117.3	1141.1	1164.8	1188.8	1212.6
28.7	1161.1	1186.7	1212.5	1238.3	1264.1	1290.0	1315.9
28.6	1252.5	1280.3	1308.1	1335.9	1363.8	1391.6	1419.5
28.5	1344.3	1374.2	1404.0	1433.8	1463.7	1493.6	1523.5
28.4	1436.4	1468.4	1500.2	1532.1	1563.9	1595.9	1627.9
28.3	1528.5	1562.9	1596.8	1630.7	1664.5	1698.6	1732.7
28.2	1621.5	1657.7	1693.7	1729.6	1765.6	1801.7	1837.9
28.1	1714.6	1752.8	1790.9	1828.9	1867.0	1905.2	1943.4
28.0	1808.1	1848.3	1888.5	1928.6	1968.8	2009.0	2049.3
27.9	1901.9	1944.2	1986.4	2028.6	2071.0	2113.2	2155.6
27.8	1996.0	2040.4	2084.7	2128.9	2173.5	2217.8	2262.3
27.7	2090.5	2136.9	2183.4	2229.6	2276.3	2322.7	2369.3
27.6	2185.2	2233.8	2282.4	2330.7	2379.4	2428.0	2476.7
27.5	2280.3	2331.1	2381.7	2432.2	2482.9	2533.6	2584.5
27.4	2375.8	2428.7	2481.4	2534.1	2586.8	2639.6	2692.7
27.3	2471.6	2526.7	2581.3	2636.2	2691.1	2746.0	2801.3
27.2	2567.8	2625.0	2681.9	2738.9	2795.9	2852.9	2910.3
27.1	2664.3	2723.6	2782.6	2841.8	2901.0	2960.2	3019.7
27.0	2761.2	2822.6	2883.9	2945.1	3006.5	3067.9	3129.5

When the station is on some hill, the name should be the popular designation of the elevation, or the name of the person who owns the property on which it is situated.

It is a great mistake to attempt to bequeath to posterity the name of one of the party locating the signal. When no name can be found to attract attention to the locality of the station, a number will answer the purpose of a name. As soon as a station is ready for occupancy it will be found advisable to write a description of the signal, its position, and the way to reach it from some well-known thoroughfare, to be sent to headquarters. This would be of especial service in case the work should cease before the completion of the observations, to be resumed at some future time by another party.

PORTER.

" This point is at the head of Blue Lick, a tributary of the Left Fork of Twelve Pole, in Wayne County, W. Va. It is on the farm of Larkin Maynerd. The signal is built in the form of a tripod, and stands on the highest point of a large field.

" A wagon can be taken up the Twelve Pole from Wayne C. H., and up Blue Lick to the signal. From this point can be seen Scaggs, Pigeon, Williamson, Vance, Runyan, and Rattlesnake."

" Station No. 24: Ford County, Ill.; corner of sections, 14, 15, 22, 23 ; township, 23 ; range, 10 east."

Each station should be provided with an underground mark, consisting, when accessible, of a stone pier with a hole drilled in the top and filled with lead bearing a cross-mark on its upper surface, the intersection forming the centre of the station. The top of the stone should not be within eighteen inches of the surface of the ground, so as to be below the action of frost, and any disturbance likely to arise from a cultivation of the soil. Occasionally it has been found convenient to build above this another pier to a height of eighteen or twenty inches above ground, to serve as a rest for the instrument when the station is occupied, and a stand for the heliotrope when the station is observed upon.

When large stone cannot be had, a section of an earthenware pipe four inches in diameter may be used by filling it with cement and broken stone. The upper surface can be marked with lines before the cement sets, or a nail driven in while it is plastic.

When it is impracticable to dig a hole of any depth for a masonry superstructure on account of a stone ledge immediately underlying the soil, it will be found sufficient to drill in the top of the rock a hole and fill it with lead. Whatever form of underground or permanent station-marks is used, it is essential to have surface, or reference-marks.

These are usually large stones set N., E., S., and W. of the centre, and at such distances that the diagonals joining those at the corners will intersect directly over the centre.

For immediate use it is well to place over the centre a surface-mark, so that should anything happen to the signal before it is finished with, it can be replaced without disturbing the permanent mark.

When the signal is a high tripod, or when it is necessary to raise the instrument at the time the station is occupied, the relative position of the centre of the station and the centre of the instrument must be tested at frequent intervals, as an unequal settling of the signal would deflect it from or towards the centre. The quickest way to determine this relative position is to set up a small theodolite at a convenient distance from the centre, and fix the intersection of the cross-wires on the centre of the underground mark, or reliable surface-mark ; then, by raising the telescope, determine two points on opposite sides of the top of the signal. Then repeat this operation from a position approximately at right angles to the first position. Draw a string from each pair of points so fixed, and the intersection of these strings will indicate the centre. If possible, the instrument should be placed directly over this point; if not, then the distance to the point, and its direction referred to one of the triangle-sides, should be carefully measured and recorded.

Sometimes it happens that, in the case of a very high signal situated on a sharp point, no position can be found from which both the top and the station-mark can be seen. To meet just this difficulty, Mr. Mosman has devised an instrument with a vertical axis resting on levelling-screws, and so adjusted that when freed from errors the telescope revolves around an imaginary axis passing through the intersection of the cross-wires.

The optical features are such as to admit of focusing it on objects at distances varying from a few inches to 150 or 200 feet. To use it, you place it on a support over the centre of the station, the support, of course, having a hole through it. After levelling the instrument, move it until the cross-wires coincide with the station-mark; then, by simply changing the focus, a point can be found in the intersection of these wires. This operation should be repeated with the telescope in different positions; and as different points are obtained, the centre of the figure formed by joining these points will be the one desired.

The reverse operation can also be successfully performed with this instrument.

It sometimes occurs that a straight tree is used as a signal, in which event it is necessary to occupy an eccentric station. This must be marked with as much care as though it were the true station. The method for reducing the observed angles will be given in full on page 143.

In the record-book must be kept a description of the markings of the stations; and when an eccentric position is occupied, the distance and direction already referred to are to be carefully entered.

The method of observing horizontal angles must depend upon the accuracy desired and upon the kind of instrument used. Regarding the maximum error in closing primary triangles to be three seconds, or six for secondary, a number of precautions must be taken. The principal ones may be classed under the following heads:

7

1. Care in bisecting the object observed upon.
2. Stability of the theodolite-support.
3. Elimination of instrumental errors.
4. Preservation of the horizontality of the circle.
5. Rapidity of pointings.
6. Observations at different times of the day.

Conditions 1 and 2 are self-apparent, and the best means of compliance therewith will readily suggest themselves to the observer.

The instructions for eliminating instrumental errors have already been given (see Chap. II.).

When the theodolite is placed in position and levelled, see that the adjustments have not been disturbed before beginning a set of readings. If, while observing, the level shows a change in the horizontality of the circle, do not disturb it until the set is finished. But if the deflection be considerable, the readings must be thrown away.

The advantage of pointing rapidly is the greater certainty of having the same state of affairs when sighting to all of the signals in the circuit, since it diminishes the interval during which there can occur unequal expansion of the circle; twist in the theodolite-support, changes in the illumination of the different signals, or flexure of the circle from any cause.

By making observations at different times of the day, errors arising from lateral reflection may be diminished because of the changes in the condition of the atmosphere.

There are two principal classes of theodolites—repeating- and direction-instruments. The former gives a number of readings in a short time, but a new source of errors is introduced by the repeated clamping and unclamping. However, if the clamps do not produce what is called travelling, the principle of repetitions renders it possible to obtain a large number of readings on all parts of the circle, and thus tends to free the average from the effect of errors of graduation, for if the divisions on one side of the circle are too far apart, there will be other parts on which the divisions are too close. In measuring an angle with a repeater, it is best to set the circle at zero; point on the first station on the left, bisect the signal, see that the circle is clamped, and then turn to the next station. Read and record both verniers, turn the entire instrument back to the initial point and bisect; then unclamp the telescope and point to the second station, clamp, and turn back to the first. Repeat this operation until the whole circle has been passed over; divide the last readings by the number of pointings, and the quotient will be the value to adopt as the average for the two verniers. The advantage of recording the first reading is that it serves as a check on the number of degrees and minutes in the final result.

If there are several angles at a station, it is advisable to read them individually and in all combinations. Calling the angles in their order, 1, 2, 3, 4, and 5, we read and repeat 1, then 2, 3, 4, and 5; afterwards 1, 2, as one angle; then 1, 2, 3, as one; 1, 2, 3, 4, as one; and 1, 2, 3, 4, 5; also 2, 3; 2, 3, 4; and 2, 3, 4, 5; then 3, 4; 3, 4, 5; and, finally, 4, 5, this closing the horizon. The advantage of this can be seen when we take up the adjustment of the angles around a station. When an instrument can be reversed in its Y's, it will be found desirable to make a similar set with the telescope reversed, and record these as *R*.

With a direction-instrument, it is not necessary to make these combinations. The plan is to make 5, 7, 11, 13, 17, 19, or 23 series, by dividing the circle into such a number of parts; as each one is prime to two or three reading-microscopes, no microscope can fall on the same part of the limb twice in measuring the same angle.

Suppose we decide to make eleven series, we first find the initial pointing for each set of the series. One eleventh of $360° = 32° 43' 38''.2$, two elevenths $= 64° 27' 16''.4$, etc.

We set the circle approximately on zero, and turn the entire instrument upon some arbitrary point that can be readily bisected, clamp on this, and make bisection perfect by moving tangent-screw of telescope if necessary. Read and record all the microscopes, taking both forward and backward micrometer-readings as already explained. Turn the telescope until the next signal is bisected; read and record as before; continue around to the last. After recording this last reading, see if the signal is bisected; if so, record the same values as just read for the first on the return set. When the initial point is reached, reverse the telescope and make a set as before, recording this set as R. Then set on the second position and make a complete set, continuing in this way until all of the positions are used.

It is desirable to sight on all of the signals every time, and also on the azimuth-mark if one has been erected; but if one should become indistinct, while all the others show well, this one can be omitted and supplied afterwards. It will be seen at once that by this method we get an angle as the difference of two directions; hence the probable error of an angle will be $\sqrt{2}$ times the probable error of a direction. The record-book should be explicit, giving the time of each pointing, position of circle at the initial point, the position of the telescope, D or R, appearance of signal (the latter is of importance in weighting angles); also, if a tin cone is sighted, the time and direction of the sun referred to the cone must be recorded as data for correcting for phase.

If the triangulation is for general topographic purposes, it will be found advisable to read angles to prominent objects that may be in view, since if one is seen from two well-determined stations its position can be approximately located. Preliminary computations should be carried along in the field, so as to apply reduction from eccentric stations to centre and deduce the probable errors of the angles.

If this falls beyond the predetermined limit, or if the triangles do not close after allowing for spherical excess within the limit prescribed, the angles should be remeasured.

The example here given is taken from record-book just as it came from the field—*d* is the forward, and *d'* the backward micrometer-reading:

HORIZONTAL DIRECTIONS.

Station: Holmes, W. Va.
Observer: A. T. M. Instrument: 114.
Date: Sept. 7, 1881.
Position: 11.

Series and No.	Objects Observed.	Time. h. m.	Tel.	Mic.	°	′	d.	d'.	Mean d.	Remarks.
10	Table Rock....	5 : 10	D	A	32	44	48	48		Weather clear, atmosphere moderately clear.
				B			25	24		
				C			25	25	32.50	
	Somerville	5 : 8	D	A	312	44	74	73		Wind S.W., light. Ther. 97°.5.
				B			50	49		
				C			53	53	58.66	
	Somerville	5 : 13	R	A	132	44	72	71		Reversed.
				B			40	39		
				C			48	47	52.83	
	Table Rock....	5 : 20	R	A	212	44	50	50		
				B			20	19		
				C			30	29	33.0	
11	Table Rock....	5 : 35	R	A	212	44	49	48		
				B			19	19		
				C			30	28	32.16	
	Piney..........	5 : 33	R	A	301	18	64	63		Heliotrope.
				B			35	34		
				C			45	43	47.33	Reversed.

In addition to the determination of the geographic positions of various points by triangulation, it is also possible to obtain with some precision their elevation, for, since we compute the distances between the stations, the only remaining term is the angle of depression or elevation from the station occupied to each that can be seen. This necessitates a determination, by levelling, of the height of the initial point only.

The field-work can be easily described as consisting of a

number of readings of the angles from the zenith to each station. In the computation given on page 90, it will be seen that vertical refraction affects this angle; but if the zenith-distances be measured from each station to the others at the same time, supposing the refraction to be equable throughout the intervening space, the uncertainty caused by the unknown deflection of the sight-line will be eliminated.

But as it is not always feasible to have all the points occupied at the same time, the zenith-distances can be measured on different days, and when possible, under such varying atmospheric conditions as to secure the same average relative refraction. The best time is between the hours 10 A.M. and 3 P.M. The height of the theodolite above ground must be known, as well as that of the signal sighted.

In 1860, Assistant Davidson organized a series of experiments to obtain a comparison of the various methods of determining altitudes. He used a Stackpole level, a rod carefully compared with a standard and levelled in both directions. The measures of zenith-distances were reciprocal. They were made seven times daily for five days. The barometric series consisted of hourly readings during five days of a mercurial barometer, attached, detached, and wet-bulb thermometers. The differences in the altitudes are :

As determined by levelling,   598.74 metres.
    "   "   zenith-distances,   598.64   "
    "   "   atmospheric pressure, 595.26   "

REFERENCES.

U. S. Coast and Geodetic Survey Reports, 1876, pp. 238–401; '80, pp. 96–109; '82, pp. 151–208.

Puissant, Géodésie, vol. i. pp. 350–376.

Bessel, Gradmessung in Ostpreussen, pp. 59–128.

Ordnance Survey, Account of the Principal Triangulation, pp. 1–61.

Struve, Arc du Méridien, vol. i. pp. 1–35.

Publications of the Prussian Geodetic Institute, especially " Das Hessische Dreiecksnetz" and " Das Rheinische Dreiecks- netz," II. Heft.

CHAPTER V.

THEORY OF LEAST SQUARES.

WHEN in the various measurements of a magnitude a number of results are obtained, it is a matter of great importance to know which to regard as correct. That all cannot be correct is apparent, and that some one is true may safely be assumed. Errors which render a magnitude too great are called negative errors, and those which make it too small are positive errors. Should, for instance, the true length of a line be 73.45 chains, and its length found by measurement to be 73.44 chains, the error would be $+$ 0.01 chain; while if the measurement show 73.46 chains the error would be $-$ 0.01 chain.

It may be accepted as a general rule that positive and negative errors are equally probable; also, that small errors are more likely to occur than great ones, since the tendency to commit a great error would be readily detected before recording it, while those smaller could not be easily distinguished from the value afterwards found to be correct.

Let the angle x be measured n times with equal care, so that in each result there is the same liability for an error to occur; let the individual values obtained be $v_1, v_2, \ldots v_n$. Since x is the true value, the errors will be: $x - v_1$, $x - v_2$, $\ldots x - v_n$; these we will denote by $dx_1, dx_2, \ldots dx_n$, and, from what has just been said, some are positive and some are negative. As there exists the same probability for the positive as for the negative errors, and since the individual errors are nearly equal to each other, their sum will nearly amount to zero, and we may put,

$$dx_1 + dx_2 + dx_3 + dx_4 + \ldots + dx_n = 0,$$

or $$(x - v_1) + (x - v_2) \ldots + (x - v_n) = 0,$$

whence $nx = v_1 + v_2 + v_3 + \ldots + v_n.$ Hence:

(1) $x = (v_1 + v_2 + v_3 + \ldots v_n) \div n$, which is simply the arithmetical mean of the n terms. This, however, gives no information as to the value of the errors. If for each positive error we had committed an equal negative error, the arithmetical mean would give the correct value, but this fortuitous elimination can only be expected in an infinite number of observations; even then it will not enable us to form any definite opinion as to the degree of accuracy attained in the individual observations. In order to accomplish this, we must find some means for preventing the positive errors from destroying the negative ones. Gauss found the way by taking into account not the errors themselves, but their squares, which are positive, and hence cannot eliminate one another.

For brevity we will write $[v_n]$ for the series of terms involving v, as $v_1, v_2, v_3, \ldots v_n$, and $S[v_n]$ for the sum of such a series. Hence we may put for the sum of the squares of the errors, $S[d_nx]^2$, or $S[x - v_n]^2$. The value of x will approach the nearest to its correct value when the arithmetical sum of the errors is the smallest, or when the sum of the squares of the errors is a minimum; that is, when $S[d_nx^2]$ is a minimum.

Let $$y = S[d_nx^2];$$

then by differentiation, $\dfrac{dy}{dx} = 2S[d_nx].$

As this is to be a minimum, we place the first differential coefficient = 0,

or $\qquad S[d_n x] = 0,$ $\qquad$ or $\qquad S[(x - v_n)] = 0.$

If $\qquad x - v_1 + x - v_2 + x - v_3 \ldots + x - v_n = 0,$

$$nx = v_1 + v_2 + v_3 \ldots + v_n, \qquad \text{or} \qquad x = \frac{v_1 + v_2 + v_3 \ldots + v_n}{n}$$

a result identical with the one previously obtained.

The converse can also be demonstrated; that is, the arithmetical mean gives to the square of the residuals the minimum,

$$[d_n x] = d_1 x + d_2 x + d_3 x \ldots + d_n x$$
$$= (x - v_1) + (x - v_2) + (x - v_3) \ldots + (x - v_n) = 0;$$

squaring this,

$$[d_n x]^2 = (x - v_1)^2 + (x - v_2)^2 + (x - v_3)^2 \ldots + (x - v_n)^2$$
$$= nx^2 - 2[v_n]x + [v_n]^2,$$

but $\qquad x = \dfrac{[v_n]}{n},$ $\qquad$ and $\qquad x^2 = \dfrac{[v_n]^2}{n^2};$

substituting these values,

$$[d_n x]^2 = \frac{[v_n]^2}{n} - \frac{2[v_n]^2}{n} + [v_n]^2 = [v_n]^2 - \frac{[v_n]^2}{n}. \quad \cdot \quad (1)$$

Suppose we now take some other value, x_1, so that $d_1 x_1, d_2 x_1$ $\ldots d_n x_1$ represent the residuals, then

$$[d_n x_1]^2 = \overline{d_1 x_1}^2 + \overline{d_2 x_1}^2 \ldots + \overline{d_n x_1}^2$$
$$= (x_1 - v_1)^2 + (x_1 - v_2)^2 \ldots + (x_1 - v_n)^2 = 0$$
$$= n x_1^2 - 2[v_n] x_1 + [v_n]^2;$$

substituting in this equation the value for $[v_n]^2$ derived from (1),

$$[d_n x_1]^2 = [d_n x]^2 + n x_1^2 - 2[v_n] x_1 + \frac{[v_n]^2}{n}$$

$$= [d_n x]^2 + n \left(\frac{[v_n]}{n} - x_1 \right)^2, \quad \text{but } \frac{[v_n]}{n} = x;$$

therefore, $\quad [d_n x_1]^2 = [d_n x]^2 + n(x - x_1)^2. \quad \ldots \quad (2)$

Since $(x - x_1)^2$ is always positive, $[d_n x_1]^2$ is greater than $[d_n x]^2$; that is, the square of the residuals when any value other than the arithmetical mean is used, is greater than when the arithmetical mean is taken. From this it is seen that the arithmetical mean is the most probable value ; but the correct value might be a little more or a little less than this mean.

When the individual results are nearly the same, we might be satisfied with any one; but when there is a great range, we accept the average even with some trepidation. Now, if we had some term that depended upon the residuals, the magnitude of this term might be taken as the *measure of precision :* this is what is known as the *probable error.*

The development of an expression for the probable error has been undertaken by many persons, and prosecuted in various ways, but all attaining the same end. The discussion that follows is taken principally from Chauvenet.

Let us recapitulate what are known as the theorems of the theory of probabilities.

1st. Equal positive and negative errors are equally probable, and, in a large series of observations, are equally frequent.

2d. There is a limit of error which the greatest accidental errors do not exceed; if l denote the absolute magnitude of this limit, all the positive errors will be comprised between o and $+ l$, and all the negative errors between o and $- l$, so that the errors are contained within $2l$.

3d. Small errors are more frequent than large ones.

So that the frequency of the error may be considered a function of the error itself. If Δ be an error of a certain magnitude, and its frequency $\varphi\Delta$, this function will be a maximum when $\Delta = 0$, and be o when $\Delta = \pm l$. If we denote the probability of an error Δ by y, we have $y = \varphi\Delta$, an equation of a curve in which Δ is the abscissa and y the ordinate; as Δ has equal values with contrary signs, the curve is symmetrical with respect to the axis y, and for $y = 0$, $\Delta = \pm \infty$.

We shall therefore consider Δ as a continuous variable, and $\varphi\Delta$ as a continuous function of it.

If there are n errors equal to Δ, $n' = \Delta' \ldots$, and the entire number equal to m, the respective probabilities are

$$\varphi\Delta = \frac{n}{m}, \qquad \varphi\Delta' = \frac{n'}{m}, \text{etc.,}$$

and the sum $\quad \varphi\Delta + \varphi\Delta' \ldots = \dfrac{n + n' \ldots}{m} = \dfrac{m}{m} = 1;$

therefore, $\quad \varphi\Delta + \varphi\Delta' + \varphi\Delta'' + \ldots = 1.$

However, the continuity of the curve requires that the successive values of Δ shall differ from one another by an infinitesimal, so that the number of values for $\varphi\Delta$ is infinite.

Let us take the smallest unit of magnitude in the observations as 1, then the probability of the error $\varDelta$ may be regarded as the same as the probability that the error falls between $\varDelta$ and $\varDelta + 1$, and the probability of an error between $\varDelta$ and $\varDelta + i$ will be the sum of the probabilities of the errors $\varDelta$, $\varDelta + 1, \varDelta + 2 \ldots \varDelta + (i - 1)$. By making i small the probability of each of the errors from $\varDelta$ to $\varDelta + i$ will be nearly the same as $\varDelta$, and their sum will approximate $i\varphi\varDelta$. When the interval between the successive errors approximates an infinitesimal, the expression becomes more nearly exact, and for i we may put $d\varDelta$, and write $\varphi\varDelta \cdot d\varDelta$ as the accurate expression for the probability that an error falls between $\varDelta$, and $\varDelta + d\varDelta$. Hence the probability that an error falls between the limits $+ \infty$ and $- \infty$ is the sum of the elements of the form $\varphi\varDelta \cdot d\varDelta$, or the integral $\int_{-\infty}^{+\infty} \varphi\varDelta \cdot d\varDelta = 1$.

Suppose the quantity M be a function of x, y, z, etc., $\varDelta, \varDelta'$, $\varDelta''$, be the errors, and $\varphi\varDelta, \varphi\varDelta', \varphi\varDelta''$, their respective probabilities.

Since the probability of M will be the product of the probabilities of the quantities of which M is a function, we may put $P = \varphi\varDelta \cdot \varphi\varDelta' \cdot \varphi\varDelta'' \ldots$

From preceding principles we know that the most probable system of values of the unknown quantities $x, y, z \ldots$ will be that which makes P a maximum; therefore we obtain the differential coefficient of P with respect to each variable and place it equal to 0. Log P varies with P, and as P is a function of $x, y, z, \ldots$, the differential coefficients of P with respect to $x, y, z, \ldots$, must separately $= 0$; or

$$\frac{1}{P} \cdot \frac{dP}{dx} = 0, \qquad \frac{1}{P} \cdot \frac{dP}{dy} = 0, \qquad \frac{1}{P} \cdot \frac{dP}{dz} = 0. \qquad (1)$$

But, $\qquad \log P = \log \varphi\varDelta + \log \varphi\varDelta' + \log \varphi\varDelta'' \ldots \qquad (2)$

Therefore, $\quad \dfrac{dP}{P} = \dfrac{d\varphi\varDelta}{\varphi\varDelta} + \dfrac{d\varphi\varDelta'}{\varphi\varDelta'} + \dfrac{d\varphi\varDelta''}{\varphi\varDelta''}\cdots$ $\qquad\qquad$ (3)

Divide (3) by dx, dy, and dz, ...

$$\left.\begin{aligned}
\frac{dP}{P \cdot dx} &= \frac{d\varphi\varDelta}{\varphi\varDelta dx} + \frac{d\varphi\varDelta'}{\varphi\varDelta' dx} + \frac{d\varphi\varDelta''}{\varphi\varDelta'' dx}\cdots = 0; \\[2mm]
\frac{dP}{P \cdot dy} &= \frac{d\varphi\varDelta}{\varphi\varDelta dy} + \frac{d\varphi\varDelta'}{\varphi\varDelta' dy} + \frac{d\varphi\varDelta''}{\varphi\varDelta'' dy}\cdots = 0; \\[2mm]
\frac{dP}{P \cdot dz} &= \frac{d\varphi\varDelta}{\varphi\varDelta dz} + \frac{d\varphi\varDelta'}{\varphi\varDelta' dz} + \frac{d\varphi\varDelta''}{\varphi\varDelta'' dz}\cdots = 0;
\end{aligned}\right\} \text{(A)}$$

$$\text{etc.,} \qquad\qquad\qquad \text{etc.;}$$

since the first members are equal to zero, from (1).

In (A) let us place for $\dfrac{d\varphi\varDelta}{\varphi\varDelta}$, $\varphi'\varDelta$. $d\varDelta$; for $\dfrac{d\varphi\varDelta'}{\varphi\varDelta'}$, $\varphi'\varDelta' \cdot d'\varDelta'$.

Then they will become

$$\left.\begin{aligned}
\varphi'\varDelta\frac{d\varDelta}{dx} + \varphi'\varDelta'\frac{d\varDelta'}{dx} + \varphi'\varDelta''\frac{d\varDelta''}{dx}\cdots = 0; \\[2mm]
\varphi'\varDelta\frac{d\varDelta}{dy} + \varphi'\varDelta'\frac{d\varDelta'}{dy} + \varphi'\varDelta''\frac{d\varDelta''}{dy}\cdots = 0; \\[2mm]
\varphi'\varDelta\frac{d\varDelta}{dz} + \varphi'\varDelta'\frac{d\varDelta'}{dz} + \varphi'\varDelta''\frac{d\varDelta''}{dz}\cdots = 0;
\end{aligned}\right\} \text{(B)}$$

$$\text{etc.,} \qquad\qquad\qquad \text{etc.}$$

If x be the correct value of M, M', M'', etc.,

$$\varDelta = M - x, \qquad \varDelta' = M' - x, \qquad \varDelta'' = M'' - x \cdots;$$

from which
$$\frac{d\Delta}{dx} = \frac{d\Delta'}{dx} = \frac{d\Delta''}{dx} \ldots = -1.$$

The first equation at (B) becomes

$$\varphi'(M - x) + \varphi'(M' - x) + \varphi'(M'' - x) \ldots = 0. \quad (4)$$

Now, if in this equation we suppose $M' = M'' \ldots = M - mN$, where m represents the number of observations, and since the arithmetical mean is the most probable value of x,

$$x = \frac{1}{m}(M + M' + M'' \ldots)$$

$$= \frac{1}{m}[M + (m - 1)(M - mN)],$$

since there will be $m - 1$ terms after the first, each equivalent to $M - mN$,

or
$$x = \frac{1}{m}(M + mM - m^2N - M + mN)$$

$$= \frac{1}{m}(mM - m^2N + mN)$$

$$= M - mN + N$$

$$= M - (m - 1)N;$$

or
$$M - x = (m - 1)N,$$

and
$$M' - x = M'' - x = M - mN - x;$$

but $\qquad x = M - mN + N$;

therefore

$$M - mN - x = M - mN - (M - mN + N)$$
$$= M - mN - M + mN - N = -N.$$

Substituting these values for x in (4), we get

$$\varphi'[(m-1)N] + (m-1)\varphi'(-N) = 0,$$

since there are $m - 1$ terms after the first each equal to $-N$. Transposing,

$$\varphi'[(m-1)N] = -(m-1)\,\varphi'(-N),$$
$$\frac{\varphi'[(m-1)N]}{m-1} = -\varphi'(-N);$$

dividing by N,

$$\frac{\varphi'[(m-1)N]}{(m-1)N} = \frac{\varphi'(-N)}{-N}.$$

This is a true expression for all values of m, or $(m - 1)$, or $N(m - 1)$. As the second term is not affected by changes in m, the expression is a constant. By putting $\Delta = (m - 1)N$, we will have $\dfrac{\varphi'\Delta}{\Delta} =$ a constant which is called K.

If $\qquad \dfrac{\varphi'\Delta}{\Delta} = K, \qquad \varphi'\Delta = K\Delta.$

But we supposed $\varphi'\varDelta = \dfrac{d\varphi\varDelta}{\varphi\varDelta \cdot d\varDelta}$ (page 110);

therefore $\dfrac{d\varphi\varDelta}{\varphi\varDelta \cdot d\varDelta} = K\varDelta,$

or $\dfrac{d\varphi\varDelta}{\varphi\varDelta} = K\varDelta \cdot d\varDelta.$

Integrating this, $\log \varphi\varDelta = \tfrac{1}{2}K\varDelta^2 + \log c,$

or $\varphi\varDelta = ce^{\tfrac{1}{2}K\varDelta\varDelta},$

in which e is the Naperian base.

Since $\varphi\varDelta$ must decrease as $\tfrac{1}{2}K$ increases, it must be negative. Placing $-h^2$ for $\tfrac{1}{2}K$, we have

likewise
$$\varphi\varDelta = ce^{-h^2\varDelta^2};$$
$$\varphi\varDelta' = ce^{-h^2\varDelta'^2},$$
$$\varphi\varDelta'' = ce^{-h^2\varDelta''^2},$$
$$\text{etc.}$$

We found that $P = \varphi\varDelta \cdot \varphi\varDelta' \cdot \varphi\varDelta'' \ldots;$
therefore $P = c(e^{-h^2\varDelta^2} + e^{-h^2\varDelta'^2} + e^{-h^2\varDelta''^2} \ldots),$

or $P = c\Sigma_\varDelta^{\varDelta^n} e^{-h^2\varDelta^2}; \ldots \ldots \ldots \quad (5)$

which represents the probabilities of all errors from $\varDelta$ to $\varDelta^n$ inclusive.

8

To determine the constant c, we will take the integral on page 109,

$$\int_{-\infty}^{+\infty} \varphi\varDelta \,.\, d\varDelta = 1,$$

and substitute for $\varphi\varDelta$, $ce^{-h^2\varDelta^2}$,

$$\int_{-\infty}^{+\infty} ce^{-h^2\varDelta^2} d\varDelta = 1.$$

We will write $\quad t^2 = h^2\varDelta^2, \quad$ and $\quad \varDelta = \dfrac{t}{h};$

then we obtain

$$\int_{-\infty}^{+\infty} ce^{-t^2} d\frac{t}{h};$$

factoring $\dfrac{c}{h}$,

$$\frac{c}{h}\int_{-\infty}^{+\infty} e^{-t^2} dt = 1.$$

Let

$$m = \int_{-\infty}^{+\infty} dt\,e^{-t^2};$$

then, since this integral is independent of the variable, we may also put

$$m = \int_{-\infty}^{+\infty} du\,e^{-u^2};$$

by multiplication,

$$m^2 = \int_{-\infty}^{+\infty} \int_{-\infty}^{+\infty} dt\,.\,du\,e^{-(t^2+u^2)}. \quad . \quad . \quad . \quad (6)$$

If we integrate between the limits ∞ and 0, then between the limits 0 and — ∞ their sums will be the value of the definite integral between the limits + ∞ and — ∞.

We shall now place $u = tv$, and $du = tdv$; then (6) becomes

$$m^2 = \int_0^\infty \int_0^\infty dv \, . \, dt \, . \, te^{-t^2(1+v^2)}$$

$$= \int_0^\infty dv \int_0^\infty dt \, . \, te^{-t^2(1+v^2)} \, ;$$

v being regarded as the variable, and t the constant,

$$\cdot \, m^2 = \int_0^\infty dv \, . \, \frac{1}{2(1+v^2)} = \tfrac{1}{2}(\tan^{-1}\infty - \tan^{-1}0) = \frac{\pi}{4} \, ;$$

$$m = \int_0^\infty dte^{-t^2} = \frac{\sqrt{\pi}}{2}$$

Without changing notation :

$$m = \int_{-\infty}^0 dte^{-t^2} = \frac{\sqrt{\pi}}{2} \, ,$$

or the total integral, $\displaystyle\int_{-\infty}^{+\infty} dte^{-t^2} = \sqrt{\pi}.$

But

$$\frac{c}{h}\int_{-\infty}^{+\infty} e^{-t^2} dt = 1 \, ;$$

therefore $\dfrac{c}{h}\sqrt{\pi} = 1,$ $c\sqrt{\pi} = h,$ $c = \dfrac{h}{\sqrt{\pi}}.$

Placing this value for c in $\varphi\Delta = ce^{-h^2\Delta^2}$,

we have $\varphi\Delta = \dfrac{h}{\sqrt{\pi}}e^{-h^2\Delta^2}.$

This method of obtaining the value for the definite integral is taken from Laplace, *Mécanique Céleste.*

Identical results are obtained by different methods by Poisson and Airy.

The probability that the error falls between Δ and $\Delta + d\Delta$ is $\dfrac{h}{\sqrt{\pi}}e^{-h^2\Delta^2}d\Delta$, and that it falls between the limits 0 and a is $\dfrac{h}{\sqrt{\pi}}\displaystyle\int_{\Delta=0}^{\Delta=a} e^{-h^2\Delta^2}d\Delta$, as already explained.

Let $t = h\Delta$,   then $\Delta = \dfrac{t}{h}$; and $a' = \Delta\dfrac{t}{h}$,   then $t = ah.$

Substitute these values in the last integral; it becomes

$$\frac{2}{\sqrt{\pi}}\int_{t=0}^{t=ah} e^{-t^2}dt$$

after multiplying by two, since the sum of negative errors is considered equal to the positive errors.

This integral has been computed for values of t. A table of these is given in Merriman's " Least Squares."

From this table it is found that the error which occupies the middle place in the series of errors, arranged in the order of their magnitude, has the same number of errors above as below; therefore, the error satisfying this condition is that for which the value of the integral is $\frac{1}{2}$. If we designate the corresponding value of t by ρ, we find from the same table that

$$\rho = 0.4769.$$

If r be the error in a series of observations whose precision is h, we can put $\rho = hr$, $r = \dfrac{\rho}{h}$, $h = \dfrac{\rho}{r}$.

MEAN OF THE ERRORS.

If we have a series of m errors $\varDelta$, $\varDelta' \ldots$; a positive, and a negative each equal to $\varDelta$, or $2a$ in all, the probabilities are that in all there will be $\dfrac{2a}{m}$, $\dfrac{2a'}{m} \ldots$ The mean of these errors, supposing each repeated a number of times proportional to the probability of its occurrence, is $\dfrac{2a\varDelta + 2a'\varDelta' + 2a''\varDelta''}{m} \ldots$

$$= 2\varDelta\frac{a}{m} + 2\varDelta'\frac{a'}{m} + 2\varDelta''\frac{a''}{m} \ldots$$

The probability of an error $\varDelta$ has been shown equal to $\varphi\varDelta \,.\, d\varDelta$. So that the above expression for an infinite number of terms approximates a series of terms of the form $2\varDelta \,.\, \varphi\varDelta \,.\, d\varDelta$. But on page 116

$$\varphi\varDelta = \frac{h}{\sqrt{\pi}}e^{-h^2\varDelta^2};$$

multiplying by $2\Delta . d\Delta$, we have

$$2\Delta\varphi\Delta . d\Delta = \frac{2h}{\sqrt{\pi}}\Delta e^{-h^2\Delta^2}d\Delta.$$

If η be the mean error,

$$\eta = \int_{0}^{\infty} \frac{2h}{\sqrt{\pi}}\Delta e^{-h^2\Delta^2}d\Delta = \frac{1}{h\sqrt{\pi}}.$$

$h = \dfrac{\rho}{r};$　　　therefore　　　$\eta = \dfrac{1}{\dfrac{\rho}{r}\sqrt{\pi}} = \dfrac{r}{\rho\sqrt{\pi}} = 1.1829r;$

or　　　　　　$r = 0.8453\eta,$　　　since　　　$\rho = 0.4769$

As was stated elsewhere, it is not feasible to obtain the mean of the error, since the negative and positive errors being theoretically equal, their sum will become zero. So we take the sum of the squares of these errors, and the square which is the mean of these squares is the square of the *mean error*.

That is, if ε be the mean error,

$$\varepsilon^2 = \int_{-\infty}^{+\infty} \frac{h}{\sqrt{\pi}}\Delta^2 e^{-h^2\Delta^2}d\Delta = \frac{1}{2h^2};$$

$$\varepsilon = \frac{1}{h\sqrt{2}} = \frac{1}{\dfrac{\rho}{r}\sqrt{2}} = \frac{r}{\rho\sqrt{2}} = 1.4826r;$$

$$r = 0.6745\varepsilon.$$

This value of r is the probable error of any one of the observed values of the unknown quantity, x.

Let us now look for an expression for the value of the arithmetical mean, r_0.

Equation (5), $P = \varphi\Delta + \varphi\Delta' + \varphi\Delta'' \ldots$
$$= c(e^{-h^2\Delta^2} + e^{-h^2\Delta'^2} + e^{-h^2\Delta''^2} \ldots$$
$$= h^m\pi^{-\frac{1}{2}m}e^{-h^2(\Delta^2 + \Delta'^2 + \Delta''^2 \ldots)}.$$

The most probable value of the observed quantity is that which makes P a maximum, or that makes $\Delta^2 + \Delta'^2 + \Delta''^2 \ldots$ a minimum.

But it has been shown that the arithmetical mean renders the sum of the squares a minimum; therefore P represents the probability of the arithmetical mean when $\Delta, \Delta', \Delta'' \ldots$ represent the residuals referred to this mean. The probability of any other value of x, as $x + dx$, will be

$$P' = h^m\pi^{-\frac{1}{2}m}e^{-h^2\{(\Delta-d)^2 + (\Delta'-d)^2 + (\Delta''-d)^2\}}$$
$$= h^m\pi^{-\frac{1}{2}m}e^{-h^2\{[\Delta^2] - 2[\Delta]d + md^2\}};$$

but $\Delta^2 = m\varepsilon^2$, $P' = h^m\pi^{-\frac{1}{2}m}e^{-h^2(m\varepsilon^2 + md^2)}$;

$[\Delta]$, being the sum of the errors, $= 0$.

$$P = h^m\pi^{-\frac{1}{2}m}e^{-h^2m\varepsilon^2},$$

since $d = 0$, when $x = x_0$,

$$P : P' :: h^m\pi^{-\frac{1}{2}m}e^{-h^2m\varepsilon^2} : h^m\pi^{-\frac{1}{2}m}e^{-h^2(m\varepsilon^2 + md^2)},$$
$$P : P' :: 1 : e^{-h^2md^2},$$

dividing the second ratio by the third term.

If $m = 1$, $P : P' :: 1 : e^{-h^2d^2}$.

In this single observation the probability of zero-error, as in the arithmetical mean, is to the probability of error, d, as $1 : e^{-h^2 d^2}$.

As h is the measure of precision of a single observation, h^2 will be the square of this measure.

In the expression for the error of the arithmetical mean we find for the *square* of the measure of precision of m observations $h^2 m$; therefore the measure of precision of the arithmetical mean of m quantities is $h \sqrt{m}$. That is, the measure of precision of the mean increases as the square root of the number of observations.

$$r_{\text{o}} = \frac{r}{\sqrt{m}}, \qquad r = 0.6745 \varepsilon, \qquad r_{\text{o}} = .6745 \varepsilon_{\text{o}};$$

therefore

$$\varepsilon_{\text{o}} = \frac{\varepsilon}{\sqrt{m}}.$$

If $v, v_1, v_2 \ldots$ be the observed values of a quantity whose mean is x, the residuals will be $u, u_{\prime}, u_{\prime\prime}$, or $x - v, x - v_{\prime}, x - v_{\prime\prime} \ldots$ If x were the correct value, $x - v, x - v_{\prime}, x - v_{\prime\prime}$ would be equal to $\Delta, \Delta', \Delta'' \ldots$

and

$$m \varepsilon^2 = [\Delta^2] = [u^2];$$

$$\varepsilon^2 = \frac{[u^2]}{m}, \qquad \varepsilon = \sqrt{\frac{[u^2]}{m}}.$$

However, this does not consider the mean errors of the residuals. Suppose $\Delta = u - d, \Delta' = u' - d, \Delta'' = u'' - d, \ldots$

$$[\Delta^2] = m\varepsilon^2 = (u - d)^2 + (u' - d)^2 + (u'' - d)^2 \ldots$$
$$= [u^2] - 2[u]d + md^2$$
$$= [u^2] + md^2, \quad \text{since } [u] = 0.$$

d^2 may be taken $= \varepsilon_0^2 = \dfrac{\varepsilon^2}{m};$

$$md^2 = m\frac{\varepsilon^2}{m} = \varepsilon^2;$$

so that
$$[\Delta^2] = [u^2] + \varepsilon^2 = m\varepsilon^2;$$

transposing
$$m\varepsilon^2 - \varepsilon^2 = [u^2];$$

$$\varepsilon^2(m - 1) = [u^2];$$

$$\varepsilon^2 = \frac{[u^2]}{m - 1}, \qquad \varepsilon = \sqrt{\frac{[u^2]}{m - 1}};$$

$$r = 0.6745\sqrt{\frac{[u^2]}{m - 1}};$$

$$\varepsilon_0 = \frac{\varepsilon}{\sqrt{m}} = \sqrt{\frac{[u^2]}{m(m - 1)}};$$

$$r_0 = \pm\, 0.6745\sqrt{\frac{[u^2]}{m(m - 1)}}.$$

To determine the probable error of the arithmetical mean, we find the difference between each individual result and the mean, square these quantities, and divide their sum by

$m(m - 1)$, where m represents the number of individual results. Extract the square root of this quotient, and multiply by 0.6745; the product will be the probable error of the arithmetical mean.

The whole operation can be performed by logarithms.

To illustrate:

Angle.	u.	u^2.
$66° - 54' - 12.''5$	$+ 1.1$	1.21
13. 5	$+ 0.1$	.01
11. 3	$+ 2.3$	5.29
16. 5	$- 2.9$	8.41
12. 3	$+ 1.3$	1.69
15. 5	$- 1.9$	3.61
Average 13. 6		$20.22 = [u^2]$

The probable error of a single determination,

$$r = \pm\, 0.6745\sqrt{\frac{20.22}{5}} = \pm\, 1''.33.$$

The probable error of the arithmetical mean,

$$r_i = \pm\, 0.6745\sqrt{\frac{20.22}{6 \times 5}} = \pm\, 0''.54.$$

If the probable errors of the means of different sets of determinations have been found, their relative weights may be readily ascertained. Let h, h_1, h_2 . . . be the measures of precision, and r, r_1, r_2 . . . the probable errors.

Suppose we compare our individual observations with a fictitious standard whose mean error is ε_1; and the actual observations with a mean error ε, need w in number to reduce the mean error of their arithmetical mean to ε_0; this gives $\varepsilon_0 = \dfrac{\varepsilon_1}{\sqrt{w}}$, or $w\varepsilon_0 = \varepsilon_1^2$. Likewise any other set would give $w_1\varepsilon_0'^2 = \varepsilon_1^2$, or $w_1\varepsilon_0'^2 = w\varepsilon^2$; that is, $w_1 : w :: \varepsilon_0^2 : \varepsilon_0'^2$. We call $w, w_1 \ldots$, etc., the weights; they are reciprocally proportional to their probable errors.

The arithmetical mean of n_1 observations of weight w, n_2 of weight w_2, etc., would be

$$x = \frac{n_1 w_1 + n_2 w_2 \ldots + n_n w_n}{w_1 + w_2 \ldots + w_n},$$

or $\quad x = \dfrac{[nw]}{[w]}, \quad$ and $\quad \varepsilon = \dfrac{\varepsilon_1}{\sqrt{(w_1 + w_2 \ldots w_n)}} = \dfrac{\varepsilon_1}{\sqrt{[w]}},$

where ε_1 is the mean error of unit weight.

Let $\quad v_1 = n_1 - x, \quad v_2 = n_2 - x, \quad v_3 = n_3 - x,$

$$\varepsilon'^2 = v_1^2 + \varepsilon_0^2; \quad \text{but} \quad w_1\varepsilon'^2 = \varepsilon_1^2 = w_1 v_1^2 + w_1 \varepsilon_0^2,$$

and $\hspace{4cm} \varepsilon_1^2 = w_2 v_2^2 + w_2 \varepsilon_0^2$, etc.

If m be the sum of such terms,

$$m\varepsilon_1^2 = [wv^2] + [w]\varepsilon_0^2 = [wv^2] + \varepsilon_1^2$$

$$\varepsilon_1 = \sqrt{\frac{[wv^2]}{m - 1}};$$

this, substituted in the value of ε_0, gives

$$\varepsilon_0 = \sqrt{\frac{[wv^2]}{[w](m-1)}}.$$

In figure- or station-adjustment, if the number of repetitions, or some other well-established reason, does not afford weights for the averages used, the reciprocals of their probable errors can be used. While in the development of the foregoing formulæ there were a number of assumptions, and some approximations to cause cautious persons to distrust the absolute rigor of the results, it will be apparent to all that the arithmetical mean deserves a confidence that varies with different cases.

Suppose in measuring an angle ten results are obtained individually differing considerably among themselves. In another measurement of the same angle ten other results are secured with a very small range; now, if the average be the same in these two cases, the latter would be more readily accepted, as the residuals are individually smaller. So we need some exponent of confidence that is a function of the residuals; and if our accepted value of the probable error is not *absolutely* correct, it will afford us some information as to the agreement of the individual results with the arithmetical mean, and in a number of different determinations it gives us all the *relative* information we need.

I shall add just here, without demonstration, other formulæ in general use in determining probable errors:

Probable error of a single observation,

$$r = 0.6745\sqrt{\frac{[u^2]}{m-1}}.$$

Probable error of the arithmetical mean,

$$r_{\bullet} = 0.6745\sqrt{\frac{[u^2]}{m(m-1)}};$$

If m = number of observed angles ;
             r = number of conditions in a chain ;

probable error of an adjusted angle $= \sqrt{\dfrac{m-r}{m}}$ times prob-

able error of an observed angle, supposing the weights approximately equal (Walker).

If an angle be determined by a direction-instrument, its value
will be the difference of two directions; so that if a is the
probable error of a direction, $a\sqrt{2}$ will be the probable error
of the angle.

If $r_1, r_2, r_3 \ldots$ be the probable errors of different segments
of a base-line, the probable error of the line as a whole, $R =$
$\sqrt{r_1^2 + r_2^2 + r_3^2} \ldots$

We have now shown how to determine the probable error
of an angle or a base-line. The next subject to consider is to
what extent these errors in an angle or in a base will affect the
computed parts. As the errors just referred to are small in
comparison with the magnitudes themselves, we may omit in
all the discussions into which they enter all products, and powers above the first. All geodetic computations are based upon
formulæ relating to triangles, so we will investigate those expressions which are of most frequent occurrence. Denoting
the sides of a plane triangle by a, b, and c, the corresponding
opposite angles by A, B, and C, and the errors with which they
may be affected by da, db, dc, dA, dB, and dC, we can find by

computation the value of any three if the values of the other three be known (provided one be a side). The following formulæ are those most frequently used :

(1) $$a \cdot \sin B = b \cdot \sin A \ ;$$

(2) $$c = a \cdot \cos B + b \cdot \cos A \ ;$$

(3) $$A + B + C = 180°.$$

As *da* represents the correction to *a*, $a + da$ will be the correct value of *a*, or $a + da$, $b + db$, $c + dc$, $A + dA$, $B + dB$, $C + dC$, will be the true values. Substituting these in equations (1), (2), (3), we shall have :

(4) $$(a + da) \sin (B + dB) = (b + db) \sin (A + dA) \ ;$$

(5) $$(c + dc) = (a + da) \cos (B + dB) + (b + db) \cos (A + dA) ;$$

(6) $$A + dA + B + dB + C + dC = 180°.$$

But $$\sin (B + dB) = \sin B + dB \cdot \cos B,$$

since $$\sin dB = dB, \quad \text{and} \quad \cos dB = 1 \ ;$$

also $$\sin (A + dA) = \sin A + dA \cos A \ ;$$
$$\cos (B + dB) = \cos B - dB \sin B \ ;$$
$$\cos (A + dA) = \cos A - dA \sin A.$$

Introducing these values in (4), (5), (6), and omitting all products of $da \cdot db$, etc., we shall get

$$a \cdot \sin B + da \cdot \sin B + a \cdot dB \cos B = b \cdot \sin A + db \cdot \sin A$$
$$+ b \cdot dA \cos A \; ;$$

$$c + dc = a \cdot \cos B + da \cdot \cos B - a \cdot dB \cdot \sin B + b \cdot \cos A$$
$$+ db \cdot \cos A - b \cdot dA \cdot \sin A;$$

$$A + B + C + dA + dB + dC = 180°.$$

Subtracting equations (1), (2), (3), from these just given, we obtain:

(7) $da \cdot \sin B + a \cdot dB \cos B = db \cdot \sin A + b \cdot dA \cos A \; ;$

(8) $dc = da \cdot \cos B - a \cdot dB \sin B + db \cdot \cos A - b \cdot dA \sin A \; ;$

(9) $$dA + dB + dC = 0.$$

In a similar way, expressions can be obtained for the other parts, as: .

(10) $dc \cdot \sin A + c \cdot dA \cos A = da \cdot \sin C + a \cdot dC \cdot \cos C;$

(11) $db \cdot \sin C + b \cdot dC \cdot \cos C = dc \cdot \sin B + c \cdot dB \cdot \cos B;$

(12) $da = dc \cdot \cos B - c \cdot dB \sin B + db \cdot \cos C - b \cdot dC \sin C;$

(13) $db = da \cdot \cos C - a \cdot dC \sin C + dc \cdot \cos A - c \cdot dA \sin A.$

Suppose that in a triangle c, A, and B are given, and by means of them the values a, b, and C are computed. Knowing the limits of errors with which these quantities are affected, it is required to find the limits of the errors with which the computed quantities are affected; that is, knowing dc, dA, and

dB, we are to determine da, db, and dC. From equations (7) and (8) we have :

(14) $dC = -dA - dB$;

(15) $da \cdot \sin B - db \cdot \sin A = -a \cdot dB \cos B + b \cdot dA \cos A$;

(16) $da \cdot \cos B + db \cdot \cos A = dc + a \cdot dB \sin B + b \cdot dA \sin A.$

Multiplying (15) by $\cos A$, (16) by $\sin A$ and adding, we get :

(17) $da(\sin A \cdot \cos B + \cos A \cdot \sin B) = dc \cdot \sin A + b \cdot dA$
$$- a \cdot dB(\cos A \cos B - \sin A \sin B),$$

or, $da \cdot \sin (A + B) = dc \cdot \sin A + b \cdot dA - a \cdot dB \cdot \cos (A + B)$,

$$da = dc \cdot \frac{\sin A}{\sin (A + B)} + \frac{b \cdot dA}{\sin (A + B)} - a \cdot dB \frac{\cos (A + B)}{\sin (A + B)}.$$

Also multiplying (15) by $\cos B$, (16) by $\sin B$, and subtracting, we get :

$$db \cdot \sin (A + B) = dc \cdot \sin B + a \cdot dB - b \cdot dA \cdot \cos (A + B),$$

$$db = dc \frac{\sin B}{\sin (A + B)} + \frac{a \cdot dB}{\sin (A + B)} - b dA \frac{\cos (A + B)}{\sin (A + B)}.$$

Since $\sin (A + B) = \sin C$, and $\cos (A + B) = -\cos C$, we can write :

$$da = dc \frac{\sin A}{\sin C} + \frac{b \cdot dA}{\sin C} + a \cdot dB \frac{\cos C}{\sin C},$$

$$db = dc\frac{\sin B}{\sin C} + \frac{a \cdot dB}{\sin C} + b \cdot dA\frac{\cos C}{\sin C}.$$

And, again, since $\sin A : \sin C :: a : c$, $\sin B : \sin C :: b : c$, and for $\cos C : \sin C$ we may put $\cot C$, the equations then reduce to the following very simple form:

$$da = dc\frac{a}{c} + \frac{b \cdot dA}{\sin C} + a \cdot dB \cot C,$$

$$db = dc \cdot \frac{b}{c} + \frac{a \cdot dB}{\sin C} + b \cdot dA \cot C;$$

or, obtaining the relation between da and a, db and b,

$$\frac{da}{a} = \frac{dc}{c} + \frac{b \cdot dA}{a \cdot \sin C} + dB \cdot \cot C,$$

$$\frac{db}{b} = \frac{dc}{c} + \frac{a \cdot dB}{b \cdot \sin C} + dA \cdot \cot C.$$

Suppose $c = 564.8$, $A = 61°\ 12'\ 12''$, $B = 74°\ 16'\ 30''$, and that the error in c referred to c, or $\frac{dc}{c}$, be less than 0.0001, and the maximum error in A and B is $1''$.

It is required to compute $\frac{da}{a}$, $\frac{db}{b}$, and dC.

$\log b = 2.8894998$	$\log a = 2.8487359$
$\log dA = 4.6855749$	$\log \sin C = 9.8458288$
7.5750747	2.6945647
2.6945647	
4.8805100 $=$ log of second term.	

9

$$\begin{array}{l} \log dB = 4.6855749 \\ \log \cot C = 0.0072518 \\ \hline 4.6928267 \quad = \log \text{ of third term.} \end{array}$$

First term $= 0.0001000$
Second term $= 0.0000076$
Third term $= 0.0000049$

$$\begin{array}{l} \hline 0.0001125 \quad = \text{ error of } a \text{ proportional to the} \\ \text{side } a. \end{array}$$

$$\begin{array}{ll} \log a = 2.8487359 & \qquad \log b = 2.8894978 \\ \log dB = 4.6855749 & \qquad \log \sin C = 9.8458288 \\ \hline 7.5343108 & \qquad 2.7353266 \\ 2.7353266 & \\ \hline 4.7989842 \quad = \log \text{ of second term.} \end{array}$$

$$\begin{array}{l} \log \cot C = 0.0072518 \\ \log dA = 4.6855749 \\ \hline 4.6928267 \quad = \log \text{ of third term.} \end{array}$$

First term $= 0.00010000$
Second term $= 0.00000629$
Third term $= 0.00000493$

$$\begin{array}{l} \hline 0.00011122 \quad = \text{ error of } b \text{ proportional to } b. \end{array}$$

The discussion of these formulæ will develop some very interesting facts concerning the best-shaped triangles to make use of in prosecuting accurate geodetic work. Upon inspecting the equations it will be seen that the denominators of each term of the second members is $\sin (A + B)$, consequently when $A + B$ is nearly 180°, or when C is very small, those terms involving $\sin C$ or $\sin (A + B)$ as a denominator will be made quite large, and will give to da or db a value unduly great.

Again, the second members will have the smallest value when sin C has its greatest value or when $C = 90°$; supposing that $C = 90°$, then placing sin $C =$ sin $90° = 1$, the equations reduce to the form

$$\frac{da}{a} = \frac{dc}{c} + \frac{b}{a}dA, \qquad \frac{db}{b} = \frac{dc}{c} + \frac{a}{b}dB.$$

Should dA and dB be of about the same value, and b be greater than a, or $b : a$ greater than 1, and $a : b$ be less than 1, we will have $da : a$ greater than $db : b$; or if b is less than a we will have $da : a$ less than $db : b$.

From which we can see that it will be best when $a = b$, consequently when $A = B$. Remembering what has just been said, we see that the right isosceles triangle is theoretically the best form of triangle to make use of.

From a similar discussion it will be apparent that if b or a were the given side, the smallest error in the other quantities would occur when B or $A = 90°$.

As all the angles cannot be each equal to $90°$, the best triangle is the equilateral. A similar value can be obtained by direct differentiation.

$$a = \frac{\sin A}{\sin B} \cdot b, \qquad da = d\left(\frac{\sin A}{\sin B} \cdot b\right) = d\left(\frac{\sin A}{\sin B}\right) \cdot b + db\frac{\sin A}{\sin B}.$$

$$d\left(\frac{\sin A}{\sin B}\right)b = \frac{b \cdot \cos A \cdot \sin B \cdot dA - b \cdot \sin A \cos B \cdot dB}{\sin^2 B}$$

$$= \frac{b \cdot \cos A \cdot dA}{\sin B} - \frac{b \cdot \sin A}{\sin B} \cdot \frac{\cos B}{\sin B} \cdot dB.$$

Since $\dfrac{b}{\sin B} = \dfrac{c}{\sin A}$, we may write for $\dfrac{b \cdot \cos A \cdot dA}{\sin B}$,

$$\dfrac{a \cdot \cos A \cdot dA}{\sin A} = a \cot A \cdot dA.$$

Also, since $a = \dfrac{b \cdot \sin A}{\sin B}$, and $\dfrac{\cos B}{\sin B} = \cot B$,

$$-\dfrac{b \sin A}{\sin B} \cdot \dfrac{\cos B}{\sin B} \cdot dB = -a \cdot \cot B \cdot dB;$$

therefore, $da = \dfrac{\sin A}{\sin B} db - a \cdot \cot B \cdot dB + a \cot A \cdot dA.$

Or, by logarithms,

$$\log a = \log \sin A + \log b - \log \sin B;$$

differentiating,

$$\dfrac{da}{a} = \dfrac{\cos A \cdot dA}{\sin A} + \dfrac{db}{b} - \dfrac{\cos B \cdot dB}{\sin B}$$

$$= \cot A \cdot dA + \dfrac{db}{b} - \cot B \cdot dB;$$

$$da = a \cot A \cdot dA + \dfrac{a}{b} \cdot db - a \cot B \cdot dB;$$

$$\dfrac{a}{b} = \dfrac{\sin A}{\sin B};$$

hence, $da = \dfrac{\sin A}{\sin B} db - a \cot B \cdot dB + a \cot A \cdot dA.$

Given in a triangle the values of c, A, and C; required to compute the values of a, b, and B, and so find the limits of errors of the latter, supposing the errors of the former are known.

From the equations already given we find:

$$dB = -dA - dC;$$
$$da \cdot \sin (A + B) = dc \cdot \sin A + b \cdot dA - a \cdot dB \cdot \cos (A + B);$$
$$db \cdot \sin (A + B) = dc \cdot \sin B + a \cdot dB - b \cdot dA \cdot \cos (A + B).$$

But $\sin (A + B) = \sin C$,   and $\cos (A + B) = -\cos C$;

hence, $da \cdot \sin C = dc \cdot \sin A + b \cdot dA + a \cdot dB \cdot \cos C;$
$\qquad db \cdot \sin C = dc \cdot \sin B + a \cdot dB + b \cdot dA \cdot \cos C;$

$$da = \frac{dc \cdot a}{c} + \frac{b \cdot dA}{\sin C} + \frac{a \cdot dB \cdot \cos C}{\sin C}.$$

Since $dB = -dA - dC$, we may write:

$$\frac{da}{a} = \frac{dc}{c} + \frac{b \cdot dA}{a \cdot \sin C} - \frac{dA \cdot \cos C}{\sin C} - \frac{dC \cdot \cos C}{\sin C},$$
$$= \frac{dc}{c} + \frac{(b - a \cos C) dA}{a \cdot \sin C} - dC \cdot \cot C;$$

since $b = a \cos C + c \cos A$, we may put $c \cos A$ for $b - a \cos C$,

then $\dfrac{da}{a} = \dfrac{dc}{c} + \dfrac{C \cdot \cos A \cdot dA}{a \cdot \sin C} - dC \cdot \cot C;$

but $a \cdot \sin C = C \cdot \sin A,$

therefore $\dfrac{da}{a} = \dfrac{dc}{c} + dA \cdot \cot A - dC \cdot \cot C.$

Likewise, $$\frac{db}{b} = \frac{dc \cdot \sin B}{b \sin C} + \frac{a \cdot dB}{b \sin C} + \frac{dA \cdot \cos C}{\sin C},$$

$$= \frac{dc}{c} - \frac{a \cdot dA}{b \sin C} - \frac{a \cdot dC}{b \sin C} + \frac{dA \cos C}{\sin C},$$

$$= \frac{dc}{c} + \frac{(b \cos C - a)dA}{b \cdot \sin C} - \frac{a \cdot dC}{b \sin C},$$

$$= \frac{dc}{c} - \frac{c \cdot \cos B \cdot dA}{b \sin C} - \frac{a \cdot dC}{b \cdot \sin C},$$

$$= \frac{dc}{c} - dA \cdot \cot B - \frac{a \cdot dC}{b \cdot \sin C}.$$

Let $c = 450$, $A = 53° 19' 16''$, $C = 61° 42' 32''$, we will find by computation $B = 64° 58' 12''$, $a = 409.855$, $b = 463.05$.

Suppose that c be reliable to within 0.0001 of its entire length, so that $dc \div c = 0.0001$, and let $dA = dC = 5''$:

log dA = 5.3845449	log dC = 5.3845449
log cot A = 9.8720420	log cot C = 9.7309796

$dA \cdot \cot A$ = 0.00001805
$dc \div c$ = 0.00010000
$dC \cdot \cot C$ = 0.00001 3047

$da \div a$ = 0.000131097
log dA = 5.3845449
log cot B = 9.6692660

log $dA \cdot \cot B$ = 5.0538109 = 0.000011319
log a = 2.6126301
log dC = 5.3845449

log $(a \cdot dC)$ = 7.9971750
log b = 2.6656276
log sin C = 9.9447545

log $(b \cdot \sin C)$ = 2.6103821, log $(a \cdot dC \div b \cdot \sin C)$ = 5.3867929

$$dA \cdot \cot B = 0.000011319$$
$$a \cdot dC \div b \cdot \sin C = 0.000024366$$

Subtracting the sum of these two quantities from $dc \div c$, we get

$$db \div b = 0.000064315, \qquad dB = -(5'' + 5'') = -10''.$$

Since dC may be either positive or negative, we may select the sign which will give the maximum value for the error $da \div a$. We have therefore added the expression $dC \cdot \cot C$.

In the following discussion, we will do the same, supposing the errors committed in measuring A and B were nearly equal and of the same sign.

When they are nearly equal and of the same sign, according to the equation already given, they will compensate one another. But should dc have the same sign as dA and dC, it would lessen the value of da when we have $dC \cdot \cot C$ greater than $dA \cdot \cot A$, since the amount of error committed in measuring the angles is less than that of the measured side.

The value, therefore, of $da \div a$ will become the least when C is less than A and acute. But if A be obtuse, consequently $\cot A$ negative (assuming dA and dC to be positive), $da \div a$ will become the least when C is acute, for then the last two terms are to be subtracted from $dc \div c$.

For $A = 90°$, the third term will disappear entirely, which circumstance will be advantageous with respect to $da \div a$.

In regard to the side a, A must, therefore, be either a right angle or obtuse, and C as small as possible.

The same reasonings apply with respect to b, with the additional circumstance that B should be also very small.

Therefore, in the present instance, a large value for A and small values for B and C will produce the least errors.

Suppose we have the two sides and the included angle with their limiting errors given, and wish to find the limiting errors of the unknown or computed parts; that, is having a, b, and C, to compute the value of the errors in c, A, and B.

From equations (7), (8), and (9) we have

(1) $$dA + dB = - dC;$$

(2) $a \cdot dB \cdot \cos B - b \cdot dA \cdot \cos A = db \cdot \sin A - da \cdot \sin B;$

(3) $dc + a \cdot dB \cdot \sin B + b \cdot dA \cdot \sin A = db \cdot \cos A + da \cdot \cos B.$

Substituting for dA, $- (dC + dB)$, (2) becomes

(4) $a \cdot dB \cdot \cos B + b \cdot \cos A \,(dB + dC) = -da \cdot \sin B + db \cdot \sin A.$

By expanding and transposing we get

(5) $(a \cdot \cos B + b \cdot \cos A)dB = - da \cdot \sin B + db \cdot \sin A$
$$- b \cdot dC \cdot \cos A.$$

Putting c for $a \cdot \cos B + b \cdot \cos A$,

(6) $c \cdot dB = - da \cdot \sin B + db \cdot \sin A - b \cdot dC \cdot \cos A,$

likewise,

(7) $c \cdot dA = dA \cdot \sin B - db \cdot \sin A - a \cdot dC \cdot \cos B.$

By transposing (3), we have

(8) $dc = da \cdot \cos B + db \cdot \cos A - a \cdot dB \cdot \sin B - b \cdot dA \cdot \sin A.$

Multiplying this through by c and substituting for $c.dA$ and $c.dB$, the values given on page 136, we get

(9) $c.dc = c.da.\cos B + c.db.\cos A$
    $\quad - a.\sin B(- da.\sin B + db.\sin A - b.dC.\cos A)$
    $\quad - b.\sin A(da.\sin B - db.\sin A - a.dC.\cos B).$
    $= c.da.\cos B + c.dB\cos A$
    $\quad + (a.\sin B - b\sin A)(da.\sin B - db\sin A)$
    $\quad + a.b.dC(\cos A.\sin B + \sin A.\cos B).$

The first factor $= 0$, and the last is $\sin(A + B)$ or $\sin C$;

therefore

(10) $c.dc = c.da.\cos B + c.db.\cos A + a.b.dc.\sin C.$

By expansion and substitution, (9) becomes

(10) $dc = da.\cos B + db.\cos A + a.b.dC.\sin C \div c$;

Dividing (6) and (7) by c, we get

(11) $dB = db.\sin A \div c - da.\sin B \div c - b.dC.\cos A \div c$;
(12) $dA = - db.\sin A \div c + da.\sin B \div c - a.dC.\cos B \div c.$

In computation this formula is used like those already illustrated, so it will be needless to give a solution of an example of this kind.

The only remaining case is when we have the three sides with their limiting errors to find the limiting errors of the computed angles. The discussion of this problem is of interest simply from a theoretical point of view, since such a case will never arise in any one's experience.

Rewriting equations already deduced (page 127), we start with

(1) $b.\sin A.dA + a.\sin B.dB = da.\cos B + db.\cos A - dc$;
(2) $b.\cos A.dA - a.\cos B.dB = da.\sin B - db.\sin A$;
(3) $\qquad\qquad dA + dB + dC = 0.$

Solving the first two equations with reference to dA and dB, and substituting in the results the values of dA and dB in (3), and putting sin C for sin $(A + B)$, — cos C for cos $(A + B)$, we will obtain

(4) $dA = da \div b . \sin C - db . \cos C \div b . \sin C - dc . \cos B$
$$\div b . \sin C \, ;$$

(5) $dB = - da . \cos C \div a . \sin C + db \div a . \sin C - dc . \cos A$
$$\div a . \sin C \, ;$$

(6) $dC = da(b . \cos C - a) \div a . b . \sin C + db(a . \cos C - b)$
$\div a . b . \sin C + dc(a . \cos B + b . \cos A) \div a . b . \sin C.$

Should we have $da \div a = db \div b = dc \div c$, the errors of the sides would be proportional to the sides themselves.

The defective triangle would then be similar to the true triangle, and the corresponding angles would be equal each to each, and we would have $dA = dB = dC = 0$.

When the three angles of a triangle are observed, the difference between their sum, after subtracting the spherical excess, and 180° is the total error of the triangle.

Let us call this E, the errors of the individual angles x, y, and z, with respective weights, u, v, w,

$$x + y + z = E.$$

By preceding theory $ux^2 + vy^2 + wz^2 =$ a minimum; differentiating with respect to x, y, and z, we get $ux = vy = wz$.

$$x = \frac{vy}{u}, \qquad z = \frac{vy}{w}; \qquad \text{therefore,} \qquad \frac{vy}{u} + y + \frac{vy}{w} = E;$$

$$wvy + wuy + uvy = wuE;$$

$$y = \frac{wuE}{wv + wu + uv}, \text{ also } x = \frac{wvE}{wv + wu + uv}, \, z = \frac{uvE}{wv + wu + uv}.$$

The limits of errors may be found in a similar manner for all combinations of triangles; hence a polygon may be decomposed into triangles and the limits of error found by the methods just described.

This method is not altogether satisfactory, since in the computation of the error in each triangle we use the errors of only two of the angles, ignoring the third.

From trigonometry, we have $a = \dfrac{\sin A}{\sin B} \cdot b$;

by differentiation, we have

$$da = a \cot A \cdot dA - a \cot B \cdot dB, \quad \ldots \quad (1)$$

b being a constant.

Let α, β, and γ be the measured angles, and A, B, and C the correct values. The triangle error, after correcting for spherical excess, is $\alpha + \beta + \gamma - 180°$, one third of which may be attributed to each angle, so the error in $\alpha = \dfrac{\alpha + \beta + \gamma - 180°}{3}$, and the correct value

$$A = \alpha - \frac{\alpha + \beta + \gamma - 180°}{3} = \frac{2\alpha - \beta - \gamma + 180°}{3}; \quad (2)$$

$$\text{also,} \quad B = \beta - \frac{\alpha + \beta + \gamma - 180°}{3} = \frac{2\beta - \alpha - \gamma + 180°}{3}; \quad (3)$$

$$C = \gamma - \frac{\alpha + \beta + \gamma - 180°}{3} = \frac{2\gamma - \beta - \alpha + 180°}{3}. \quad (4)$$

As A and B depend upon α, β, and γ, the total error in the side a, or ϵ_a will be a function of α, β, and γ;

or,
$$\varepsilon_a{}^2 = \left(\frac{da}{d\alpha}\right)^2 \varepsilon_a{}^2 + \left(\frac{da}{d\beta}\right)^2 \varepsilon_\beta{}^2 + \left(\frac{da}{d\gamma}\right)^2 \varepsilon_\gamma{}^2. \qquad (5)$$

In which ε_a, ε_β, and ε_γ are the probable errors in α, β, and γ,

and in (1) $\quad da = a \cot A . dA - a . \cot B . dB.$,

so we must obtain dA from (2), in terms of α, β, and γ.
Likewise, dB from (3), or we may write (1)

$$da = a \cot A . d\left(\frac{2\alpha - \beta - \gamma + 180°}{3}\right)$$
$$- a \cot B . d\left(\frac{2\beta - \alpha - \gamma + 180°}{3}\right). \quad . \quad . \quad . \quad (6)$$

Differentiating (6) with respect to α, β, and γ, we have

$$\frac{da}{d\alpha} = \frac{2}{3}a . \cot A + \frac{1}{3}a . \cot B = a\left(\frac{2}{3}\cot A + \frac{1}{3}\cot B\right); \quad (7)$$

$$\frac{da}{d\beta} = -\frac{1}{3}a \cot A - \frac{2}{3}a . \cot B = a\left(-\frac{1}{3}\cot A - \frac{2}{3}\cot B\right); (8)$$

$$\frac{da}{d\gamma} = -\frac{1}{3}a \cot A + \frac{1}{3}a \cot B = a\left(-\frac{1}{3}\cot A + \frac{1}{3}\cot B\right). \quad (9)$$

Squaring (7), (8), and (9),

$$\left(\frac{da}{d\alpha}\right)^2 = \frac{4}{9}a^2 \cot^2 A + \frac{4}{9}a^2 \cot A . \cot B + \frac{1}{9}a^2 \cot^2 B;$$

$$\left(\frac{da}{d\beta}\right)^2 = \frac{1}{9}a^2 \cot^2 A + \frac{4}{9}a^2 \cot A . \cot B + \frac{4}{9}a^2 \cot^2 B;$$

$$\left(\frac{da}{d\gamma}\right)^2 = \frac{1}{9}a^2 \cot^2 A - \frac{2}{9}a^2 \cot A . \cot B + \frac{1}{9}a^2 \cot^2 B;$$

therefore, supposing $\varepsilon_a = \varepsilon_\beta = \varepsilon_\gamma = \varepsilon$, we have

$$\varepsilon_a{}^2 = \left(\frac{da}{d\alpha}\right)^2 + \left(\frac{da}{d\beta}\right)^2 + \left(\frac{da}{d\gamma}\right)^2$$

$$= \varepsilon^2[\tfrac{2}{3}a^2 \cot^2 A + \tfrac{2}{3}a^2 \cot A \cdot \cot B + \tfrac{2}{3}a^2 \cot^2 B]$$

$$= \tfrac{2}{3}\varepsilon^2 a^2(\cot^2 A + \cot A \cdot \cot B + \cot^2 B);$$

$$\varepsilon_a = \varepsilon a \sqrt{\tfrac{2}{3}(\cot^2 A + \cot A \cdot \cot B + \cot^2 B)}.$$

As ε_a is small, the second member can be converted into a linear unit by writing it equal to its algebraic value times sin 1″.

$$\varepsilon_a = \varepsilon a \cdot \sin 1'' \sqrt{\tfrac{2}{3}(\cot^2 A + \cot A \cdot \cot B + \cot^2 B)}. \quad (10)$$

This is a rigorous expression for the probable error of a side, as computed from a base supposed to be free from error. The side a of the first triangle may be regarded as the accurate value of the base of the next triangle, and the probable error of another side computed, and so on through the entire chain. So we may put for ε_n, the error of the last side,

$$\varepsilon_n = \varepsilon a \sin 1'' \sqrt{\tfrac{2}{3}\Sigma(\cot^2 A + \cot A \cdot \cot B + \cot^2 B)}. \quad (11)$$

In which Σ represents the sum. In determining the angles to be used in this formula, it must be remembered that A is opposite the side whose error is being determined, and B is opposite the side whose error was last computed.

To illustrate:

Starting with the base b, we first pass to u;

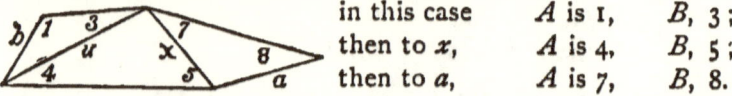

in this case	A is 1,	B, 3;
then to x,	A is 4,	B, 5;
then to a,	A is 7,	B, 8.

Hence, $\Sigma \cot^2 A = \cot^2(1) + \cot^2(4) + \cot^2(7) \ldots$ et

In (11), ε is the average angle-error in the chain. If the probable error of the base be ε_b', this error will be carried through the chain without augmentation or diminution, owing to inaccuracies in the angles, but it will be increased in the ratio of the length of the computed line to the base. In the first computed side a, the error from this source will be $\frac{a}{b}\varepsilon_b'$. Suppose this be ε_x', then in the next triangle, if c is computed from a, the error $\varepsilon_y' = \frac{c}{a}\cdot\varepsilon_x' = \frac{c}{a}\cdot\frac{a}{b}\cdot\varepsilon_b' = \frac{c}{b}\varepsilon_b'$, and so on through the entire chain; so if n be the last line, $\varepsilon_n' = \frac{n}{b}\cdot\varepsilon_b'$. The total error, E, from both sources, will be $E = \sqrt{\varepsilon_n'^2 + \varepsilon_n^2}$. If each side of each triangle has been computed by two different routes, the value for E must be divided by $\sqrt{2}$, or, $E = \sqrt{\frac{1}{2}(\varepsilon_n'^2 + \varepsilon_n^2)}$.

CHAPTER VI.

CALCULATION OF THE TRIANGULATION.

HAVING assumed in the field that we had a line of known or approximately known length for a base-line, we measured the angles of all the triangles of our net a sufficient number of times to eliminate instrumental errors ; and now wish to compute the distances of all the stations from one another, as far as possible.

When the three angles of a triangle are measured with the same care, it will be found that their sum will not equal 180° + spherical excess, and when two individual angles are measured separately and then as a whole, the sum of the two will not equal the two when treated as a single angle; and, again, the sum of the angles that complete the horizon will always differ from 360°.

The problem then is to find results from a number of observed values that will approach the nearest to the truth, and at the same time eliminate those discrepancies just referred to.

There are two classes of conditions that should be fulfilled :

(*a*) the sum of the individual angles should equal the measured whole ;

(*b*) the sum of all the angles completing the horizon should equal 360°.

The operation of filling these conditions is called *station-adjustment.*

(*c*) The three angles of a triangle should equal 180° ;

(*d*) The length of every side should be the same, regardless of the route by which it is computed.

The filling of these conditions is called *figure-adjustment*. These two adjustments are to be effected simultaneously, since the same quantities occur in each.

The method of adjustment will depend on the way in which the angles are read; whether with a repeating-theodolite, or direction-instrument. If with the former, the average value obtained for each angle will be the quantity that enters the equations formed by the expressed conditions.

Before writing these equations we must correct the angles for run of micrometers, as already explained on page 35, and for phase.

The latter is the effect of sighting to the illuminated portion of a signal instead of the centre; it is only appreciable when a tin cone, or some large reflecting surface, is observed on. This bright spot will be exactly in the line to the centre when the sun is directly behind the observer, and furthest from the centre when the sun is at an angle of 90° with the cone and observer.

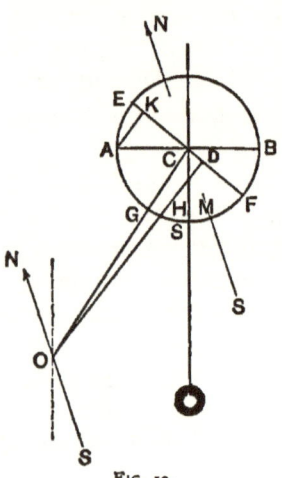

FIG. 12.

Let C be the centre of the signal and O the the position of the observer, the distance in the figure being greatly shortened, proportioned to the size of the signal.

The rays of the sun may be regarded as parallel and illuminating half of the signal, as ASB. Of this the observer sees only ASF; this he bisects, sighting to D instead of C. This causes an error equal to the angle COD.

Let $SCG = x$, $EC = r$, $OC = D$, and $COD = \theta$. KF is the projection of the visible arc, and $CD = \frac{1}{2}EK$. AK, being perpendicular to EF, and FAE a right triangle, $\overline{AK}^2 = EK \cdot KF = EK \cdot 2EC$ (nearly), or,

$$EK = \frac{\overline{AK}^2}{2EC}; \quad \text{but} \quad AK = EC \cdot \sin ACE,$$

hence, $\overline{AK}^2 = \overline{EC}^2 \cdot \sin^2 ACE$,

and $$EK = \frac{\overline{EC}^2 \cdot \sin^2 ACE}{2\overline{EC}} = \frac{EC \cdot \sin^2 ACE}{2}.$$

As ACE is small, we can write $\sin^2 ACE = 4 \sin^2 \frac{1}{2}ACE$, $EK = 2r \cdot \sin^2 \frac{1}{2}ACE$, but $ACE = GCS$, both being complements of ACG, or, $ACE = x$; also $CD = \dfrac{EK}{2}$; substituting, $CD = r \sin^2 \frac{1}{2}x$. In the right triangle OCD, $\sin \theta = \dfrac{CD}{D} = \dfrac{r \sin^2 \frac{1}{2}x}{D}$. As θ is small, $\sin \theta = \theta \cdot \sin 1''$, or, $\theta = \dfrac{r \cdot \sin^2 \frac{1}{2}x}{D \cdot \sin 1'''}$.

This correction is to be subtracted, when the sun is to the right of the observer, and added when the sun is to the left. In the case of independent angles, if both objects observed need a correction for phase, the two individual corrections are to be subtracted if they have opposite signs, and added when they have the same signs.

In the principle of directions, each direction should be corrected for phase, using only the average direction in applying the correction, and at all times measuring the angle x about the mean time of the series of observations.

A similar correction is to be applied when an eccentric sig-

10

nal was sighted; in this case it is necessary to know the perpendicular distance from the centre of the signal to the line
joining the observed and observing stations. This will form a
right triangle in which $\sin \theta = \dfrac{r}{D}$, or $\theta = \dfrac{r}{D \cdot \sin 1''}$, in which
θ = correction; r, the perpendicular, and D, the distance be-
tween the stations. This correction is additive when the point
observed is within the angle formed by the centres of the two
stations, and subtractive when it falls without.

This is but a special case of reduction to centre, discussed
on page 196, and like the latter can be applied later as well
as at this point.

With the average angles corrected we wish to find those
values that will fulfil the required conditions and at the same
contain the largest element of truth. We have seen that the
arithmetical mean renders the sum of the squares of the residuals a minimum, and that the most probable value of a number of disagreeing results is the one that makes the squares of
the errors a minimum. So we shall now look for *that* most
probable value which will fulfil the conditions.

Suppose we have a series of a observations, giving m for the
arithmetical mean, and a series of b, giving n for the mean; the
relative value of these two means would be to each other as
$a : b$.

Consequently the larger number of equally good observations we have, the better relative value we will get for the
mean. If, therefore, the first arithmetical mean, v_1, be obtained
from a series of a_1, the second, v_2, from a_2 ... the nth, v_n, from
a_n, we will have for the most probable value of x,

$$x = \frac{S[(av)_n]}{S[a_n]} = S\left[\frac{(av)_n}{a_n}\right].$$

If an angle be measured

> 10 times with the result 18° 18′ 12″,
> 8 times with the result 18° 18′ 2″,
> 5 times with the result 18° 18′ 21″,
> 4 times with the result 18° 18′ 30″,

$$x = \frac{10(18°18'12'') + 8(18°18'2'') + 5(18°18'21'') + 4(18°18'30'')}{10 + 8 + 5 + 4}$$

$$= \frac{494° \ 12' \ 1''}{27} = 18° \ 18' \ 13''.37.$$

On page 123 it was shown that the residuals, or individual errors, squared were multiplied by their weights, and these products summed, to give the square of the probable error of the observations as a whole. Then, since this probable error is obtained by taking that value which reduces the residuals squared to a minimum, the sum of the individual errors squared, each multiplied by its respective weight, must assume the form which renders it a minimum.

By way of illustration, let us take the following example : Suppose A, B, and C, be three angles in a plane around a point as a common vertex, and amounting to 360°. Suppose the measured values be A, B, and C; $a_{,}$, $b_{,}$, and $c_{,}$ their true values, and a, b, and c the errors of A, B, and C, so that we have $A + a = a_{,}$, $B + b = b_{,}$, $C + c = c_{,}$; also, $a_{,} + b_{,} + c_{,} = 360°$.

> From a set of 10 measurements $A = 120° \ 15' \ 20''$;
> From a set of 12 measurements $B = 132° \ 16' \ 30''$;
> From a set of 15 measurements $C = 107° \ 28' \ 19''$.

$$A + B + C = \quad 360° \ 00' \ 09''$$
$$a, + b, + c, = \quad 360° \ 00' \ 00''$$
$$\overline{a + b + c = - \quad 00° \ 00' \ 09''} \tag{1}$$

Taking the sum of the squares of these errors, $a^2 + b^2 + c^2$, and multiplying each by its respective weight,

$$10a^2 + 12b^2 + 15c^2. \tag{2}$$

From (1) $c = -a - b - 9$;
$$c^2 = a^2 + b^2 + 81 + 2ab + 18a + 18b;$$
$$15c^2 = 15(81 + a^2 + b^2 + 2ab + 18a + 18b);$$
$$15c^2 = 1215 + 15a^2 + 15b^2 + 30ab + 270a + 270b;$$

substituting this value for $15c^2$ in (2), we get

$$25a^2 + 27b^2 + 30ab + 270a + 270b + 1215. \tag{3}$$

According to principles already explained, we obtain the differential coefficient with respect to a and b, and place each result equal to zero;

$$50a + 30b + 270 = 0; \qquad 5a + 3b + 27 = 0;$$
$$54b + 30a + 270 = 0; \qquad 5a + 9b + 45 = 0;$$

therefore, $b + 3'' = 0$, $b = -3''$, $a = -3''.6$; substituting in (1), $c = -2''.4$.

The same result may be obtained by using an indeterminate coefficient, and afterwards eliminating it,

$$10a^2 + 12b^2 + 15c^2 + 2\varphi(a + b + c),$$

we take 2φ to avoid the use of fractions. Differentiating this with respect to *a*, *b*, and *c*, and placing the results equal to zero, we get

$$20a + 2\varphi = 0 \quad \text{or} \quad 10a + \varphi = 0;$$
$$24b + 2\varphi = 0 \quad\quad\quad 12b + \varphi = 0;$$
$$30c + 2\varphi = 0 \quad\quad\quad 15c + \varphi = 0.$$

Eliminating φ from two of these equations, we get

$$10a - 12b = 0;$$
$$'12b - 15c = 0;$$

also,
$$a + b + c + 9 = 0.$$

By the simple elimination, we get

$$a = -3''.6, \quad b = -3'', \quad c = -2''.4.$$

$$A = 120° \; 15' \; 20'' - 3''.6 = 120° \; 15' \; 16''.4;$$
$$B = 132 \;\; 16 \;\; 30 \;\; - 3 \;.0 = 132 \;\; 16 \;\; 27 \;.0;$$
$$C = 107 \;\; 28 \;\; 19 \;\; - 2 \;.4 = 107 \;\; 28 \;\; 16 \;.6;$$
$$a_, + b_, + c_, \quad\quad\quad = 360° \; 00' \; 00''.$$

The above is the simplest case in practice; that is, when only one condition is to be fulfilled. Let us pass to a more complicated case, or when several conditions are to be fulfilled.

Suppose, in Fig. 13, we have from repeated measurements the following results:

(1) $MON = \;\; 68° \; 37' \;\; 1''$ with the weight 5;
. (2) $MOP = 140 \;\;\; 2 \;\; 19$ with the weight 10;
(3) $NOQ = 134 \;\; 15 \;\; 41$ with the weight 20;

(4) $NOR = 211\ 56\ 10$ with the weight 15 ;
(5) $POR = 140\ 30\ 40$ with the weight 12 ;
(6) $MOQ = 202\ 52\ 46$ with the weight 18 ;
(7) $NOP = \ \ 71\ 25\ 38$ with the weight 16 ;
(8) $QOR = \ \ 77\ 40\ \ 6$ with the weight 20.

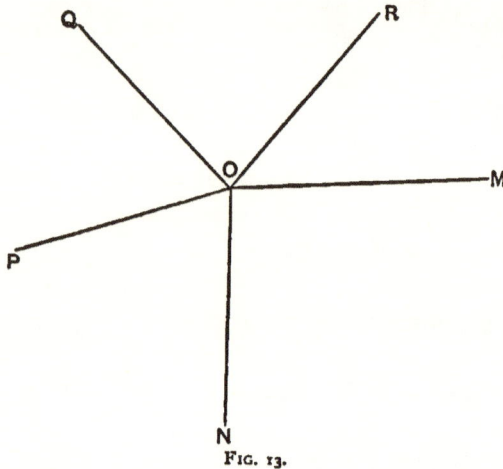

Fig. 13.

Upon inspection it will be seen that the following conditions should be fulfilled :

(1)   (2) − (1) = (7);
(2)   (4) − (3) = (8);
(3)   (5) + (7) = (4);   . . . . . . (A)
(4)   (6) − (3) = (1).

Denoting the corrections to the angles by $a, b, c, \ldots h$,

(1) $[(2) + b] - [(1) + a] = [(7) + g]$;
(2) $[(4) + d] - [(3) + c] = [(8) + h]$;
(3) $[(5) + e] + [(7) + g] = [(4) + d]$;   . . (B)
(4) $[(6) + f] - [(3) + c] = [(1) + a]$.

Substituting in these equations the angles designated by (1), (2), ... (8), they reduce to

$$
\begin{array}{ll}
(1) & b - a - g = -20''; \\
(2) & d - c - h = 23; \\
(3) & e + g - d = 8; \\
(4) & f - c - a = 4.
\end{array}
\left.\rule{0pt}{36pt}\right\} \quad \cdots \cdots \text{(C)}
$$

These are the relations that must exist between the corrections that are to be applied to the different angles.

Squaring each symbolic correction and multiplying each by its respective weight, we have

$$5a^2 + 10b^2 + 20c^2 + 15d^2 + 12e^2 + 18f^2 + 16g^2 + 20h^2. \quad \text{(D)}$$

From the equations at (C) we obtain

(1), $b = a + g - 20$; (2), $c = d - h - 23$;
(3), $e = d - g + 8$; (4), $f = a + c + 4 = a + d - h - 23 + 4.$

Substituting these in (D),

$$
\begin{aligned}
5a^2 &+ 10(a + g - 20)^2 + 20(d - h - 23)^2 + 15d^2 \\
&+ 12(d - g + 8)^2 + 18(a + d - h - 19)^2 + 16g^2 + 20h^2,
\end{aligned}
$$

must be a minimum.

The square, omitting constants, gives:

$$
\begin{aligned}
5a^2 &+ 10a^2 + 10g^2 + 20ag - 400a - 400g + 20d^2 + 20h^2 \\
&- 40dh - 920d + 920h + 15d^2 + 12d^2 + 12g^2 - 24dg \\
&+ 192d - 192g + 18a^2 + 18d^2 + 18h^2 + 36ad - 36ah \\
&- 36dh - 684a - 684d + 684h + 16g^2 + 20h^2.
\end{aligned}
$$

Differentiating this and placing the coefficient of each equal to zero, we have

$$33a + 18d + 10g - 18h = 542 ;$$
$$18a + 65d - 12g - 38h = 706 ;$$
$$5a - 6d + 19g \qquad = 148 ;$$
$$9a + 19d \qquad - 29h = 401.$$

The solution of these equations gives $a = 6.46$, $d = 5.89$, $g = 7.95$, and $h = -7.97$, which values substituted in C, give $b = -5.59$, $c = -9.14$, $e = 5.94$, and $f = 1.32$. Since the errors are to be obliterated in applying the correction, each correction must have the opposite sign to its error; so that if the above represent the errors, they are to be applied with contrary signs to the respective angles, which reduce the angles to :

$$(1) = \quad 68° \ 36' \ 54''.54 ;$$
$$(2) = 140 \quad 2 \ 24 \ .59 ;$$
$$(3) = 134 \ 15 \ 50 \ .14 ;$$
$$(4) = 211 \ 56 \quad 4 \ .11 ;$$
$$(5) = 140 \ 30 \ 34 \ .06 ;$$
$$(6) = 202 \ 52 \ 44 \ .68 ;$$
$$(7) = \quad 71 \ 25 \ 30 \ .05 ;$$
$$(8) = \quad 77 \ 40 \ 13 \ .97.$$

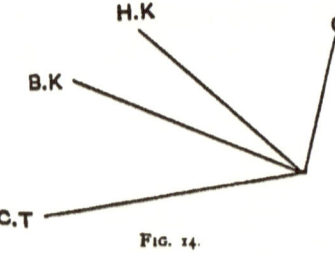

Fig. 14.

In order to furnish practice, the following observed angles are taken from the author's record-book. The corrected results are given, so that those adjusting them can verify their work. This, however, can be done by seeing if the conditions are fulfilled when the corrected values are taken. The weights are equal, and so can be omitted.

	Observed.					Corrected.			
(1)	CT to BK =	36°	24′	23″.25	=	36°	24′	22″.75 ;
(2)	CT to HK =	49	53	49 .36	=	49	53	51 .61 ;
(3)	CT to C =	95	06	40 .80	=	95	06	39 .05 ;
(4)	BK to HK =	13	29	31 .11	=	13	29	28 .86 ;
(5)	BK to C =	58	42	14 .55	=	58	42	16 .30.

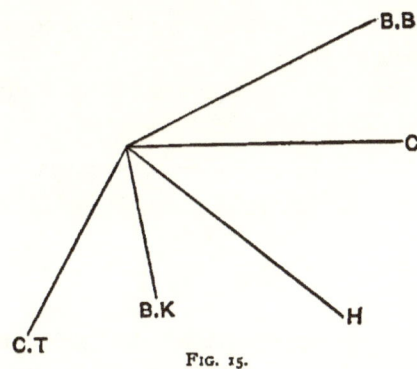

FIG. 15.

	Observed.					Corrected.			
(1)	BB to C =	26°	44′	50″.57	=	26°	44′	57″.82 ;
(2)	BB to H =	62	55	56 .14	=	62	55	47 .315 ;
(3)	BB to BK =	85	08	27 .43	=	85	08	29 .005 ;
(4)	C to H =	36	10	41 .57	=	36	10	49 .495 ;
(5)	C to BK =	58	23	31 .86	=	58	23	31 .185 ;
(6)	H to BK =	22	12	40 .79	=	22	12	41 .69 ;
(7)	H to CT =	53	09	11 .98	=	53	09	10 .18 ;
(8)	BK to CT =	30	56	26 .69	=	30	56	28 .49.

In a large number of condition equations the above operation may be considered long and tedious, so that one of the following methods may be found preferable.

Suppose we have, as the result of the same number of related quantities x, y, and z, the values N_1, N_2, and N_3, giving the equations :

$$\left.\begin{array}{l} a_1x + b_1y + c_1z \ldots = N_1; \\ a_2x + b_2y + c_2z \ldots = N_2; \\ a_3x + b_3y + c_3z \ldots = N_3; \\ a_nx + b_ny + c_nz \ldots = N_n; \end{array}\right\} \quad \ldots \ldots \text{(A)}$$

in which the coefficients are known. As the number of unknown quantities is less than the number of equations, a direct solution is impossible.

Designating the errors by u, we can write equations at (A),

$$\left.\begin{array}{l} a_1x + b_1y + c_1z - N_1 = u_1; \\ a_2x + b_2y + c_2z - N_2 = u_2; \\ \quad \cdot \quad \cdot \quad \cdot \quad \cdot \\ a_nx + b_ny + c_nz - N_n = u_n. \end{array}\right\} \quad \ldots \ldots \text{(B)}$$

By the principles already stated, the most probable values for these various quantities are those which render the sum of the squares of the errors, $u_1^2 + u_2^2 \ldots + u_n^2$, a minimum. Placing all terms but those depending upon x, equal to M_1, M_2 $\ldots M_n$, equations at (B) will take the form

$$\left.\begin{array}{l} a_1x + M_1 = u_1; \\ a_2x + M_2 = u_2; \\ \quad \cdot \quad \cdot \quad \cdot \\ a_nx + M_n = u_n. \end{array}\right\} \quad \ldots \ldots \text{(C)}$$

Taking the sum of the squares of both members of the equations at (C), we obtain

$$(a_1x + M_1)^2 + (a_2x + M_2)^2 \ldots + (a_nx + M_n)^2 = u_1^2 + u_2^2 \ldots u_n^2.$$

Differentiating this with respect to x, and placing the first differential coefficient equal to zero, we have, after dividing by 2,

$$a_1(a_1x + M_1) + a_2(a_2x + M_2) \ldots + a_n(a_nx + M_n) = 0.$$

From this, we see that to form the most probable value for x, we multiply each equation by the coefficient of x in that equation, add these products, and place the sum equal to zero. By doing this with y and z we will obtain one equation for each unknown quantity, from which each can be found by the ordinary methods of elimination.

To illustrate:

$$x + 2y + 2z - 2 = 0; \ldots \ldots (1)$$
$$-2x + y + z + 4 = 0; \ldots \ldots (2)$$
$$3x + y - z - 3 = 0; \ldots \ldots (3)$$
$$x - 2y + 2z - 8 = 0. \ldots \ldots (4)$$

Multiply (1) by 1, $x + 2y + 2z - 2 = 0;$
multiply (2) by -2, $4x - 2y - 2z - 8 = 0;$
multiply (3) by 3, $9x + 3y - 3z - 9 = 0;$
multiply (4) by 1, $x - 2y + 2z - 8 = 0;$
by adding, $15x + y - z - 27 = 0. \ldots \ldots (5)$

Multiply (1) by 2, $2x + 4y + 4z - 4 = 0;$
multiply (2) by 1, $-2x + y + z + 4 = 0;$
multiply (3) by 1, $3x + y - z - 3 = 0;$
multiply (4) by -2, $-2x + 4y - 4z + 16 = 0;$
by adding, $x + 10y + 13 = 0. \ldots \ldots (6)$

Likewise by multiplying (1) by 2, (2) by 1, (3) by -1, and (4) by 2, and adding, we get

$$-x + 10z - 13 = 0. \ldots \ldots (7)$$

Eliminating (5), (6), and (7), which are called the *normal equations*, by the usual algebraic method, we find $x = 2$, $y = -1.5$, and $z = 1.5$.

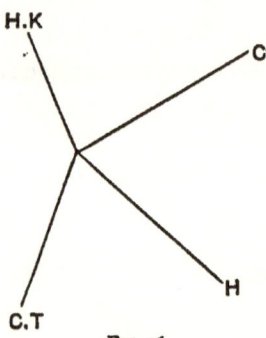

FIG. 16.

To further illustrate this method, we will take another example:

(1)	*H.K* to *C*	=	87°	47′	42″.5 ;
(2)	*H.K* to *H*	=	144	17	47 .5 ;
(3)	*C* to *H*	=	56	30	09 .0 ;
(4)	*C* to *C.T*	=	148	04	22 .5 ;
(5)	*H* to *C.T*	=	91	34	14 .5 ;
(6)	*C.T* to *H.K*	=	124	07	29 .5.

In this figure there are three conditions to be fulfilled:

$$(3) + (5) = (4),\ (1) + (3) = (2),\ \text{and}\ (2) + (5) + (6) = 360°.$$

As the changes in these values will not likely affect anything beyond the seconds, suppose we designate the seconds of the angles by $a, b \ldots f$, so that we will write the angles:

$$(1) = 87° 47′ + a'';$$
$$(2) = 144\ 17 + b;$$
$$\cdot \quad \cdot \quad \cdot \quad \cdot \quad \cdot \quad \cdot$$
$$(6) = 124\ 07 + f.$$

$(3) + (5) = (4)$, $(3) = 56° 30′ + c$;
       $(5) = 91° 34′ + e$;

$(3) + (5) =$ $148° 04′ + c + e$, $(4) = 148° 04′ + d$;

therefore, $c + e = d.$

Also $(1) + (3) = (2)$, $(1) = 87°47' + a$;

$\qquad\qquad\qquad (3) = 56°30' + c$,

$\quad (1) + (3) = \qquad\qquad 144°17' + a + c$, $(2) = 144° 17' + b$;

therefore, $\qquad\qquad\qquad a + c = b.$

$\quad (2) + (5) + (6) = 360°$, $\qquad (2) = 144° 17' + b$;

$\qquad\qquad\qquad\qquad\qquad\qquad (5) = 91\ 34 + e$;

$\qquad\qquad\qquad\qquad\qquad\qquad (6) = 124\ 07 + f$;

$\quad (2) + (5) + (6) = 359° 58' + b + e + f = 360°$;

therefore, $\qquad\qquad b + e + f = 120''.$

By observation, $\qquad a = 42''.5$;

$\qquad\qquad\qquad\qquad b = 47''.5$;

$\qquad\qquad\qquad\qquad c = 09''\ $;

$\qquad\qquad\qquad\qquad d = 22''.5$;

$\qquad\qquad\qquad\qquad e = 14''.5$;

$\qquad\qquad\qquad\qquad f = 29''.5.$

From condition, $\qquad c + e = d$;

$\qquad\qquad\qquad\qquad a + c = b$;

$\qquad\qquad\qquad b + e + f = 120''.$

Substituting in observation equations the values of d, and b as determined by the conditional equations, we can write

$$a = \quad 42''.5\ ;$$
$$a + c = \quad 47''.5 \qquad (a + c) = b;$$
$$c = \quad 9''\ \ ;$$
$$c + e = \quad 22''.5 \qquad (c + e) = d;$$
$$e = \quad 14''.5\ ;$$
$$f = \quad 29''.5\ ;$$
$$b + e + f = 120''.$$

From these we obtain the following normal equations:

$$2a + c = 90;$$
$$b + e + f = 120;$$
$$a + 3c + e = 79;$$
$$b + c + 3e + f = 157;$$
$$b + e + 2f = 149.5.$$

Solving for a, b, c, e, and f, by ordinary method of elimination, we find $a = 41''.125$, $b = 48''.875$, $c = 7''.75$, $d = c + e = 49''.375$, $e = 41''.625$, and $f = 29''.5$.

This gives for the angles the following as the most probable values:

$$(1) = 87° 47' 41''.125;$$
$$(2) = 144\ 17\ 48\ .875;$$
$$(3) = 56\ 30\ 7\ .75;$$
$$(4) = 148\ 04\ 49\ .375;$$
$$(5) = 91\ 34\ 41\ .625;$$
$$(6) = 124\ 07\ 29\ .5.$$

Observations with different weights can be adjusted by this method. Since we do not use in this case the *square* of the error, or some quantity involving the error squared, but only the first power, we must therefore multiply the error, or quantity involving the error, by the square root of the weight. The weight can be determined from the probable error as explained on page 123, if not taken directly from the number of measurements.

When it is desired to make use of this method for adjusting observations of different weights, the outline of the method may be given as follows.

For each of the observations write an observation equation.

For each condition write a conditional equation.

From the conditional equations obtain as many values as possible for one unknown quantity in terms of others, and substitute in the observation equations. Multiply each observation equation by the square root of its weight. Form the normal equations and solve as in ordinary cases.

While normal equations will afford an excellent solution for any number of observation and conditional equations, the labor becomes quite great when we have a large number of equations, or large quantities to handle.

In such cases the method of *correlatives* as developed by Gauss will afford the readiest solution. This method pertains to equations of condition only, and in terms of corrections that are to be applied to the various quantities in order to make them fulfil the required conditions.

Suppose α, β, γ . . . represent the corrections, and the conditional equations expressed in terms of these corrections with coefficients whose values are known, as well as the absolute term; for instance, in the last example we had the condition $(3) + (5) = (4)$, but in reality $(3) + (5) = (4) + 1''$, or $(3) + (5) - (4) = 1''$. So if α, β, and γ represent the corrections applied to (3), (4), and (5), their algebraic sum should equal $-1''$, to counteract the error $+ 1''$; that is, $\alpha + \gamma - \beta = -1''$. In this case the known coefficients are 1, and the absolute term $-1''$. So that, in general, we may express the conditional equations in terms of known coefficients, and absolute terms, with the corrections as the unknown quantities; as

$$a_1\alpha + a_2\beta + a_3\gamma \ldots = M_1;$$
$$b_1\alpha + b_2\beta + b_3\gamma \ldots = M_2;$$
$$c_1\alpha + c_2\beta + c_3\gamma \ldots = M_3;$$
$$. \quad . \quad .$$
$$n_1\alpha + n_2\beta + n_3\gamma \ldots = M_n.$$

Since the most favorable results are obtained by making the sum of the squares of the errors a minimum, if we take $a_i\alpha^2$ $+ a_i\beta^2 + a_i\gamma^2 \ldots a_n\varphi^2 = M$, and differentiate it with respect to each variable, and making the first differential equal to zero, we will have, after dividing by 2,

$$\left.\begin{array}{l} a_i d\alpha + a_i d\beta + a_i d\gamma \ldots + a_n d\varphi = 0\,; \\ b_i d\alpha + b_i d\beta + b_i d\gamma \ldots + b_n d\varphi = 0\,; \\ \qquad \cdot \qquad \cdot \qquad \cdot \qquad \qquad \cdot \qquad \cdot \\ m_i d\alpha + m_i d\beta + m_i d\gamma \ldots + m_n d\varphi = 0. \end{array}\right\} \quad \cdot \cdot \text{ (A)}$$

Also, $\alpha^2 + \beta^2 + \gamma^2 \ldots + \varphi^2 = $ a minimum, or

$$\alpha \cdot d\alpha + \beta \cdot d\beta + \gamma \cdot d\gamma \ldots + \varphi \cdot d\varphi = 0. \quad \cdot \cdot \text{ (B)}$$

As the number of equations is less than the number of unknown quantities, a part, as M, can be found in terms of the others ; with these values substituted in equations (A), we will have M less than originally, and each of these may be made equal to zero. Chauvenet accomplishes this result in the following way : multiply the first equation at (A) by k_i, the second by k_2, the third by k_3, and the nth by k_n and equation (B) by -1 ; then add these products. Now, supposing k_i, k_2, $\ldots$ etc., are such that M of the differentials disappear, the final equation will contain $M' - M$ (calling M' the original number) differentials with M' equations. Making them severally equal to zero, we get

$$a_i k_i + b_i k_2 + c_i k_3 \ldots m_i k_m - \alpha = 0\,;$$
$$a_i k_i + b_i k_2 + c_i k_3 \ldots m_i k_m - \beta = 0\,;$$
$$\qquad \cdot \qquad \cdot \qquad \cdot \qquad \qquad \cdot \qquad \cdot \qquad \cdot$$
$$a_n k_n + b_n k_n + c_n k_n \ldots m_n k_n - \varphi = 0.$$

Now, by multiplying the first by a_i, the second by a_2, etc., and adding the products, expressing the sum of like terms by Σ, we get

$$\Sigma a^2 k_1 + \Sigma abk_2 \ldots = a_1 \alpha + a_2 \beta \ldots = M_1.$$

Likewise, multiplying the first equation by b_1, the next by $b_2 \ldots b^n$, we have

$$\Sigma abk_1 + \Sigma b^2 k_2 \ldots = b_1 \alpha + b_2 \beta \ldots = M_2.$$

This will give as many normal equations as there are unknown quantities k_1, k_2, etc.; so that we obtain α, β, γ, etc., in terms of k_1, k_2, etc. While the theory of this is quite complicated and involves a knowledge of differential equations, in practice it is exceedingly simple, as the appended example will show:

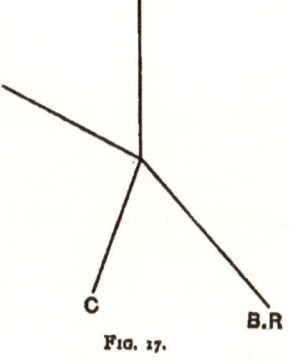

Fig. 17.

(1)   B.R to $C =$ 75° 31′ 53″.44 ;
(2)   B.R to $R =$ 144   36   49   .01 ;
(3)   B.R to $G =$ 239   35   03   .46 ;
(4) C to $R =$ 69   05   00   .57 ;
(5) C to $G =$ 164   02   51   .52 ;
(6) R to $G =$ 94   58   05   .44.

The conditions to be fulfilled are:

$$(1) + (4) - (2) = 0 ;$$
$$(2) + (6) - (3) = 0 ;$$
$$(4) + (6) - (5) = 0.$$

However, we find that

$$(1) + (4) - (2) = \quad 5'' \quad ;$$
$$(2) + (6) - (3) = - \quad 9''.01 ;$$
$$(4) + (6) - (5) = \quad 14''.49 ;$$

and the corrections necessary to neutralize these errors will be -5, $+9.01$, and -14.49. Indicating the corrections by the same symbols we have used for the angles, and transposing the constant needed, we will write the above equations,

$$(1) + (4) - (2) + 5 \quad = 0, \quad (a)$$
$$(2) + (6) - (3) - 9.01 = 0, \quad (b)$$
$$(4) + (6) - (5) + 14.49 = 0, \quad (c)$$

Now we rule as many vertical columns as there are conditions in this case, three, and as many horizontal ones as there are quantities to correct,—in this case six.

In the first condition we have $+ (1)$ $+ (4) - (2)$, so we write $+ k_1$ opposite 1, $+ k_1$ opposite 4, and $- k_1$ opposite 2.

	1st.	2d.	3d.
1	$+ k_1$		
2	$- k_1$	$+ k_2$	
3		$- k_2$	
4	$+ k_1$		$+ k_3$
5			$- k_3$
6		$+ k_2$	$+ k_3$

The second condition has $(2) + (6) - (3)$; so we put $+ k_2$ opposite 2, and 6, and $- k_2$ opposite 3.

The third condition involves $(4) + (6) - (5)$; so we put $+ k_3$ opposite 4 and 6, and $- k_3$ opposite 5.

The first equation of correlative is to contain the contents of the 1st and 4th horizontal columns, and minus the contents of the 2d; this is determined by that equation having $(1) + (4) - (2)$.

1st column contains $+ k_1$;
2d column contains $+ k_1 - k_2$; [signs changed as it is $- (2)$]
4th column contains $+ k_1 \qquad + k_3$;
1st correlative contains $3k_1 - k_2 + k_3$.

In the second conditional equation, we have $(2)+(6)-(3)$, so we take the contents of the 2d and 6th horizontal columns and the 3d with signs changed.

2d contains	$-k_1+k_2$;
6th contains	$+k_2+k_3$;
3d contains (sign changed)	$+k_2$;
$(2)+(6)-(3)$ contains	$-k_1+3k_2+k_3$,

2d correlative equation.

Likewise for the 3d we get $k_1+k_2+3k_3$.

Placing these correlatives in the equations involving the corrections, (a), (b), and (c), we get

$$3k_1 - k_2 + k_3 + 5 = 0;$$
$$-k_1 + 3k_2 + k_3 - 9.01 = 0,$$
$$k_1 + k_2 + 3k_3 + 14.49 = 0.$$

By ordinary process of elimination, we find $k_1 = 3''.37$, $k_2 = 6''.87$, $k_3 = -8''.24$.

Angle.	1st.	2d.	3d.	Correction.	Corrected Angles.
1	$+k_1$			$+3.37$	75° 31′ 56″.81
2	$-k_1$	$+k_2$		$-3.37+687$	144 36 52 .51
3		$-k_2$		-6.87	239 34 56 .58
4	$+k_1$		$+k_3$	$+3.37-8.24$	69 04 55 .70
5			$-k_3$	$+8.24$	164 02 59 .76
6		$+k_2$	$+k_3$	$+6.87-8.24$	94 58 04 .07

These corrections are determined in this way:

(1) is in the first condition and positive, so it is affected by $+k_1$;

(2) is in the first and second,—negative in the first, and positive in the second; therefore it is affected by $-k_1$ and $+k_2$;

(3) is negative in the second so it is corrected by $- k_2$;

(4) is positive in the first and third, so its correction will be $+ k_1 + k_3$;

(5) is negative in the third, therefore its correction is $- k_3$;

(6) is positive in the second and third, so it will be corrected by $+ k_2 + k_3$.

These values of k_1, k_2, and k_3, applied as just indicated to the observed angles, will give the most probable values for the angles that will make them conformable to the conditions.

It may be noticed that the method of forming the equations of correlatives is the same as forming normal equations. To illustrate, let us take (a) of the conditional equations; the coefficient of (1) is $+ 1$, of (4) is $+ 1$, and of (2) is $- 1$.

Multiply horizontal column 1 by $+ 1$, $= + k_1$;

multiply horizontal column 4 by $+ 1$, $= + k_1 \qquad + k_3$;

multiply horizontal column 2 by $- 1$, $= + k_1 - k_2$;

$(1) + (4) - (2) \qquad\qquad\qquad\qquad = \overline{\quad 3k_1 - k_2 + k_3};$

therefore $\qquad\qquad 3k_1 - k_2 + k_3 + 5 = 0.$

This is the better plan when the coefficients are not unities. When the observations have different weights, the operation is somewhat complicated and can be best explained by solving an example;

FIG. 18.

(1) C to $P = 107° 53' 00''.07$ weight 5;
(2) C to $A = 171\ 42\ 02\ .18$ weight 4;
(3) C to $B = 198\ 10\ 28\ .22$ weight 6;
(4) P to $A = 63\ 49\ 05\ .86$ weight 2;
(5) P to $B = 90\ 17\ 16\ .02$ weight 3;
(6) A to $B = 26\ 28\ 04\ .54$ weight 1.

The conditional equations are :

$$(1) + (4) - (2) + 3.75 = 0; \quad \cdots \cdots \quad (a)$$
$$(1) + (5) - (3) - 12.13 = 0; \quad \cdots \cdots \quad (b)$$
$$(4) + (6) - (5) - 5.62 = 0; \quad \cdots \cdots \quad (c)$$

designating the corrections by the same symbols as the angles.

If the equations on page 159 had been weighted before differentiation, α', β' ... φ' would have been multiplied by the respective weights of the observation to which they were to form corrections. These weights, say $w_1, w_2 \ldots w_n$, being constant factors, would remain in the differentials; so that the equations just referred to would have for their last term $- w_1\alpha$, $- w_2\beta \ldots - w_n\varphi$. Then afterwards, when multiplied by $a_1, a_2,$ etc., before summing the products, in order to get $\alpha, \beta \ldots \varphi$ freed from factors, since we only know the values of these errors unaffected by their weights, we must divide the first equation by w_1, second by w_2, etc.

We make the arrangement as though there were no weights so far as the position and signs of the correlatives are concerned, but take the reciprocal of the weight of the angle as the coefficient.

Angle.	k_1.	k_2.	k_3.
1	$+ \tfrac{1}{5}k_1$	$+ \tfrac{1}{5}k_2$	
2	$- \tfrac{1}{2}k_1$		
3		$- \tfrac{1}{2}k_2$	
4	$+ \tfrac{1}{4}k_1$		$+ \tfrac{1}{4}k_3$
5		$+ \tfrac{1}{4}k_2$	$- \tfrac{1}{2}k_3$
6			$+ \tfrac{1}{5}k_3$

To illustrate : the first condition equation involves a correction to be applied positively to (1) and (4), and negatively to (2). And since the reliability of these angles is proportional to 5, 2, and 4, it is apparent that the corrections they should receive would be in the inverse proportion, or $\tfrac{1}{5}$, $\tfrac{1}{2}$, and $\tfrac{1}{4}$.

Therefore for the correction, this equation suggests that for (1) we should write $\frac{1}{3}k_1$; for (4), $\frac{1}{2}k_1$; and for — (2), — $\frac{1}{4}k_1$.

Second conditional equation involves corrections to (1)+ (5)—(3). These angles are in point of accuracy proportional to their weights, 5, 3, and 6; therefore the corrections will have the inverse proportion, $\frac{1}{5}$, $\frac{1}{3}$, and $\frac{1}{6}$. So we write the corrections; the second conditional equation suggests for (1), + $\frac{1}{5}k_2$; for (5), + $\frac{1}{3}k_2$; and for — (3), — $\frac{1}{6}k_2$.

Likewise in the third, for (4), + $\frac{1}{2}k_3$; for (6), + $\frac{1}{1}k_3$; and for — (5), — $\frac{1}{3}k_3$.

Now, to form the equations, the first condition requires the sum of the quantities in the first and fourth horizontal column, and the negative of the second.

$$
\begin{array}{lll}
(1) \text{ contains} & \frac{1}{3}k_1 + \frac{1}{5}k_2 & ; \\
(4) \text{ contains} & \frac{1}{2}k_1 & + \frac{1}{2}k_3; \\
-(2) \text{ contains} & \frac{1}{4}k_1 & ; \\
(1)+(4)-(2) \text{ contains} & (\frac{1}{3}+\frac{1}{2}+\frac{1}{4})k_1 + \frac{1}{5}k_2 + \frac{1}{2}k_3 = & (e)
\end{array}
$$

The second condition requires (1)+(5) — (3).

$$
\begin{array}{lll}
(1) \text{ contains } \frac{1}{3}k_1 & + \frac{1}{5}k_2 & ; \\
(5) \text{ contains} & + \frac{1}{3}k_2 - \frac{1}{3}k_3; \\
-(3) \text{ contains} & + \frac{1}{6}k_2 & ; \\
(1)+(5)-(3) \text{ contains } \frac{1}{3}k_1 + (\frac{1}{5}+\frac{1}{3}+\frac{1}{6})k_2 - \frac{1}{3}k_3. & (f)
\end{array}
$$

Likewise,
$$
\begin{array}{lll}
(4) \text{ contains } \frac{1}{2}k_1 & + \frac{1}{2}k_3; \\
(6) \text{ contains} & + \ k_3; \\
-(5) \text{ contains} \quad - \frac{1}{3}k_2 & + \frac{1}{3}k_3; \\
(4)+(6)-(5) \text{ contains } \frac{1}{2}k_1 - \frac{1}{3}k_2 + (\frac{1}{2}+1+\frac{1}{3})k_3. & (g)
\end{array}
$$

Clearing equations (e), (f), and (g) of fractions and substituting them for the values of the corrections in (a), (b), and (c), we get

$$\tfrac{57}{60}k_1 + \tfrac{12}{60}k_2 + \tfrac{30}{60}k_3 + 3.75 = 0; \quad \ldots \ldots \quad (h)$$

$$\tfrac{6}{30}k_1 + \tfrac{21}{30}k_2 - \tfrac{10}{30}k_3 - 12.13 = 0; \quad \ldots \ldots \quad (i)$$

$$\tfrac{3}{6}k_1 - \tfrac{2}{6}k_2 + \tfrac{11}{6}k_3 - 5.62 = 0; \quad \ldots \ldots \quad (k)$$

Reducing
$$57k_1 + 12k_2 + 30k_3 + 225.00 = 0;$$
$$6k_1 + 21k_2 - 10k_3 - 363.90 = 0;$$
$$3k_1 - 2k_2 + 11k_3 - 33.72 = 0.$$

Eliminating by the usual process, we find that

$$k_1 = -16''.50, \quad k_2 = 28''.08, \quad k_3 = 12''.68.$$

The plan for applying these values can be best exhibited:

Angle.	1st.	2d.	3d.	Correction.	Corrected Angle.
1	$\tfrac{1}{6}k_1$	$\tfrac{1}{6}k_2$		$-3.30 + 5.61$	107° 53′ 02″.38
2	$-\tfrac{1}{4}k_1$			$-(-4.12)$	171 42 06 .30
3		$-\tfrac{1}{6}k_2$		-4.68	198 10 23 .54
4	$\tfrac{1}{4}k_1$		$\tfrac{1}{6}k_3$	$-8.25 + 6.34$	63 49 03 .95
5		$\tfrac{1}{6}k_2$	$-\tfrac{1}{6}k_3$	$9.36 - 4.22$	90 17 21 .16
6			k_3	12.68	26 28 17 .22

(1) is corrected by $\tfrac{1}{6}k_1$ and $\tfrac{1}{6}k_2$, or $-3.30 + 5.61$;

(2) is corrected by $-\tfrac{1}{4}k_1$ or $-\tfrac{1}{4}(-16.50) = 4.12$, etc.

In the case of weighted observation, the method of correlatives is far the simplest.

While station adjustment is of somewhat frequent occurrence, yet the angles regarded as forming parts of a triangle more frequently require attention. The geometric requirement that the three angles of a triangle equal 180° furnishes a condition to begin with ; likewise, these angles as individuals may form a part of a station condition. In this case—which is the rule—we combine station-adjustment with what is known as *figure-adjustment;* that is, bringing the angles into conformity with the geometric requirements of the figure.

The first geometric condition is that the angles of the triangles equal $180°$ + spherical excess, or $A + B + C - \varepsilon = 180°$, in which, A, B, and C are the measured angles of the triangle, and ε = spherical excess. To find what the errors are in the case of each triangle, it is necessary to determine the value of ε. By geometry we know that the three angles of a spherical triangle bear the same relation to four right angles that its area bears to a hemisphere; that is, $\varepsilon : 2\pi :: \text{area} : 2\pi r^2$,

$\varepsilon = \dfrac{\text{area}}{r^2}$. ε being small, ε in seconds = . $\sin 1''$, $\varepsilon = \dfrac{\text{area}}{r^2 \sin 1''}$.

As the triangle is small compared with the surface of the sphere, it may be regarded as equivalent to a plane triangle = $\frac{1}{2}a . b . \sin C$, hence $\varepsilon = \dfrac{a . b . \sin C}{2r^2 \sin 1''}$, in which a, b, and C represent the two sides and included angle, and r the radius of a sphere. r can be considered a mean proportional between the radius of curvature of a meridian and the normal of a point whose position is the centre of the triangle.

On page 207, $R = \dfrac{a(1 - e^2)}{(1 - e^2 \sin^2 L)^{\frac{3}{2}}}$, $N = \dfrac{a}{(1 - e^2 \sin^2 L)^{\frac{1}{2}}}$, $r^2 = N . R = \dfrac{a^2(1 - e^2)}{(1 - e^2 \sin^2 L)^2}$; dividing by $1 - e^2$ and neglecting terms involving powers of e above the fourth, $r^2 = \dfrac{a^2}{1 + e^2 - 2e^2 \sin^2 L}$

$= \dfrac{a^2}{1 + e^2(1 - 2 \sin^2 L)} = \dfrac{a^2}{1 + e^2 \cos 2L}$. Substituting this value for r^2, $\varepsilon = \dfrac{a . b \sin C (1 + e^2 \cos 2L)}{2a^2 \sin 1''}$. The factor $\dfrac{1 + e^2 \cos 2 L}{2a^2 \sin 1''}$ varies with $2L$, and can be computed with L as the variable for every $30'$ and tabulated; calling this term n, $\varepsilon = a . b . \sin C . n$.

The most elaborate spheroidal triangle-computation for spherical excess shows that the result obtained by using the above formula will differ from the correct value, only in the thousandth part of a second. For preliminary field computation the excess may be taken as 1″ for every 200 square kilometres, or 75.5 square miles; and when the sides are 4 miles or under, it can be disregarded. The following table contains n for L, from 24° to 53° 30′, based upon Clarke's spheroid. The table must be entered with the average latitude of the triangle approximately.

Latitude.	Log n.	Latitude.	Log n.	Latitude.	Log n.
24° 00′	1.40596	34° 00′	1.40509	44° 00′	1.40410
24 30	92	34 30	05	44 30	05
25 00	88	35 00	00	45 00	00
25 30	84	35 30	495	45 30	395
26 00	80	36 00	91	46 00	90
26 30	76	36 30	86	46 30	85
27 00	72	37 00	81	47 00	80
27 30	68	37 30	76	47 30	75
28 00	64	38 00	71	48 00	69
28 30	1.40559	38 30	1.40466	48 30	1.40364
29 00	55	39 00	61	49 00	59
29 30	51	39 30	56	49 30	54
30 00	47	40 00	51	50 00	49
30 30	42	40 30	46	50 30	44
31 00	37	41 00	41	51 00	39
31 30	33	41 30	36	51 30	34
32 00	28	42 00	31	52 00	29
32 30	24	42 30	26	52 30	24
33 00	19	43 00	20	53 00	19
33 30	1.40514	43 30	1.40415	53 30	1.40314

The spherical excess computed by this formula is for the entire triangle; and, unless there is considerable difference in the lengths of the opposite sides, one third of the excess is to be deducted from each angle of the triangle; but this reduced value is used only in the *triangle* condition, and not in the station condition.

If in this figure we have measured the angles numbered and have the averages, which we will designate by the numbers, it

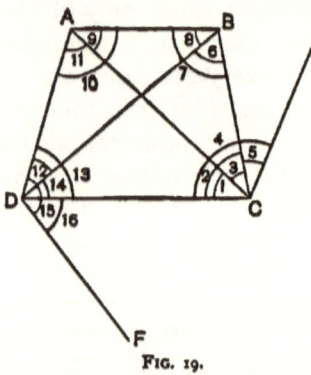

FIG. 19.

will be seen that a great variety of conditions may be written. But upon examination it will become apparent that some of the angles are indirectly two or more times subjected to the same or equivalent conditions. For instance, if $(3) + (7) + (9) = 180°$, and $(11) + (13) + (1) = 180°$, the condition that $(2) + (7) + (10) + (13) = 360°$ is already fulfilled. Also, if $(1) + (3) = (2)$, and $(2) +$ $(5) = (4)$, the condition $(1) + (3) + (5) = (4)$ is unnecessary; and, again, if $(3) + (7) + (9) = 180°$, $(11) + (13) + (1) = 180°$, and $(14) + (2) + (6) = 180°$, then $(1) + (3) = (2)$ is unnecessary. If we have the most probable value for (6) and (7), their difference will be (8) without involving (8) in the adjustment; or if we have the best values for (8) and (6), their sum will give (7); or if we have (1), (2), and (4), we can find by subtraction the most probable value for (3) and (5).

From this we learn that it is useless to involve whole angles and all of their parts in different conditions. With such a figure the following conditions would be sufficient:

$$(2) + (5) = (4);$$
$$(3) + (7) + (9) = 180°;$$
$$(8) + (10) + (12) = 180°;$$
$$(2) + (7) + (10) + (13) = 360°;$$
$$(13) + (16) = (15).$$

Other combinations could also be used.

In such adjustments the method of correlatives should be used, as the labor does not increase rapidly in proportion to the increased number of conditions.

The equations like those given so far are called *angle* or *angular* equations. The theorem in trigonometry that the ratio of sides is equal to the ratio of the sines of the opposite angles gives us $\dfrac{AB}{AC} = \dfrac{\sin (3)}{\sin (7)}$. Since A, B, and C are fixed points, the distances AB and AC are constant; therefore $\dfrac{AB}{AC}$ represents a constant quantity, so that if (3) and (7) are changed at all, the sine of (3) and its correction must have the same ratio to the sine of (7) and its correction that sin (3) has to sin (7). This involves another condition, which will now be elaborated.

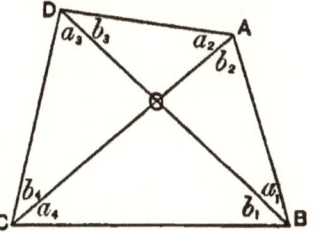

FIG. 20.

From the theorem just referred to, we obtain the following equations:

$$\frac{OB}{OA} = \frac{\sin b_3}{\sin a_1}, \quad \frac{OA}{OD} = \frac{\sin b_3}{\sin a_2}, \quad \frac{OD}{OC} = \frac{\sin b_4}{\sin a_3}, \quad \frac{OC}{OB} = \frac{\sin b_1}{\sin a_4}.$$

Multiplying these equations together, member by member, we obtain

$$\frac{OB . OA . OD . OC}{OA . OD . OC . OB} = 1 = \frac{\sin b_2 . \sin b_3 . \sin b_4 . \sin b_1}{\sin a_1 . \sin a_2 . \sin a_3 . \sin a_4};$$

or, $\sin a_1 . \sin a_2 . \sin a_3 . \sin a_4 = \sin b_1 . \sin b_2 . \sin b_3 . \sin b_4.$

But these are the values after correction, so we will put M_1, M_2, M_3, M_4, for a_1, a_2, a_3, a_4; N_1, N_2, N_3, and N_4 for b_1, b_2, b_3, and b_4; and denote the necessary corrections by v_1, v_2, v_3, v_4, and x_1, x_2, x_3, and x_4. Substituting these values in the last equation, we have

$$\sin(M_1+v_1) \cdot \sin(M_2+v_2) \cdot \sin(M_3+v_3) \cdot \sin(M_4+v_4)$$
$$= \sin(N_1+x_1) \cdot \sin(N_2+x_2) \cdot \sin(N_3+x_3) \cdot \sin(N_4+x_4);$$

or, passing to logs,

$$\log\sin(M_1+v_1) + \log\sin(M_2+v_2) + \log\sin(M_3+v_3)$$
$$+ \log\sin(M_4+v_4)$$
$$= \log\sin(N_1+x_1) + \log\sin(N_2+x_2) + \log\sin(N_3+x_3)$$
$$+ \log\sin(N_4+x_4).$$

Since v_1, v_2, v_3, v_4, x_1, x_2, x_3, x_4, are very small, we may develop each of the above terms by Taylor's theorem, stopping with the first power of the correction :

$$\log\sin(M_1+v_1) = \log\sin M_1 + \left(\frac{d \log \sin M_1}{dM_1}\right)v_1 \, ;$$

$$\log\sin(M_2+v_2) = \log\sin M_2 + \left(\frac{d \log \sin M_2}{dM_2}\right)v_2,$$

etc.,   etc.;

$$\log\sin(N_1+x_1) = \log\sin N_1 + \left(\frac{d \log \sin N_1}{dN_1}\right)x_1,$$

etc.,   etc.;

in which v_1, v_2, v_3, v_4, x_1, x_2, x_3, x_4, are expressed in seconds, so that $\dfrac{d \log \sin M_1}{dM_1}$ is the log difference for one tabular unit for the angle M_1, or the tabular difference for M_1; let us call this difference d_1, d_2, d_3, d_4, for M_1, M_2, M_3, M_4, and $\delta_1, \delta_2, \delta_3, \delta_4$, for N_1, N_2, N_3, N_4.

Substituting these values in the last equation, we have

$$\log \sin M_1 + d_1 v_1 + \log \sin M_2 + d_2 v_2 + \log \sin M_3 + d_3 v_3 \\ + \log \sin M_4 + d_4 v_4 \\ = \log \sin N_1 + \delta_1 x_1 + \log \sin N_2 + \delta_2 x_2 + \log \sin N_3 + \delta_3 x_3 \\ + \log \sin N_4 + \delta_4 x_4.$$

When transposed,

$$\log \sin M_1 + \log \sin M_2 + \log \sin M_3 + \log \sin M_4 \\ - \log \sin N_1 - \log \sin N_2 - \log \sin N_3 - \log \sin N_4 \\ = \delta_1 x_1 + \delta_2 x_2 + \delta_3 x_3 + \delta_4 x_4 - d_1 v_1 - d_2 v_2 - d_3 v_3 - d_4 v_4$$

—an equation in which the unknown quantities are the corrections to the angles, or the same quantities that are sought in the adjusting equations.

This gives directly an equation of condition, for since the sum of the log sines of M_1, M_2, M_3, and M_4 should equal the sum of the log sines of N_1, N_2, N_3, and N_4, the corrections $d_1 v_1 + d_2 v_2 + d_3 v_3 + d_4 v_4$ should equal $\delta_1 x_1 + \delta_2 x_2 + \delta_3 x_3 + \delta_4 x_4$. But if the log sines of (M) differ from the log sines of (N), then that amount of difference must be corrected in $d_1 v_1 + d_2 v_2 \ldots$ etc. This is called the *linear* equation.

By way of illustration, suppose we have the appended figure with the average angles as given :

(1) = 50° 31′ 13″.68 ;
(2) = 14 51 47 .88 ;
(3)   not needed ;

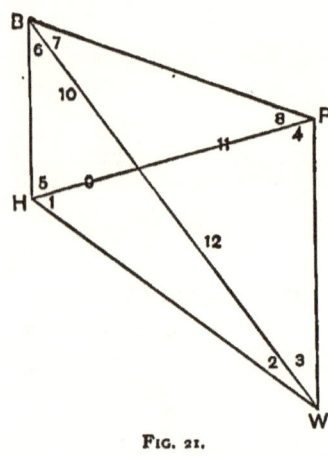

FIG. 21.

(4) = 71° 46′ 16″.36 ;
(5) = 82 32 49 .52 ;
(6) = 32 04 12 .49 ;
(7)   not needed ;
(8) = 30 03 29 .39 ;
(9) = 133 03 52 .48 ;
(10) = 67 23 18 .99 ;
(11)   not needed ;
(12) = 57 42 49 .56.

We first deduce the linear equation :

$$HW . \sin (2) = HB . \sin (6) ;$$
$$HB . \sin (10) = HP . \sin (8) ;$$
$$HP . \sin (4) = HW . \sin (12) ;$$

by multiplication,

$$\sin (2) . \sin (10) . \sin (4) = \sin (6) . \sin (8) . \sin (12).$$

Writing for tabular difference $\delta(2)$, $\delta(10)$, etc., and [2], [10], etc. as the corrections for (2), (10), etc., we have

$$\log \sin (2) + \delta(2) [2] + \log \sin (10) + \delta(10) [10]$$
$$+ \log \sin (4) + \delta(4) [4]$$
$$= \log \sin (6) + \delta(6) [6] + \log \sin (8) + \delta(8) [8]$$
$$+ \log \sin (12) + \delta(12) [12].$$

From the table of logs, we find :

log sin (6) = 9.72505722,	δ (6) = .00000336 ;
log sin (8) = 9.69978200,	δ (8) = 364 ;
log sin (12) = 9.92705722,	$\delta(12) =$ 133 ;
sum = 29.35189644.	

log sin (2) = 9.40910559,   δ (2) = .00000794 ;
log sin (4) = 9.97763813,   δ (4) =   69 ;
log sin (10) = 9.96526395,   δ(10) =   87 ;
sum   = 29.35200767.

log sin (2) + log sin (4) + log sin (10)
    = log sin (6) + log sin (8) + log sin (12) + 0.00011123.

As the corrections are to neutralize this difference, we write

δ(2)[2] + δ(4)[4] + δ(10)[10]
    = δ(6)[6] + δ(8)[8] + δ(12)[12] − 0.00011123.

Substituting for δ(2), δ(4), etc., their values, we have, after multiplying by 1000000 to avoid decimals,

7.94[2] + .87[10] + .69[4]
    = 1.33[12] + 3.64[8] + 3.36[6] − 111.23.

Transposing and passing to our usual notation,
7.94(2) + .87(10) + .69(4) − 1.33(12) − 3.64(8) − 3.36(6)
                                  + 111.23 = 0.

The angle equations are those involving the angles that will not be doubly adjusted. In the present case they will be, when expressed in terms of their corrections,

(5) + (1) − (9) + 10.72 = 0 ;
(9) + (2) + (6) − 7.15 = 0 ;
(1) + (4) + (12) + 19.60 = 0 ;
(5) + (8) + (10) − 22.10 = 0 ;

$$7.94(2) + .87(10) + .69(4) - 1.33(12) - 3.64(8) - 3.36(6)$$
$$+ 111.23 = 0.$$

In this (3) is omitted, since if (2) and (12) are known, (3) can be found by subtraction. Likewise, (11) is the sum of (8) and (4); also (7), the difference between (10) and (6). So we now simply form the correlative equations from these five conditional equations.

	1st.	2d.	3d.	4th.	5th.
1	k_1		k_3		
2		k_2			$7.94k_5$
4			k_3		$.69k_5$
5	k_1			k_4	
6		k_2			$-3.36k_5$
8				k_4	$-3.64k_5$
9	$-k_1$	k_2			
10				k_4	$.87k_5$
12			k_3		$-1.33k_5$

The formation of the first four normal equations follows the principles repeatedly given, but as something new may appear in obtaining the fifth equation, it will be formed in detail.

7.94 times column 2 =	$7.94k_2$	$+63.0436k_5$;
.87 times column 10 =		$.87k_4 + .7569k_5$;
.69 times column 4 =	$.69k_3$	$+ .4761k_5$;
− 1.33 times column 12 =	$-1.33k_3$	$+ 1.7689k_5$;
− 3.64 times column 8 =		$-3.64k_4 + 13.2496k_5$;
− 3.36 times column 6 = $-3.36k_2$		$+11.2896k_5$;
Total,	$4.58k_2 - .64k_3 - 2.77k_4 + 90.5847k_5$.	

Barlow's table of squares will facilitate work, as the coefficients of the terms in the side equation are squared in finding the coefficient of the correlative corresponding to the equation of condition formed by the side equation. In this case, the fifth conditional equation is the side equation, and the coefficients of k_s in the fifth normal equation are the squares of 7.94, etc.

The normal equations are :

$$3k_1 - k_2 + k_3 + k_4 + 10.72 = 0;$$
$$- k_1 + 3k_2 + 4.58k_5 - 7.15 = 0;$$
$$+ k_1 + 3k_3 - .64k_5 + 19.60 = 0;$$
$$k_1 + 3k_4 - 2.77k_5 - 9.29 = 0;$$
$$4.58k_2 - .64k_3 - 2.77k_4 + 90.58k_5 + 111.23 = 0.$$

The solution of these equations gives $k_1 = -''.53$, $k_2 = 4''.40$, $k_3 = -6''.66$, $k_4 = 1''.94$, $k_5 = -1''.43$.

These values are applied to the various angles as indicated in the table just given. For instance, (2) is to be corrected by k_2 and 7.94 times k_5.

The best rule that can be given for the formation of side equations is to regard one of the vertices as the vertex of a pyramid, with the figure formed by the other points as the base, and take the product of the sines of the angles in one direction, equal to the product of the sines in the opposite direction.

Take *H* as the vertex, and *WPB* as the base; then,

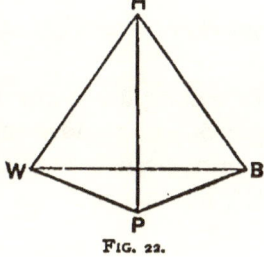

FIG. 22.

$$\sin HWP . \sin HPB . \sin HBW$$
$$= \sin HBP . \sin HPW . \sin HWB. ;$$

that is, $\sin (12) . \sin (8) . \sin (6) = \sin (10) . \sin (4) . \sin (2)$, as was otherwise obtained. The angles at the point used as the ver-

12

tex are not involved in this equation, so they must be involved in a station adjustment, or in a triangle condition.

If one should find it difficult to conceive a pyramid constructed in this way, he can without trouble secure the side equation in the manner made use of on page 174, in which we started from $HW \cdot \sin(2) = HB \cdot \sin(6)$.

In the next equation obtain a value of HB. in another triangle, as $HB \cdot \sin(10) = HP \cdot \sin(8)$; then in terms of HP., as $HP \cdot \sin 4 = HW \cdot \sin 12$.

This is as far as we can go, as we have returned to the starting-point. Suppose we start from WP.

$$WP \cdot \sin(11) = WB \cdot \sin(7);$$
$$WB \sin(6) = WH \cdot \sin(9);$$
$$WH \cdot \sin(1) = WP \cdot \sin(4);$$

by multiplying, $\sin(11) \cdot \sin(6) \cdot \sin(1) = \sin(7) \cdot \sin(9) \cdot \sin(4)$. The same can be obtained by taking W as the vertex, and BHP as the base, the angles in one direction will give

$$\sin WPH \cdot \sin WHB \cdot \sin WBP = \sin WBH \cdot \sin WHP \cdot \sin WPB.$$

In writing down the equations to be used, a good plan is to put down the sides emanating from the pole to all the other points, putting the line first in the first member, and then in the second; as,

$$WP \sin(\ ) = WB \sin(\ );$$
$$WB \cdot \sin(\ ) = WH \cdot \sin(\ );$$
$$WH \cdot \sin(\ ) = WP \sin(\ );$$

coming back to the first line used. Then we put in the angle that is opposite the side in the other term; as, (11) opposite

WB, (7) opposite *WP*, in accordance with the trigonometric theorem.

The following rule, so frequently quoted, is taken from Schott (C. S. Report, 1854).

The only choice in selecting the station to be used as the vertex, or pole, as it is sometimes called, is to take that vertex at which the triangles meet which form the triangle equations of condition, and to avoid small angles, since the tabular differences, being large, will give unwieldy coefficients. It is sometimes difficult to determine the precise number of condition equations that can be formed.

The least number of lines necessary to form a closed figure by connecting p points is p, and gives one angular condition. Every additional line, which must necessarily have been observed in both directions, furnishes a condition; hence a system of l lines between p points, $l - p + 1$ angle equations, where it must be borne in mind that each of the l lines must have both a forward and a backward sight.

When, in any system, the first two points are determined in reference to one another by the measurement of the line joining, then the determination of the position of any additional station requires two sides, or necessarily two directions; hence in any system of triangles between p points, we have to determine $p - 2$ points, which require $2(p - 2)$ directions, or by adding the first $2p - 3$. Consequently, in a system of l lines, $l - (2p - 3)$, or $l - 2p + 3$ sides are supernumerary, and give an equal number of side equations.

We have, therefore,

$$l - p + 1 \text{ angle equations;}$$
$$l - 2p + 3 \text{ side equations;}$$
$$2l - 3b + 4 \text{ in all.}$$

It is apparent that each point may be taken as the pole, and as many side equations formed as there are vertices. In a quadrilateral, for instance, if four side equations are formed, the fourth equation would involve the identical corrections contained in the others. Since there are only 12 angles in all, these can be incorporated in two equations, each of which contains 6 angle corrections.

From the formulæ just given, it will be seen that 4 conditional equations will be sufficient in a quadrilateral; 1 side and 3 angle equations, or 2 side and 2 angle equations, but never more than 2 side equations.

The method of station adjustment differs somewhat from the foregoing when the values of the angles depend upon directions.

In nearly all refined geodetic work angles are so determined ; that is, the zero of the circle is set at any position, the telescope is pointed upon the first signal to the left, and the micrometers or verniers read ; the telescope is then pointed to each in succession and the readings recorded. After reading the circle at the last pointing, this signal is again bisected and readings made, likewise with the others in the reverse order. The telescope is reversed in its Y's and a similar forward and backward set of pointings and readings made. These form a set. The circle is then shifted into a new position and another set observed, as already described. The average of the direct and reversed readings of each series is taken as a single determination of a direction.

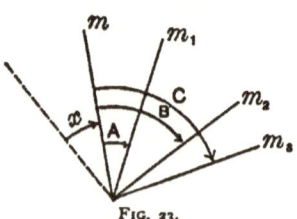

Fig. 23.

Let x be the angle between the zero of the instrument and the direction of the first line, A, B, C, etc., the angles the other lines make with the first, whose most probable values are to be determined, and let m_1, m_1', m_1' . . . be the reading of the circle when pointing to the signals in order, of which x_1 is the most probable, and the errors of observation $m_1 - x_1$. Supposing no errors existed, we should have the following equations:

$$m_1 - x_1 = 0; \quad m_1^1 - x_1 - A = 0;$$
$$m_1^2 - x_1 - B = 0; \quad m_1^3 - x_1 - C = 0.$$

The second series would give

$$m_2 - x_2 = 0; \quad m_2^1 - x_2 - A = 0;$$
$$m_2^2 - x_2 - B = 0; \quad m_2^3 - x_2 - C = 0;$$

and the nth, $\quad m_n - x_n = 0; \quad m_n^1 - x_n - A = 0;$
$$m_n^2 - x_n - B = 0; \quad m_n^3 - x_n - C = 0.$$

The most probable values will be those the sum of the squares of whose errors is a minimum. Also, the errors squared must be multiplied by the corresponding weights, p_1, $p_1^1, p_1^2 \ldots p_2, p_2^1 \ldots$ which will give

$$p_1(m_1 - x_1)^2 + p_1^1(m_1^1 - x_1 - A)^2 + p_1^2(m_1^2 - x_1 - B)^2$$
$$+ p_1^3(m_1^3 - x_1 - C)^2;$$

$$p_2(m_2 - x_2)^2 + p_2^1(m_2^1 - x_2 - A)^2 + p_2^2(m_2^2 - x_2 - B)^2$$
$$+ p_2^3(m_2^3 - x_2 - C)^2;$$

$$p_3(m_3 - x_3)^2 + p_3^1(m_3^1 - x_3 - A)^2 + p_3^2(m_3^2 - x_3 - B)^2$$
$$+ p_3^3(m_3^3 - x_3 - C)^2;$$

etc.,   etc.

Differentiating with respect to $x_1, x_2, x_3 \ldots A, B, C \ldots$ and placing the differential coefficients separately equal to zero, we shall have

$$\left.\begin{aligned}
&p_1 m_1 + p_1'm_1' + p_1^2 m_1^2 + p_1^3 m_1^3 \ldots \\
&\quad = (p_1 + p_1' + p_1^2 + p_1^3 \ldots)x_1 + p_1'A + p_1^2 B + p_1^3 C \ldots; \\
&p_2 m_2 + p_2'm_2' + p_2^2 m_2^2 + p_2^3 m_2^3 \ldots \\
&\quad = (p_2 + p_2' + p_2^2 + p_2^3 \ldots)x_2 + p_2'A + p_2^2 B + p_2^3 C \ldots; \\
&p_3 m_3 + p_3'm_3' + p_3^2 m_3^2 + p_3^3 m_3^3 \ldots \\
&\quad = (p_3 + p_3' + p_3^2 + p_3^3 \ldots)x_3 + p_3'A + p_3^2 B + p_3^3 C \ldots,
\end{aligned}\right\} \text{(A)}$$

etc.,   etc.;

$$\left.\begin{aligned}
&p_1'm_1' + p_2'm_2' + p_3'm_3' + \ldots \\
&\quad = (p_1' + p_2' + p_3' \ldots)A + p_1'x_1 + p_2'x_2 + p_3'x_3 \ldots; \\
&p_1^2 m_1^2 + p_2^2 m_2^2 + p_3^2 m_3^2 + \ldots \\
&\quad = (p_1^2 + p_2^2 + p_3^2 \ldots)B + p_1^2 x_1 + p_2^2 x_2 + p_3^2 x_3 \ldots; \\
&p_1^3 m_1^3 + p_2^3 m_2^3 + p_3^3 m_3^3 + \ldots \\
&\quad = (p_1^3 + p_2^3 + p_3^3 \ldots)C + p_1^3 x_1 + p_2^3 x_2 + p_3^3 x_3 \ldots.
\end{aligned}\right\} \text{(B)}$$

In these equations $x_1 - m_1$, $x_2 - m_2$, $x_3 - m_3 \ldots$ are the errors of observation; calling these x_1, x_2, $x_3 \ldots$ they will represent the corrections of the first, second, third ... pointings from the zero-mark—usually a small quantity.

By multiplying out the parenthesis in the second member of (A), and transposing all the terms from the first, we have

$$0 = p_1 x_1 - p_1 m_1 + p_1'x_1 - p_1'm_1' + p_1^2 x_1 - p_1^2 m_1^2 + p_1^3 x_1 - p_1^3 m_1^3 \\ + p_1'A + p_1^2 B + p_1^3 C \ldots;$$

$$0 = p_1(x_1 - m_1) + p_1'(x_1 - m_1') + p_1^2(x_1 - m_1^2) + p_1^3(x_1 - m_1^3) \ldots \\ + p_1'A + p_1^2 B + p_1^3 C.$$

Introduce into each parenthesis $m_1 - m_1$, except the first,

$$0 = p_1(x_1 - m_1) + p_1'(x_1 - m_1' - m_1 + m_1) + p_1^2(x_1 - m_1^2 + m_1 - m_1) \\ + p_1^3(x_1 - m_1^3 + m_1 - m_1) \ldots + p_1'A + p_1^2 B + p_1^3 C \ldots;$$

$$0 = p_1(x_1 - m_1) + p_1'[(x_1 - m_1) - (m_1' - m_1)]$$
$$+ p_1^2[(x_1 - m_1) - (m_1^2 - m_1)] + p_1^3[(x_1 - m_1) - (m_1^3 - m_1)]$$
$$+ p_1'A + p_1^2B + p_1^3C \ldots .$$

For $x_1 - m_1$ substitute x_1, and for $m_1' - m_1$ write m_1'; remembering that m_i^s, which is to take the place of $m_i^s - m_i$, does not mean the tth reading on the sth arc, as recorded, but the recorded reading *minus* the reading of the zero on that arc.

This will reduce the last equation to

$$0 = p_1x_1 + p_1'x_1 - p_1'm_1' + p_1^2x_1 - p_1^2m_1^2 + p_1^3x_1 - p_1^3m_1^3$$
$$+ p_1'A + p_1^2B + p_1^3C \ldots$$

$$p_1'm_1' + p_1^2m_1^2 + p_1^3m_1^3$$
$$= (p_1 + p_1' + p_1^2 + p_1^3)x_1 + p_1'A + p_1^2B + p_1^3C \ldots \left.\vphantom{\begin{array}{c}1\\1\\1\\1\end{array}}\right\}$$

In the same manner the other equations (A) reduce to

$$p_2'm_2' + p_2^2m_2^2 + p_2^3m_2^3 \ldots \qquad \left.\vphantom{\begin{array}{c}1\\1\end{array}}\right\} \text{(C)}$$
$$= (p_2 + p_2' + p_2^2 + p_2^3 \ldots)x_2 + p_2'A + p_2^2B + p_2^3C \ldots ;$$
$$p_3'm_3' + p_3^2m_3^2 + p_3^3m_3^3 \ldots$$
$$= (p_3 + p_3' + p_3^2 + p_3^3 \ldots)x_3 + p_3'A + p_3^2B + p_3^3C \ldots .$$

Likewise, equations (B) reduce to

$$p_1'm_1' + p_2'm_2' + p_3'm_3' \ldots$$
$$= (p_1' + p_2' + p_3' \ldots)A + p_1'x_1 + p_2'x_2 + p_3'x_3 \ldots ;$$
$$p_1^2m_1^2 + p_2^2m_2^2 + p_3^2m_3^2 \ldots \qquad \left.\vphantom{\begin{array}{c}1\\1\\1\end{array}}\right\} \text{(D)}$$
$$= (p_1^2 + p_2^2 + p_3^2 \ldots)B + p_1^2x_1 + p_2^2x_2 + p_3^2x_3 \ldots ;$$
$$p_1^3m_1^3 + p_2^3m_2^3 + p_3^3m_3^3 \ldots$$
$$= (p_1^3 + p_2^3 + p_3^3 \ldots)C + p_1^3x_1 + p_2^3x_2 + p_3^3x_3 \ldots .$$

When the signals observed upon are numerous, the solution of equations (C) and (D) would be very laborious.

Captain Yollond, of the Ordnance Survey of Great Britain, found the method of successive approximations sufficiently accurate.

Suppose x_1, x_2, x_3 ... severally equal to zero in (D), from which we find the first approximation :

$$A' = \frac{p_1'm_1' + p_2'm_2' + p_3'm_3' \cdots}{p_1' + p_2' + p_3' \cdots};$$

$$B' = \frac{p_1'm_1^2 + p_2'm_2^2 + p_3'm_3^2 \cdots}{p_1' + p_2' + p_3' \cdots};$$

$$C' = \frac{p_1'm_1^3 + p_2'm_2^3 + p_3'm_3^3 \cdots}{p_1' + p_2' + p_3' \cdots}.$$

Substituting these values in (C), we obtain a new value for x_1, x_2, x_3 ...

$$x_1 = \frac{p_1'(m_1' - A') + p_1^2(m_1^2 - B') + p_1^3(m_1^3 - C') \cdots}{p_1 + p_1' + p_1^2 + p_1^3 \cdots};$$

$$x_2 = \frac{p_2'(m_2' - A') + p_2^2(m_2^2 - B') + p_2^3(m_2^3 - C') \cdots}{p_2 + p_2' + p_2^2 + p_2^3 \cdots};$$

$$x_3 = \frac{p_3'(m_3' - A') + p_3^2(m_3^2 - B') + p_3^3(m_3^3 - C') \cdots}{p_3 + p_3' + p_3^2 + p_3^3 \cdots}.$$

Substituting these values in (D), we obtain the second approximation, or

$$A'' = \frac{p_1'(m_1' - x_1) + p_2'(m_2' - x_2) + p_3'(m_3' - x_3) \cdots}{p_1' + p_2' + p_3' \cdots};$$

$$B'' = \frac{p_1^{\,2}(m_1^{\,\prime} - x_1) + p_2^{\,2}(m_2^{\,\prime} - x_2) + p_3^{\,2}(m_3^{\,\prime} - x_3) \cdots}{p_1^{\,2} + p_2^{\,2} + p_3^{\,2} \cdots};$$

$$C'' = \frac{p_1^{\,2}(m_1^{\,\prime} - x_1) + p_2^{\,2}(m_2^{\,\prime} - x_2) + p_3^{\,2}(m_3^{\,\prime} - x_3) \cdots}{p_1^{\,2} + p_2^{\,2} + p_3^{\,2} \cdots}.$$

The values can be further substituted in (C) and the resulting values of x_1, x_2, x_3 ... placed in (D) for the third approximation for A, B, C ... However, the second has been found sufficient in good work.

The weights for observed directions is unity, and zero for any directions that could not be observed. The work can be materially shortened by pointing on the first object on the left, as the beginning of each series; and in each successive series the readings of the first direction should be diminished by the preceding direction, in this way taking as a zero the first direction of each series.

In the ordnance survey, the readings on the initial object were made the same in the different series by adding to the average readings of the microscopes on each signal such a quantity, positive or negative, as to make the initial readings the same.

Considering the weights unity,

$$A' = \frac{m_1^{\,\prime} + m_2^{\,\prime} + m_3^{\,\prime} \cdots}{n},$$

where n represents the number of series, or $A' =$ the arithmetical mean, say M_1; in the same way we find

$$B' = M_2, \qquad C' = M_3 \cdots$$

Substituting these values in the expressions for x_1, x_2 ... we have

$$x_1 = \frac{1}{n}(m_1{}^1 - M_1 + m_1{}^2 - M_2 + m_1{}^3 - M_3 \ldots),$$

or, $\quad -x_1 = \frac{1}{n}(M_1 - m_1{}^1 + M_2 - m_1{}^2 + M_3 - m_1{}^3 \ldots) = -M_1{}^1,$

and similarly for $x_2, x_3 \ldots$ we get $-M_2{}^1, -M_3{}^1 \ldots$
Placing these values in the second approximation,

$$A'' = \frac{1}{n}(m_1{}^1 - M_1{}^1 + m_2{}^1 - M_2{}^1 + m_3{}^1 - M_3{}^1 \ldots);$$

$$B'' = \frac{1}{n}(m_1{}^2 - M_1{}^1 + m_2{}^2 - M_2{}^1 + m_3{}^2 - M_3{}^1 \ldots);$$

$$C'' = \frac{1}{n}(m_1{}^3 - M_1{}^1 + m_2{}^3 - M_2{}^1 + m_3{}^3 - M_3{}^1 \ldots).$$

We have first obtained a constant reading for the initial direction, either its angular distance from an azimuth-mark, or by making the first direction zero. We then found the average of each direction, giving $A' = M_1, B' = M_2, \ldots$ or the arithmetical mean as the first approximation. Next we subtracted each average from each reading, giving a set of errors —the average of those in the same series giving $M_1{}^1, M_2{}^1 \ldots$

Afterwards these are taken from the readings of the corresponding series, giving diminished values of each direction; and the average of these diminished directions gives the second approximation.

A symbolic analysis can be seen in the appended table, followed by an example taken from the Report of the Ordnance Survey, 1858, page 65:

Initial Object.	A.	B.	C.	Averages.
m m m . . .	$m_1{}^1$ $m_2{}^1$ $m_3{}^1$ . . .	$m_1{}^2$ $m_2{}^2$ $m_3{}^2$ . . .	$m_1{}^3$ $m_2{}^3$ $m_3{}^3$ . . .	
Average	$\dot{M}_1$	$\dot{M}_2$	$\dot{M}_3$	
	$m_1{}^1 - M_1$ $m_2{}^1 - M_1$ $m_3{}^1 - M_1$ . . .	$m_1{}^2 - M_2$ $m_2{}^2 - M_2$ $m_3{}^2 - M_2$ . . .	$m_1{}^3 - M_3$ $m_2{}^3 - M_3$ $m_3{}^3 - M_3$ . . .	$M_1{}^1$ $M_2{}^1$ $M_3{}^1$ . .
	$m_1{}^1 - M_1{}^1$ $m_2{}^1 - M_2{}^1$ $m_3{}^1 - M_3{}^1$ . . .	$m_1{}^2 - M_1{}^1$ $m_2{}^2 - M_2{}^1$ $m_3{}^2 - M_3{}^1$ . . .	$m_1{}^3 - M_1{}^1$ $m_2{}^3 - M_2{}^1$ $m_3{}^3 - M_3{}^1$ . . .	
Averages....	$\dot{A}''$	$\dot{B}''$	$\dot{C}'$	

No. of Series.	Initial O.	$A = 11°\,7'$.	$B = 37°\,34'$.	$C = 97°\,54'$.	$D = 220°\,3'$.	Average Errors.
1	$4°21'29''.21$	$36''.04$	$14''.07$	$47''.84$	$19''.00$	
2	29.21	35.91	....	....	18.18	
3	29.21	34.21	11.86	....	....	
4	29.21	32.41	10.71	46.05	16.30	
5	29.21	....	11.91	48.30	14.17	
6	29.21	....	....	....	18.59	
Average	$29''.21$	$34''.64$	$12''.14$	$47''.40$	$17''.25$	
Errors.	$00''.00$ $.00$ $.00$ $.00$ $.00$ $.00$	$+\ 1''.40$ $+\ 1.27$ $-\ 0.43$ $-\ 2.23$ 	$+\ 1''.93$ .... $-\ 0.28$ $-\ 1.43$ $-\ 0.23$ 	$+\ 0''.44$ .... $-\ 1.35$ $+\ 0.90$	$+\ 1''.75$ $+\ 0.93$ .... $-\ 0.95$ $-\ 3.08$ $+\ 1.34$	$+1''.10$ $+0.73$ -0.23 -1.19 -0.60 $+0.67$
	$28''.11$ 28.48 29.44 30.40 29.81 28.54	$34''.94$ 35.18 34.44 33.60 	$12''.97$ 12.09 11.90 12.51 	$46''.74$ 46.28 48.90	$17''.90$ $17\ 45$ 17.49 14.77 17.92	
Average	$29''.13$	$34''.54$	$12''.37$	$47''.31$	$17''.11$	

This gives the directions as follows:

$$
\begin{aligned}
\text{Initial object} &= \quad 4°\ 21'\ 29''.13\,; \\
\text{direction } A'' &= \quad 11 \quad 7 \quad 34\ .54\,; \\
\text{direction } B'' &= \quad 37 \quad 34 \quad 12\ .37\,; \\
\text{direction } C'' &= \quad 97 \quad 54 \quad 47\ .31\,; \\
\text{direction } D'' &= 220 \quad 3 \quad 17\ .11.
\end{aligned}
$$

The third approximation, obtained in the same way, gave, omitting degrees and minutes: initial object $= 29''.12$, $A''' = 34''.55$, $B''' = 12''.40$, $C''' = 47''.34$, $D''' = 17''.08$, values differing from the above in the hundredths place only.

The angles depending upon these directions will be involved in the figure-adjustment, so their corrected values should be written $A + (1)$, $B + (2)$, $C + (3) \dots$ in which (1), (2), $(3) \dots$ are the corrections obtained in the figure-adjustment. In this operation the directions obtained at different stations have not the same weight; however, this can be computed from the formula already given on page 125, where we found $p = \dfrac{1}{2\epsilon^2}$

$$
= \frac{1}{\dfrac{2\Sigma(\epsilon^2)}{n^2}} = \frac{n^2}{2\Sigma(\epsilon^2)}.
$$

So we find the residuals by taking the difference between the individual diminished measures and the average, and divide the number of readings on that direction squared by twice the sum of the squares of the residuals; in the case of

$$
A,\ p = \frac{16}{3.1284}.
$$

To illustrate the formation of the equations of geometric condition let us take an example.

The angles adjusted at stations are:

at T, $M =$ 00° 00′ 00″ .;
$\quad\quad F =$ 83 30 34 .866 + (1) ;
$\quad\quad W =$ 287 14 13 .822 + (2) ;
at M, $T =$ 00 00 00 ;
$\quad\quad W =$ 66 56 10 .619 + (4) ;
$\quad\quad F =$ 293 57 16 .395 + (6) ;
at F, $W =$ 00 00 00 ;
$\quad\quad M =$ 20 00 09 .436 + (7) ;
$\quad\quad T =$ 349 33 27 .528 + (11);
at W, $F =$ 00 00 00 ;
$\quad\quad T =$ 13 17 05 .983 + (12);
$\quad\quad M =$ 332 59 01 .843 + (15).

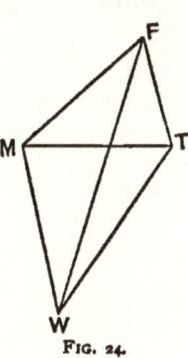

FIG. 24.

In the triangle MTF, we are to find the angles at each vertex, as follows:

$83°30'34''.866 + (1)$ $\quad\quad\quad\quad = MTF$;
$66\ \ 2\ 43\ .605 - (6)$ $\quad\quad\quad\quad = FMT$, or 360° − direction
$\quad\quad\quad\quad\quad\quad\quad\quad\quad\quad\quad\quad\quad\quad\quad F$ from T;
$\underline{30\ 26\ 41\ .908 + (7) - (11)}\quad\quad = MFT$;
$180°00'00''.379 + (1) - (6) + (7) - (11) =$ sum;
$\underline{180\ 00\ 00\ .015}\quad\quad\quad\quad\quad\quad\quad = 180° +$ spherical excess;
$0 = 0''.364 + (1) - (6) + (7) - (11).\quad\quad\quad$ Equation (I)

To find MFT, we subtract the direction of T from W, from 360°; this gives angle WFT; to this add the direction of M from W, or the angle WFM.

In the triangle TMW,

$72°45'46''.178 - (2)$ $\quad\quad\quad\quad = MTW$;
$66\ 56\ 10\ .619 + (4)$ $\quad\quad\quad\ = WMT$;
$\underline{40\ 18\ \ 4\ .140 + (12) - (15)}\quad = MWT$;
$180°00'00''.937 - (2) + (4) + (12) - (15) =$ sum;
$\underline{180\ 00\ 00\ .011}\quad\quad\quad\quad\quad\quad\quad = 180° +$ spherical excess;
$0 = + 0''.926 - (2) + (4) + (12) - (15).\quad\quad$ Equation (II)

In the triangle *WTF*,

$$13°17'05''.983+(12) \qquad\qquad = `TWF;$$
$$156\ 16\ 21\ .044+(1)-(2) \qquad = WTF;$$
$$10\ 26\ 32\ .472-(11) \qquad\qquad = TFW;$$
$$\overline{179°59'59''.499+(1)-(2)-(11)+(12)} = \text{sum};$$
$$180\ 00\ 00\ .009 \qquad\qquad\qquad = 180°+\text{spherical excess};$$
$$\overline{0 = -\ 0''.510 + (1)-(2)-(11)+(12).} \qquad\qquad \text{Equation (III)}$$

In the quadrilateral *TMFW*, the side equation is

$$1 = \frac{\sin TMW . \sin FWT . \sin TFM}{\sin MWT . \sin TFW . \sin FMT};$$

$$\sin TMW = \quad 9.9638207,6 + \quad 8.965(4)\ (8.965 = \text{tab. dif.});$$
$$\sin FWT = \quad 9.3613403,1 + \quad 89.174(12);$$
$$\sin TFM = \quad \underline{9.7047600,1 + \quad 35.824[(7)-(11)]};$$
$$\qquad\qquad\quad 29.0299210,8.$$

$$\sin MWT = \quad 9.8107734,2 + \quad 24.826[(12)-(15)];$$
$$\sin TFW = \quad 9.2582687,7 - \quad 114.245(11);$$
$$\sin FMT = \quad \underline{9.9608833,6 - \quad 9.354(6)};$$
$$\qquad\qquad\quad 29.0299255,5.$$

$$0 = -\ 44.7 + 8.965(4) + 9.354(6) + 35.824(7) + 78.421(11)$$
$$+\ 64.348(12) + 24.826(15).\ \text{Equation (IV)}$$

These four equations are solved for the unknowns, which are applied to the given directions with their proper signs, or to the angles directly, as just deduced.

In an extended triangulation, the position of every point is influenced to a certain extent by the directions at the adjacent signals; consequently, it is advisable to include in the equations of condition as many directions as possible. The influence of these directions upon an initial point diminishes with the distance, and finally becomes inappreciable, so that the triangulation can be divided into segments, each containing a convenient number of conditional equations. The corrections of the first are computed, and, as far as they go, these corrected values are substituted in the equations of condition in the second figure, and the sum of the squares of the remaining errors, each multiplied by its corresponding weight, made a minimum.

The equations of condition (I), (II), (III), (IV) . . . may be written

$$\left. \begin{array}{l} 0 = a + a_1 x_1 + a_2 x_2 \ldots ; \\ 0 = b + b_1 x_1 + b_2 x_2 \ldots ; \\ 0 = c + c_1 x_1 + c_2 x_2 \ldots ; \\ \cdot \quad \cdot \\ \cdot \quad \cdot \end{array} \right\} \quad \cdots \cdots \quad (E)$$

If $p_1, p_2 \ldots$ be the weights, corresponding to the corrections $x_1, x_2 \ldots$, the requirement that the sum of the squares of the errors be a minimum is

$$p_1 x_1^2 + p_2 x_2^2 + p_3 x_3^2 \ldots = \text{a minimum.} \quad \cdot \cdot \quad (F)$$

Differentiating (E) and (F), we have

$$0 = a_1 dx_1 + a_2 dx_2 + a_3 dx_3 \ldots ;$$
$$0 = b_1 dx_1 + b_2 dx_2 + b_3 dx_3 \ldots ;$$
$$0 = c_1 dx_1 + c_2 dx_2 + c_3 dx_3 \ldots ;$$
$$ \cdot \quad \cdot$$
$$ \cdot \quad \cdot$$
$$0 = p_1 x_1 dx_1 + p_2 x_2 dx_2 + p_3 x_3 dx_3 \ldots .$$

Solving these equations as explained on page 160, we have

$$
\left.
\begin{aligned}
p_1 x_1 &= a_1 I_1 + b_1 I_2 + c_1 I_3 \ldots ; \\
p_2 x_2 &= a_2 I_1 + b_2 I_2 + c_2 I_3 \ldots ; \\
p_3 x_3 &= a_3 I_1 + b_3 I_2 + c_3 I_3 \ldots .
\end{aligned}
\right\} \quad \ldots \quad \text{(G)}
$$

Substituting the values of x_1, x_2, x_3 ... as found in these equations in (E), we have

$$
0 = a + \frac{a_1}{p_1}(a_1 I_1 + b_1 I_2 + c_1 I_3 \ldots) + \frac{a_2}{p_2}(a_2 I_1 + b_2 I_2 + c_2 I_3 \ldots),
$$

or, $0 = a + \left(\dfrac{a^2}{p}\right)I_1 + \left(\dfrac{ab}{p}\right)I_2 + \left(\dfrac{ac}{p}\right)I_3 \ldots$

In the same way, remembering that (a^2) is the sum of the squares of quantities like a, as $a_1^2 + a_2^2 + a_3^2 \ldots$ and $(ab) = a_1 b_1 + a_2 b_2 + a_3 b_3 \ldots ,$

$$
\left.
\begin{aligned}
0 &= b + \left(\dfrac{ab}{p}\right)I_1 + \left(\dfrac{bb}{p}\right)I_2 + \left(\dfrac{bc}{p}\right)I_3 \ldots ; \\
0 &= c + \left(\dfrac{ac}{p}\right)I_1 + \left(\dfrac{bc}{p}\right)I_2 + \left(\dfrac{cc}{p}\right)I_3 \ldots .
\end{aligned}
\right\} \quad \ldots \quad \text{(H)}
$$

I_1, I_2, I_3 ..., being auxiliary multipliers, have their values obtained from (H) and substituted in (G), giving the numerical values of x_1, x_2, x_3 ...

Instead of using I_1, I_2 ... the Roman numerals I, II, III ... will be found more convenient, especially when the conditional equations are so numbered. The normal equations can be more readily formed.

To illustrate, suppose we have the following equations of condition:

$$\left.\begin{array}{l}
\text{I, } 0 = -\ 1.4042-(2)+(5)-(7)+(8)\,; \\
\text{II, } 0 = -\ 2.7737-(2)+(4)\,; \\
\text{III, } 0 = -\ 0.9595-(8)+(11)\,; \\
\text{IV, } 0 = -\ 1.2157-(3)+(4)\,; \\
\text{V, } 0 = -\ 0.9204-(3)+(5)-(7)+(10)\,; \\
\text{VI, } 0 = -\ 0.8424-(1)+(4)\,; \\
\text{VII, } 0 = -\ 0.3201-(1)+(5)-(7)+(9)\,; \\
\text{VIII, } 0 = +\ 0.999\ -(1)+(3)\,; \\
\qquad\cdot \qquad\qquad \cdot \\
\qquad\cdot \qquad\qquad \cdot \\
\text{X, } 0 = -\ 4.0567-(6)+(9)\,; \\
\text{XXV, } 0 = +\ 3.2980-0.00015(2)+15.5719(4)-15.571(5) \\
\qquad\qquad\qquad\qquad\qquad\qquad\qquad -\ 6.188(7)\,; \\
\quad\ \text{etc.,} \qquad\qquad\qquad\quad \text{etc.}
\end{array}\right\} \text{(I)}$$

(1), (2), (3) . . . represent the corrections to directions of the same number; then we multiply the terms involving (1), (2), by the reciprocals of their weights, giving

$$(1) = -\ 0.0800\text{VI} - 0.0800\text{VII} - 0.0800\text{VIII}$$

((1) occurs in VI, VII, and VIII, and 0.800 is the reciprocal of its weight);

$$\left.\begin{array}{l}
(2) = -0.2060\text{I} - 0.2060\text{II} - 0.0000309\text{XXV}\,; \\
(3) = -0.1580\text{IV} - 0.1580\text{V} + 0.1580\text{VIII}\,; \\
(4) = +0.3380\text{II}+0.3380\text{IV}+0.3380\text{VI}+5.263302\text{XXV}\,; \\
(5) = +0.2260\text{I} +0.2260\text{V} + 0.2260\text{VII}-3.51922\text{XXV}\,; \\
\quad\ \text{etc.,} \qquad\qquad\qquad\qquad \text{etc.}
\end{array}\right\} \text{(K)}$$

These values of (1), (2), (3) . . . are substituted in the equations of condition (I), giving numerical values for I, II, III . . .;

13

then these values substituted in equations (K) give the values of the corrections (1), (2), (3) . . . , which, when applied to the directions, will give their most probable values, satisfying the geometric conditions.

For the various methods of adjustments, see :

Jordan, Handbuch der Vermessungskunde, vol. i., pp. 339–346.

Bessel, Gradmessung in Ostpreussen, pp. 52–205.

Clarke, Geodesy, pp. 216–243.

Wright, Treatise on the Adjustments of Observations, pp. 250–348.

Ordnance Survey, Account of Principal Triangulation, pp. 354–416.

C. and G. Survey Report for 1854, pp. 63–95.

Die Königliche Preussische Landes-Triangulation, I., II., and III. Theile.

When a number of normal equations are to be solved, it is found, by some, desirable to eliminate by means of logarithms; but, as logarithms are never exact, there will always remain small residuals when the corrections are applied. Direct elimination is preferable, unless the coefficients are large; then the logarithmic plan is somewhat shorter. We will illustrate with an algebraic equation :

$$3u + x + 2y - z - 22 = 0; \quad . \quad . \quad . \quad (1)$$
$$4x - y + 3z - 35 = 0; \quad . \quad . \quad . \quad (2)$$
$$4u + 3x - 2y \quad\quad - 19 = 0; \quad . \quad . \quad . \quad (3)$$
$$2u \quad\quad + 4y + 2z - 46 = 0. \quad . \quad . \quad . \quad (4)$$

If the first equation were multiplied by $\frac{4}{3}$, the coefficient of u would be the same as in (3), and upon subtraction the u's would disappear. To multiply by $\frac{4}{3}$ is simply adding log 4 — log 3 to the logarithms of the coefficients of (1), omitting $3u$; we write, then, the logs of these coefficients :

	x.	*y.*	*z.*	22.
Log of coef.,	0.0000	0.3010	*n*0.0000	*n*1.3424 = 0 ;
log 4 − log 3,	0.1248	0.1248	0.1248	0.1248 ;
add	0.1248	0.4258	*n*.1248	*n*1.4672 ;
nat. numbers,	1.333	2.666	− 1.333	− 29.33 ;
coef. of (2),	3	− 2	+	− 19 ;
subtract	− 1.667	+ 4.666	− 1.333	− 10.33. . (5)

Take a factor that will make the coefficient of *u* in another equation equal to its coefficient in one of the other equations, multiply (4) by 2, or add to the logs of the coefficient in (4), the log of 2 = 0.3010.

	x.	*y.*	*z.*	46.
Logs of coef. of (4),	....	0.6020	0.3010	*n*1.6627 ;
log 2,	....	.03010	.03010	.03010 ;
add	....	0.9030	0.6020	*n*1.9637 ;
nat. numbers,	....	8	4	− 92 ;
coef. of (3),	3	− 2		− 19 ;
subtract	− 3	10	4	− 73. . . (6)

Continue to eliminate the same quantity from all the remaining equations until one equation remains with one unknown quantity.

The only advantage that this method suggests is, that only one quantity is used as a multiplier to make the coefficients identical; that factor is usually a fraction, whose log is simply the difference between the logs of the numerator and denominator.

Mr. Doolittle, of the Coast Survey, has developed another method of elimination, which can be found in the Report for 1878, page 115.

REDUCTION TO CENTRE OF STATION.

With the directions adjusted it is necessary, when an eccentric position has been occupied, to reduce the corrected observed directions to their equivalents at the centre, before computing the distances and co-ordinates.

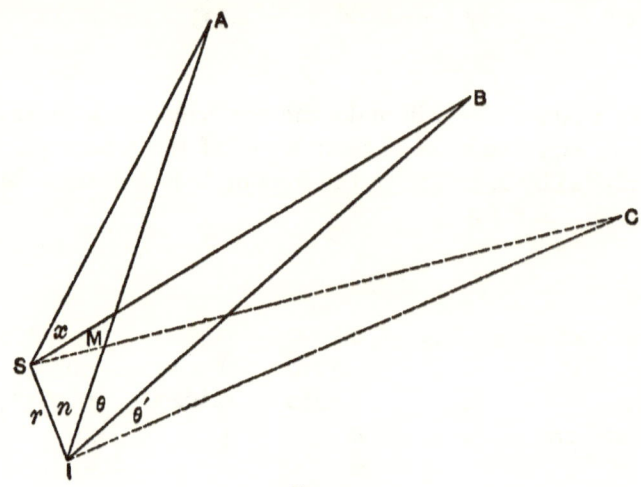

Fig. 25.

$$\theta = \text{observed angle};$$
$$x = \text{desired angle}.$$

Angle from signal to $A = a$, to $B = b$.

$$\text{Angle } m = A + x = \theta + B.$$

$$x = \theta + B - A.$$

$$\sin B : \sin (\theta + n) :: r : b, \quad \sin B = \frac{r \sin (\theta + n)}{b};$$

$$\sin A = \frac{r \sin n}{a}.$$

As B and A are always very small, they may be regarded as equal to B sin $1''$, and A sin $1''$, $B = \dfrac{r \sin (\theta + n)}{b \sin 1''}$, $A = \dfrac{r \sin n}{a \sin 1''}$;

hence, $\qquad x = \theta + \dfrac{r \sin (\theta + n)}{b \sin 1''} - \dfrac{r \sin n}{a \sin 1''}$.

Also,

angle between B and $C = AOC + \dfrac{r \cdot \sin (n + \theta + \theta')}{c \cdot \sin 1''} - \dfrac{r \sin n}{a \sin 1''}$.

From the above equations it will be seen that all angles that are read from the same initial point have for their corrections the same last term ; so this term can be computed for each initial direction and applied to the various angles. In both terms of the corrections there are two constants for each station, r and sin $1''$; so the work can be facilitated by tabulating their values. The signs of the terms will depend upon the sign of the sine function.

It will assist in the computation to take the angle between the signal and the first point to the right and continue in that direction.

Signal 23 feet from instrument. Angle between H and $C.T = 71°$.

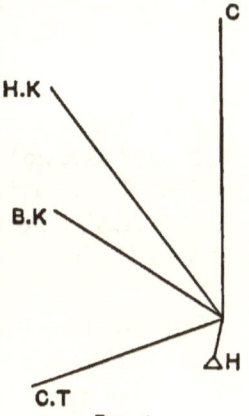

Fig. 26.

Log dist. H to $C.T$ in $M. = 4.7534757$;
log dist. H to $B.K$ in $M. = 4.6503172$;
log dist. H to $H.K$ in $M. = 4.8385482$;
log dist. H to $\quad C$ in $M. = 4.6145537$.

	Sig. to C.T.+ C.T to B.K.	Sig. to C.T+ C.T to H.K.	Sig. to C.T + C.T to C.	Sig. to B.K+ B.K to H.K.	Sig. to B.K+ B.K to C.
Direction	107° 24' 17"	120° 53' 55"	166° 06' 57"	120° 53' 59"	166° 06' 55"
Log sin......	9.9796466	9.9335264	9.3801384	9.9335214	9.3801555
Log r(M)....	0.8457389	0.8457389	0.8457389	0.8457389	0.8457389
Co. log dist..	5.3496828	5.1614518	5.3854463	5.1614518	5.3854463
Co. log sin 1"	5.3144251	5.3144251	5.3144251	5.3144251	5.3144251
	1.4894934	1.2551442	0.9257487	1.2551372	0.9257658
Cor	30".86	17".99	8".42	17".99	8".43

	Signal to C.T.	Signal to B.K.
Direction........	71 — 00 — 00	107 — 24 — 17
Log sin..........	9.9756701	9.9796466
Log r(M)........	0.8457389	0.8457389
Co. log dist......	5.2465243	5.3496828
Co. log sin 1"....	5.3144251	5.3144251
	1.3823584	1.4894934
Cor............ ...	24".12	30".87

CORRECTED ANGLES.

$C.T.$ to $B.K =$ 36° 24' 17"+30".86—24".12=36° 24' 23".74 ;

$C.T.$ to $H.K =$ 49° 53' 55"+17".99—24".12=49° 53' 48".87 ;

$C.T$ to $C.$ = 95° 06' 57"+ 8".42—24".12=95° 06' 41".30 ;

$B.K.$ to $H.K =$ 13° 29' 42"+17".99—30".87=13° 29' 29".12 ;

$B.K$ to $C.$ = 58° 42' 38"+ 8".42—30".87=58 °42' 15".55.

The distances used above were obtained from the observed values of the angles, and are, therefore, only approximate. In the case of refined work, it will be necessary to use these corrected values and again compute the distances ; then, with the correct distances, recompute the reduction to centre.

With the most probable value for all the directions, the angles of all the triangles can be found by taking a given direction from 360°, or by adding or subtracting two or more directions.

Then with a base, measured, or previously computed, each side can be found by the trigonometric formulæ $a =$ $\dfrac{b \sin \left(A - \dfrac{\varepsilon}{3}\right)}{\sin \left(B - \dfrac{\varepsilon}{3}\right)}$, and $c = \dfrac{b \cdot \sin \left(C - \dfrac{\varepsilon}{3}\right)}{\sin \left(B - \dfrac{\varepsilon}{3}\right)}$, in which ε is the computed spherical excess, as obtained from using approximate lengths and angles.

If there are more than one base in the triangulation-net, the most satisfactory method is to compute each base from all the others, and take the mean of the logarithmic values so found; or, if the entire scheme is involved in a single figure, the absolute term in the side equation can be made equal to the ratio of the two bases, $\dfrac{B_1}{B_2}$, instead of unity.

We can also find the length of any line as influenced by two or more bases. Let $B_1, B_2, B_3 \ldots$ be the bases, x the most probable value of any side in the triangulation, and $r_1, r_2, r_3 \ldots$ be the ratio of each side respectively to x; the errors then will be

$$(r_1x - B_1), \qquad (r_2x - B_2), \qquad (r_3x - B_3) \ldots$$

Now, if $p_1, p_2, p_3 \ldots$ be the weights of the bases, then

$$p_1(r_1x - B_1)^2 + p_2(r_2x - B_2)^2 + p_3(r_3x - B_3)^2 \ldots = \text{a minimum.}$$

Placing the differential coefficient with respect to $x = 0$, we find

$$x = \frac{p_1 r_1 B_1 + p_2 r_2 B_2 + p_3 r_3 B_3 \ldots}{p_1 r_1^2 + p_2 r_2^2 + p_3 r_3^2 \ldots}.$$

From this we can find the most probable length of one base from all the others. To do this we suppose x to be one of the bases, say B_1, then $r_1 = 1$,

$$x = \frac{p_1 B_1 + p_2 r_2 B_2 + p_3 r_3 B_3 \cdots}{p_1 + p_2 r_2^2 + p_3 r_3^2},$$

the correction will be $x - B_1$, or

$$x - B_1 = \frac{p_1 B_1 + p_2 r_2 B_2 + p_3 r_3 B_3 \cdots}{p_1 + p_2 r_2^2 + p_3 r_3^2} - B_1$$

$$= \frac{p_1 B_1 + p_2 r_2 B_2 + p_3 r_3 B_3 - p_1 B_1 - p_2 r_2^2 B_1 - p_3 r_3^2 B_1}{p_1 + p_2 r_2^2 + p_3 r_3^2 \cdots}$$

$$= \frac{p_2 r_2 (B_2 - r_2 B_1) + p_3 r_3 (B_3 - r_3 B_1) \cdots}{p_1 + p_2 r_2^2 + p_3 r_3^2 \cdots}.$$

The adjustments so far considered affect the geometric conditions, and in their operations may, by changing the directions of the lines, change the azimuth, making a greater or less difference between the observed and computed azimuths. In refined geodetic work, the azimuth is observed at least twice in each figure, and sometimes twice in each quadrilateral.

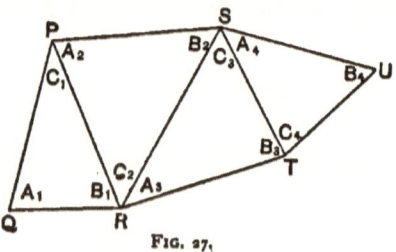

FIG. 27.

Using Wright's figure and notation, we take PQ and TU as two lines whose azimuths have been observed with the simplest and most approved connections. PQ, as a known line, enables one to compute PR, and from PR we can go direct to SR, thence to ST; so these lines are called sides of continuation.

Let $A_1, A_2, A_3, \ldots$ be the angles opposite the sides of continuation;

$B_1, B_2, B_3, \ldots$ the angles opposite the sides taken as bases;

$C_1, C_2, C_3, \ldots$ the angles opposite those sides not used;

$Z_1, Z_2,$ the measured azimuths of PQ and TU, supposed to be correct, and therefore subject to no change;

Z' the computed azimuth of TU, reckoning from the south around by the west. $C_1, C_2, C_3, C_4,$ are the only angles that enter into this computation; and the excess, E, of the observed over the computed azimuth gives

$$-(C_1) + (C_2) - (C_3) + (C_4) = E, \quad . \quad . \quad \text{Eq. (L)}$$

in which (C_1), (C_2) ... represent the corrections to $C_1, C_2 \ldots$ Now, since the triangles have had their angles adjusted to the conditions imposed upon them, their total corrections must be zero.

$$\left.\begin{array}{l} (A_1) + (B_1) + (C_1) = 0; \\ (A_2) + (B_2) + (C_2) = 0; \\ (A_3) + (B_3) + (C_3) = 0. \end{array}\right\} \quad \ldots \quad \text{(M)}$$

Also, the sum of the errors squared

$$(A_1)^2 + (B_1)^2 + (C_1)^2 \ldots = \text{a minimum.}$$

The solution of these equations would give

$$A_1 = \tfrac{1}{8}E, \qquad A_3 = -\tfrac{1}{8}E \ldots;$$
$$B_1 = \tfrac{1}{8}E, \qquad B_3 = -\tfrac{1}{8}E \ldots;$$
$$C_1 = -\tfrac{1}{4}E, \qquad C_3 = +\tfrac{1}{4}E \ldots.$$

If there were n intervening triangles, we would find

$$A_1 = \frac{1}{2n}E, \qquad A_3 = -\frac{1}{2n}E;$$

$$B_1 = \frac{1}{2n}E, \qquad B_3 = -\frac{1}{2n}E;$$

$$C_1 = -\frac{1}{n}E, \qquad C_3 = +\frac{1}{n}E.$$

From which the following rule is deduced:

· "Divide the excess of the observed over the computed azimuth by the number of triangles, and apply one half of this quantity to each of the angles adjacent to the unused side, and the total quantity with its sign changed to the third angle. In each following triangle the signs are reversed."

The discrepancies between the observed and computed latitudes and longitudes are very slight, and can be adjusted arbitrarily.

CHAPTER VII.

FORMULÆ FOR THE COMPUTATION OF GEODETIC LATITUDES, LONGITUDES AND AZIMUTHS.

WHEN we know the geographical position of a point, and the distance and direction to another, the co-ordinates of the second can be computed from the data just named, by using formulæ for the difference in the latitudes, longitudes and azimuths.

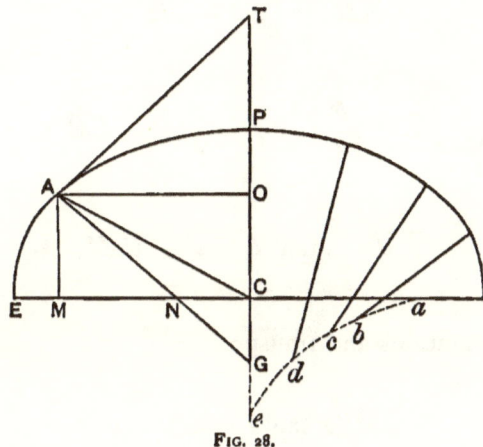

FIG. 28.

In the above meridian section, let A be a point whose latitude is L. By definition it is equal to the angle ANE, formed by the normal AN and the equatorial radius EC.

$AG = N$, $e^2 = \dfrac{a^2 - b^2}{a^2}$, in which a is the semi-major axis, and b the semi-minor.

The subnormal in an ellipse $MN = CM \cdot \dfrac{b^2}{a^2}$.

$$AM = NM \cdot \tan L = CM \cdot \frac{b^2}{a^2} \cdot \tan L,$$

squaring, $\overline{AM}^2 = \overline{CM}^2 \cdot \dfrac{b^4}{a^4} \tan^2 L.$ $\hspace{2cm}$ (1)

The equation of an ellipse gives

$$\overline{AM}^2 = \frac{b^2}{a^2}(a^2 - \overline{CM}^2),$$

therefore $\overline{CM}^2 \cdot \dfrac{b^4}{a^4} \tan^2 L = \dfrac{b^2}{a^2}(a^2 - \overline{CM}^2),$

$$\overline{CM}^2 \cdot \frac{b^2}{a^2} \tan^2 L = a^2 - \overline{CM}^2;$$

clearing of fractions and transposing,

$$\overline{CM}^2(b^2 \tan^2 L + a^2) = a^4;$$

hence $\overline{CM}^2 = \dfrac{a^4}{b^2 \tan^2 L + a^2},$

substituting $\dfrac{\sin^2 L}{\cos^2 L}$ for $\tan^2 L,$

$$\overline{CM}{}^{2} = \frac{a^{4}\cos^{2}L}{b^{2}\sin^{2}L + a^{2}\cos^{2}L} = \frac{a^{4}\cos^{2}L}{b^{2}(1 - \cos^{2}L) + a^{2}\cos^{2}L}$$

$$= \frac{a^{4}\cos^{2}L}{(a^{2} - b^{2})\cos^{2}L + b^{2}},$$

$$CM = \frac{a^{2}\cos L}{\sqrt{(a^{2} - b^{2})\cos^{2}L + b^{2}}}.$$

From definition $a^{2}e^{2} = a^{2} - b^{2}$,

$$CM = \frac{a^{2}\cos L}{\sqrt{a^{2}e^{2}\cos^{2}L + b^{2}}} = \frac{a^{2}\cos L}{\sqrt{a^{2}e^{2}(1 - \sin^{2}L) + a^{2} - a^{2}e^{2}}}$$

$$= \frac{a^{2}\cos L}{\sqrt{a^{2} - a^{2}e^{2}\sin^{2}L}} = \frac{a^{2}\cos L}{a\sqrt{1 - e^{2}\sin^{2}L}} = \frac{a\cos L}{\sqrt{1 - e^{2}\sin^{2}L}},$$

which is the radius of a meridian.

In the triangle AGO, $AG = \dfrac{AO}{\sin AGO} = \dfrac{AO}{\cos L} = \dfrac{a}{\sqrt{1 - e^{2}\sin^{2}L}}$

$= N$, or the normal produced to the minor axis.

The ordinate AM can be found from the equation of the ellipse, $a^{2} \cdot \overline{AM}{}^{2} + b^{2} \cdot \overline{CM}{}^{2} = a^{2}b^{2}$,

$$\overline{AM}{}^{2} = \frac{a^{2}b^{2} - b^{2}\overline{CM}{}^{2}}{a^{2}} = \frac{a^{2}b^{2}}{a^{2}} - \frac{b^{2}\,a^{2}\cos^{2}L}{a^{2}(1 - e^{2}\sin^{2}L)}$$

$$= b^{2} - \frac{b^{2}\cos^{2}L}{1 - e^{2}\sin^{2}L} = b^{2} - \frac{b^{2}(1 - \sin^{2}L)}{1 - e^{2}\sin^{2}L}$$

$$= \frac{b^{2} - b^{2}e^{2}\sin^{2}L - b^{2} + b^{2}\sin^{2}L}{1 - e^{2}\sin^{2}L}$$

$$= \frac{b^2 \sin^2 L(1 - e^2)}{1 - e^2 \sin^2 L} = \frac{a^2 \sin^2 L(1 - e^2)^2}{1 - e^2 \sin^2 L};$$

therefore

$$AM = \frac{a(1 - e^2) \sin L}{\sqrt{1 - e^2 \sin^2 L}}.$$

To find the normal AN, we take the triangle AMN, in which

$$AN = \frac{AM}{\sin L} = \frac{a(1 - e^2)}{\sqrt{1 - e^2 \sin^2 L}}.$$

The radius of curvature, $R = \dfrac{-\left[1 + \left(\dfrac{dy}{dx}\right)^2\right]^{\frac{3}{2}}}{\dfrac{d^2y}{dx^2}}.$

In the general equation, $\dfrac{d^2y}{dx^2} = -\dfrac{b^4}{a^2y^3}$, $\left(\dfrac{dy}{dx}\right)^2 = \dfrac{b^4x^2}{a^4y^2}$,

substituting these values,

$$R = \frac{-\left[1 + \dfrac{b^4x^2}{a^4y^2}\right]^{\frac{3}{2}}}{-\dfrac{b^4}{a^2y^3}} = \frac{a^2y^3}{b^4}\left[\frac{a^4y^2 + b^4x^2}{a^4y^2}\right]^{\frac{3}{2}} = \frac{(a^4y^2 + b^4x^2)^{\frac{3}{2}}}{a^4b^4}.$$

In this expression we place for x the value we found for CM, and for y that of AM; this gives

$$R = \frac{\left[\dfrac{a^{6}(1-e^{2})^{2}\sin^{2}L}{1-e^{2}\sin^{2}L} + \dfrac{a^{6}(1-e^{2})^{3} - a^{6}(1-e^{2})^{3}\sin^{2}L}{1-e^{2}\sin^{2}L}\right]^{\frac{3}{2}}}{a^{6}b^{6}}$$

$$= \frac{\left[\dfrac{a^{6}(1-e^{2})^{3}}{1-e^{2}\sin^{2}L}\right]^{\frac{3}{2}}}{a^{6}b^{6}} = \frac{a^{9}(1-e^{2})^{3}}{a^{6}(1-e^{2})^{2}} \cdot \frac{1}{(1-e^{2}\sin^{2}L)^{\frac{3}{2}}};$$

$$R = \frac{a(1-e^{2})}{(1-e^{2}\sin^{2}L)^{\frac{3}{2}}}.$$

The terminal points *a, b, c, d* and *e* of the radii of curvature form an evolute ; at the equator,

$$L = 0°, \qquad \sin L = 0, \qquad R = a(1-e^{2}) = \frac{b^{2}}{a}.$$

At the pole,

$$L = 90°, \qquad R = \frac{a(1-e^{2})}{(1-e^{2})^{\frac{3}{2}}} = \frac{a}{(1-e^{2})^{\frac{1}{2}}} = \frac{a^{2}}{b}.$$

The above formulæ are in terms of geographic latitude; the geocentric latitude is equal to the angle formed at the centre by the equator and radius. In the figure it is the angle *ACM*. Calling it θ, we have

$$\tan \theta = \frac{AM}{MC} = \frac{a(1-e^{2})\sin L}{(1-e^{2}\sin^{2}L)^{\frac{1}{2}}} \div \frac{a\cos L}{(1-e^{2}\sin^{2}L)^{\frac{1}{2}}}$$

$$= \frac{(1-e^{2})\sin L}{\cos L} = (1-e^{2})\tan L = \frac{b^{2}}{a^{2}}\tan L.$$

It is always less than the geographic latitude, the difference being greatest at those places where $a^2 - b^2$ is the greatest, or at latitude 45°, N. or S., where the difference is about 11′ 30″.

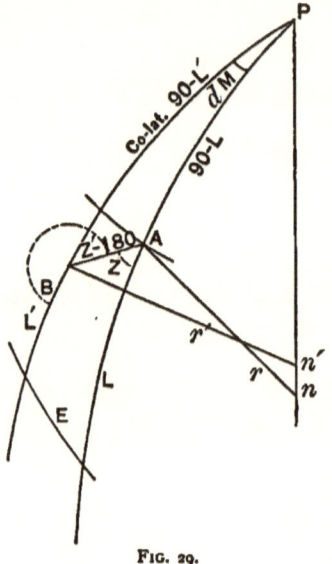

FIG. 29.

In the adjoining figure, P is the pole, E the plane of the equator, A and B two points on the earth's surface whose latitudes are L and L', co-latitudes λ and λ', and the geodesic line AB is l. An and Bn', the normals, are N and N', and R and R' the radii of curvature.

The azimuth is estimated from the south around by the west; the angle $PAB = 180° - Z$, will be designated x, and the angle between the two meridians AP and BP is the difference of longitude, dM.

In the spherical triangle APB,

$$\cos \lambda' = \cos \lambda \cos l + \sin \lambda \sin l \cos x.$$

In relation to λ and λ', l is very small, so that a series involving l will converge, so we write $\lambda' = f(\lambda + l)$.

Developing this by Taylor's formula, we have

$$\lambda' = \lambda + \frac{d\lambda}{dl}l + \frac{d^2\lambda}{2 \cdot dl^2}l^2 + \frac{d^3\lambda}{2 \cdot 3 \cdot dl^3}l^3 \cdot \ldots \quad (1)$$

In order to find these differential coefficients, some relation must be established between λ, $\lambda + d\lambda$ and dl. Taking these as sides of a differential spherical triangle having the angle between the first and third sides, we have

$$\cos(\lambda + d\lambda) = \cos dl \cos \lambda + \sin \lambda \sin dl \cos x.$$

Obtaining the differential coefficients of λ with respect to l, we substitute them in (1); this is accomplished by expanding the last equation so as to have

$$\cos \lambda \cos d\lambda - \sin \lambda . \sin d\lambda = \cos dl \cos \lambda$$
$$+ \sin \lambda \sin dl \cos x;$$
$$\cos d\lambda = 1,$$

and $\sin d\lambda = d\lambda$. This reduces the equation to

$$\cos \lambda - \sin \lambda \, d\lambda = \cos \lambda \, dl + \sin \lambda \, dl \cos x.$$

Cos λ may be assumed equal to $\cos \lambda . dl$, and therefore they eliminate each other, leaving $\dfrac{d\lambda}{dl} = -\cos x$.

$$\frac{d^2\lambda}{dl} = \sin x . dx \qquad \frac{d^2\lambda}{dl^2} = \sin x \frac{dx}{dl} ; \text{ but } \frac{dx}{dl} = -\sin x . \cot \lambda ;$$

$$\frac{d^2\lambda}{dl^2} = \sin^2 x \cot \lambda, \qquad \text{also } \frac{d^3\lambda}{dl^3} = \sin^2 x \cos x(1 + 3\cot^2 \lambda).$$

Substituting L' and L for λ' and λ, and remembering that cot $\lambda = \tan L$, we obtain from (1),

$$L' - L = -l\cos x - \tfrac{1}{2}l^2 \sin^2 x \tan L$$
$$+ \tfrac{1}{6}l^3 \sin^2 x \cos x(1 + 3\tan^2 L),$$

14

$$x = 180° - Z, \quad \cos x = -\cos Z, \quad \sin x = \sin Z,$$
$$L' - L = -dL,$$

$$L' - L = l \cos Z + \tfrac{1}{2}l^2 \sin^2 Z \tan L$$
$$- \tfrac{1}{6}l^3 \sin^2 Z \cos Z(1 + 3\tan^2 L);$$

or, $\ - dL = l \cos Z + \tfrac{1}{2}l^2 \sin^2 Z \tan L$
$$- \tfrac{1}{6}l^3 \sin^2 Z \cos Z(1 + 3\tan^2 L).$$

The value of l has been considered as expressed in arc, while in computation it will be given in linear measure. Therefore $l = \dfrac{K}{N}$, where K is the length of the line, and N the radius of the imaginary sphere on which L is a point

$$-dL = \frac{K \cos Z}{N} + \frac{K^2 \sin^2 Z \tan L}{2N^2} - \frac{K^3 \sin^2 Z \cos Z}{6N^3}(1 + 3\tan^2 L).$$

This needs a further transformation, to refer the formula to an ideal sphere whose radius is the radius of curvature of the middle meridian. This, however, cannot be known until L' is computed; however, we can start with the value of R for the initial latitude, and apply a correction. The reduction is made by multiplying by the ratio of $\dfrac{N}{R}$; we also divide by arc $1''$ to convert the arc dL into a linear multiple of $1''$. This gives

$$- dL = \frac{K}{R . \text{arc } 1''} \cos Z + \frac{K^2}{2R . N \text{ arc } 1''} \sin^2 Z . \tan L$$
$$- \frac{K^3}{6RN^2 \text{ arc } 1''} \sin^2 Z \cos Z(1 + 3\tan^2 L). \quad (2)$$

Denoting the radius of curvature of the mean meridian by R_m, dL must be increased by $\dfrac{R - R_m}{R_m} \cdot dL$;

$$R - R_m = \frac{a(1 - e^2)}{(1 - e^2 \sin^2 L)^{\frac{3}{2}}} - \frac{a(1 - e^2)}{(1 - e^2 \sin^2 L_m)^{\frac{3}{2}}}$$

$$= a(1 - e^2)\frac{(1 - e^2 \sin^2 L_m)^{\frac{3}{2}} - (1 - e^2 \sin^2 L)^{\frac{3}{2}}}{(1 - e^2 \sin^2 L)^{\frac{3}{2}}(1 - e^2 \sin^2 L_m)^{\frac{3}{2}}}.$$

Expanding by binomial formula,

$$(1 - e^2 \sin^2 L_m)^{\frac{3}{2}} = 1 - \tfrac{3}{2}e^2 \sin^2 L_m + \tfrac{3}{4}e^4 \sin^4 L_m \ldots;$$
$$(1 - e^2 \sin^2 L)^{\frac{3}{2}} = 1 - \tfrac{3}{2}e^2 \sin^2 L + \tfrac{3}{4}e^4 \sin^4 L_m \ldots;$$

subtracting $\qquad\qquad = \tfrac{3}{2}e^2 \sin^2 L - \tfrac{3}{2}e^2 \sin^2 L_m \ldots,$

omitting higher powers of e; or, $\tfrac{3}{2}e^2(\sin^2 L - \sin^2 L_m)$.
This can be reduced as follows:

$$\sin(L - L_m) \qquad\qquad = \sin L \cos L_m - \cos L \sin L_m;$$
$$\sin(L + L_m) \qquad\qquad = \sin L \cos L_m + \cos L \sin L_m;$$
$$\sin(L - L_m)\sin(L + L_m) = \sin^2 L \cos^2 L_m - \cos^2 L \sin^2 L_m$$
$$= \sin^2 L(1 - \sin^2 L_m) - (1 - \sin^2 L)\sin^2 L_m$$
$$= \sin^2 L - \sin^2 L_m.$$

L_m is the mean latitude between L and $L + dL$,

$$L_m = \tfrac{1}{2}(L + L + dL),$$
$$\sin(L - L_m)\sin(L + L_m) = \sin(L - L - \tfrac{1}{2}dL)\sin(2L + \tfrac{1}{2}dL)$$
$$= dL \sin L \cdot \cos L, \text{ nearly.}$$

Then, $\dfrac{R - R_m}{R_m}$

$$= \tfrac{3}{2}e^2 \frac{a(1 - e^2)dL \cdot \sin L \cdot \cos L}{(1 - e^2 \sin^2 L)^{\frac{1}{2}} \cdot (1 - e^2 \sin^2 L^m)^{\frac{3}{2}}} \times \frac{(1 - e^2 \sin^2 L_m)^{\frac{3}{2}}}{a(1 - e^2)}$$

$$= \tfrac{3}{2}e^2 \frac{dL \cdot \sin L \cdot \cos L}{(1 - e^2 \sin^2 L)^{\frac{1}{2}}}.$$

As this is a small quantity, it can be converted into a linear function by dividing it by arc $1''$, giving

$$\frac{R - R_m}{R_m}dL = \tfrac{3}{2}e^2 \frac{(dL)^2 \sin L \cdot \cos L}{(1 - e^2 \sin^2 L)^{\frac{1}{2}} \operatorname{arc} 1''}.$$

Introducing this into (2), we have, after placing

$$B = \frac{1}{R \cdot \operatorname{arc} 1'''}, \qquad C = \frac{\tan L}{2R \cdot N \cdot \operatorname{arc} 1'''}, \qquad E = \frac{1 + 3\tan^2 L}{6N^2},$$

$$h = \frac{K}{R \cdot \operatorname{arc} 1''} \cdot \cos Z, \qquad D = \frac{\tfrac{3}{2}e^2 \sin L \cos L}{(1 - e^2 \sin^2 L)^{\frac{3}{2}} \operatorname{arc} 1'''},$$

$$-dL = K\cos Z \cdot B + K^2 \sin^2 Z \cdot C - hK^2 \sin^2 Z \cdot E + D \cdot (dL)^2.$$

The last term was devised by Professor Hilgard, in 1846.

The factors B, C, D, E, are given in the last pages computed for Clarke's (1866) Spheroid.

When the line is not more than fifteen miles, the third term can be omitted, and h^2 put for $(dL)^2$, giving as an abbreviated formula

$$- dL = K\cos Z \cdot B + K^2 \sin^2 Z \cdot C + h^2 D.$$

Francoeur has given a purely trigonometric method for deriving the formula just obtained.

Using the same figure, we write $PA = 90° - L$, $PB = 90° - L'$.

In the spherical triangle PAB, we know PA, $AB = l$, and the angle $PAB = 180° - Z$.

$$\cos PB = \cos PA \cos l + \sin PA \sin l \cos PAB;$$
$$\cos (90° - L') = \cos (90° - L) \cos l$$
$$+ \sin (90° - L) \sin l \cos (180° - Z);$$
$$\sin L' = \sin L \cos l - \cos L \sin l \cos Z.$$

Subtracting both sides from $\sin L$,

$$\sin L - \sin L' = \sin L - \sin L \cos l + \cos L \sin l \cos Z$$
$$= \sin L(1 - \cos l) + \cos L \sin l \cos Z$$
$$= 2 \sin L \sin^2 \tfrac{1}{2}l + \cos L \sin l \cos Z.$$

$$\sin L - \sin L' = 2 \sin \tfrac{1}{2}(L - L') \cos \tfrac{1}{2}(L + L');$$

suppose $L - L' = d$, then $L + L' = 2L - (L - L') = 2L - d$,

and $\quad \tfrac{1}{2}(L - L') = \tfrac{1}{2}d, \quad \tfrac{1}{2}(2L - d) = L - \tfrac{1}{2}d,$

therefore $\sin L - \sin L' = 2 \sin \tfrac{1}{2}d \cos(L - \tfrac{1}{2}d)$
$$= 2 \sin \tfrac{1}{2}d(\cos L \cos \tfrac{1}{2}d + \sin L \sin \tfrac{1}{2}d);$$

that is, $2 \sin \tfrac{1}{2}d \cos \tfrac{1}{2}d \cos L + 2 \sin^2 \tfrac{1}{2}d \sin L$
$$= 2 \sin L \sin^2 \tfrac{1}{2}l + \cos L \sin l \cos Z.$$

Dividing by $2 \cos L \cos^2 \tfrac{1}{2}d$, we obtain

$$\frac{\sin \tfrac{1}{2}d}{\cos \tfrac{1}{2}d} + \frac{\sin^2 \tfrac{1}{2}d \sin L}{\cos^2 \tfrac{1}{2}d \cos L} = \frac{\sin L \sin^2 \tfrac{1}{2}l}{\cos L \cos^2 \tfrac{1}{2}d} + \frac{\cos L \sin l \cos Z}{2 \cos L \cos^2 \tfrac{1}{2}d};$$

$$\tan \tfrac{1}{2}d + \tan^2 \tfrac{1}{2}d \tan L = \frac{\tan L \sin^2 \tfrac{1}{2}l}{\cos^2 \tfrac{1}{2}d} + \frac{\sin l \cos Z}{2 \cos^2 \tfrac{1}{2}d};$$

$$\tan \tfrac{1}{2}d(1 + \tan \tfrac{1}{2}d \tan L) = \frac{1}{\cos^2 \tfrac{1}{2}d}(\tan L \sin^2 \tfrac{1}{2}l + \tfrac{1}{2}\sin l \cos Z).$$

Placing H for the last parenthesis, we may write

$$\tan \tfrac{1}{2}d(1 + \tan \tfrac{1}{2}d \tan L) = \frac{H}{\cos^2 \tfrac{1}{2}d} = H(1 + \tan^2 \tfrac{1}{2}d);$$

$$\tan \tfrac{1}{2}d + \tan^2 \tfrac{1}{2}d \tan L = H + H \tan^2 \tfrac{1}{2}d;$$

$$\tan \tfrac{1}{2}d + (\tan L - H)\tan^2 \tfrac{1}{2}d = H. \quad . \quad . \quad . \quad (1)$$

In the expression for H, l is small; so we can write for $\sin l$ its serial value, $\sin l = l - \dfrac{l^3}{6}$, also $\sin^2 \tfrac{1}{2}l = \dfrac{l^2}{4}$, which will give

$$H = \tfrac{1}{2}l \cos Z + \tfrac{1}{4}l^2 \tan L - \tfrac{1}{12}l^3 \cos Z.$$

We must now solve (1) for $\tfrac{1}{2}d$; for short we will put $\tfrac{1}{2}d = c$, and $\tan L - H = h$, so (1) reduces to

$$\tan c + \tan^2 c \cdot h = H, \quad \text{or} \quad \tan c = \frac{H}{1 + h \cdot \tan c}. \quad (2)$$

Neglecting $h \cdot \tan c$, we have $\tan c = H$, as the value of first approximation. Substituting this value for $\tan c$ in the second member of (2),

$$\tan c = \frac{H}{1 + h \cdot H} = H - hH^2, \text{ by division.}$$

Again, substituting this second approximation in (1), we have as the third approximation

$$\tan c = H - hH^2 + 2h^2H^3 ;$$

by continuing to the fourth, we get
$$\tan c = H - hH^2 + 2h^2H^3 - 5h^3H^4 \ldots$$

The development of an arc in terms of its tangent gives

$$c = \tan c - \tfrac{1}{3}\tan^3 c + \tfrac{1}{5}\tan^5 c \ldots$$

Placing in this the value of tan c, just found, we have

$$c = H - hH^2 + 2h^2H^3 - 5h^3H^4 - \tfrac{1}{3}(H - hH^2 \ldots)^3 , \ldots$$
$$= H - hH^2 + (2h^2 - \tfrac{1}{3})H^3 + (1 - 5h^2)hH^4 \ldots$$

Resuming our notation, we have $c = \tfrac{1}{2}d$, and $h = \tan L - H$; this gives

$$h = \tan L - \tfrac{1}{2}l\cos Z - \tfrac{1}{4}l^2\tan L + \tfrac{1}{12}l^3\cos Z ;$$
$$\tfrac{1}{2}d = \tfrac{1}{2}l\cos Z + \tfrac{1}{4}l^2\tan L - \tfrac{1}{12}l^3\cos Z$$
$$\qquad - (\tan L - \tfrac{1}{2}l\cos Z - \tfrac{1}{4}l^2\tan L + \tfrac{1}{12}l^3\cos Z \ldots)$$
$$\qquad (\tfrac{1}{2}l\cos Z + \tfrac{1}{4}l^2\tan L - \tfrac{1}{12}l^3\cos Z)^2 \ldots$$

Multiplying this out and retaining terms of l to l^3,

$$\tfrac{1}{2}d = \tfrac{1}{2}l\cos Z + \tfrac{1}{4}l^2\tan L - \tfrac{1}{4}l^2\tan L\cos^2 Z - \tfrac{1}{12}l^3\cos Z$$
$$\qquad + \tfrac{1}{12}l^3\cos^3 Z - \tfrac{1}{4}l^3\tan^2 L\cos Z + \tfrac{1}{4}l^3\tan^2 L\cos^3 Z$$
$$= \tfrac{1}{2}l\cos Z + \tfrac{1}{4}l^2\tan L(1 - \cos^2 Z) - \tfrac{1}{12}l^3\cos Z(1 - \cos^2 Z)$$
$$\qquad - \tfrac{1}{4}l^3\cos Z\tan^2 L(1 - \cos^2 Z)$$
$$= \tfrac{1}{2}l\cos Z + \tfrac{1}{4}l^2\tan L\sin^2 Z - \tfrac{1}{12}l^3\cos Z\sin^2 Z$$
$$\qquad - \tfrac{1}{4}l^3\cos Z\sin^2 Z\tan^2 L$$
$$= \tfrac{1}{2}l\cos Z + \tfrac{1}{4}l^2\tan L\sin^2 Z - \tfrac{1}{12}l^3\cos Z\sin^2 Z(1 + 3\tan^2 L) ;$$

$$d = l\cos Z + \tfrac{1}{2}l'\tan L\sin'Z - \tfrac{1}{4}l'\cos Z\sin'Z(1 + 3\tan'L).$$

Remembering that $d = L - L'$, we have here the identical formula given on page 210.

There is still another form to which this can be reduced, involving more factors that can be tabulated, and at the same time occurring in the computation of longitude and azimuth.

Take (2) and substitute u'' for $\dfrac{K}{N\sin 1''} = \dfrac{K(1 - e'\sin'L)^{\frac{1}{2}}}{a\sin 1''}$;

multiply this by $\dfrac{N}{R}$, it becomes $\dfrac{1 - e'\sin'L}{1 - e'}$; reducing this fraction and omitting terms above e',

$$= 1 + e' - e'\sin'L = 1 + e'(1 - \sin'L) = 1 + e'\cos'L.$$

The first term becomes

$$(1 + e'\cos'L)u''\cos Z;$$

likewise the second term

$$:= (1 + e'\cos'L)(u''\sin Z)'\tan L\,\frac{\sin 1''}{2};$$

substituting, it becomes

$$L' = L - (1 + e'\cos'L)u''\cos Z - \tfrac{1}{2}\sin 1''(1 + e'\cos'L)(u''\sin Z)'.$$

This formula gives good results for distances of twenty miles and under.

The algebraic sign of the different terms depends upon the trigonometric functions of Z.

Whenever the sides are more than a hundred miles long, this method of difference of latitude will introduce some errors.

In that case, the method to be followed is to solve the spheroidal triangle formed by the two points and the pole, involving as trigonometric functions the sought co-latitude, azimuth and difference of longitude.

LONGITUDE.

Referring to the figure on page 208, and using the same notation, we get in the triangle ABP, $\sin \lambda' : \sin x :: \sin l : \sin dM$. Supposing the radius of the sphere to be $Bn' = N$, $l = \dfrac{K}{N'}$, and that l and dM are proportional to their sines

$$\sin \lambda' : \sin Z :: \frac{K}{N'} : dM \text{ arc } 1'', \qquad dM = \frac{K \cdot \sin Z}{N' \cos L' \text{ arc } 1'''}$$

λ' and L' being complementary, $\sin \lambda' = \cos L'$.

If very accurate geodetic computations are to be made, a small correction must be applied, owing to the difference between the arcs and sines of small angles. This correction can be taken from the table on page 274.

The quantity dM increases towards the west. The algebraic sign of the equation depends upon $\sin Z$, which is $+$ between $0°$ and $180°$.

$$\text{If we place } u'' = \frac{K}{N \sin 1'''}, \qquad dM = \frac{u'' \sin Z}{\cos L};$$

this, however, supposes that $\dfrac{K}{N} = \dfrac{K}{N'}$, which is only approximately so.

AZIMUTH.

The initial azimuth of the base or initial line being known, that of any line emanating from either extremity can be known by adding to or subtracting from the azimuth of this base the angle between the two lines.

Let $A\,B$ be the base, and C a point making angle m with AB at A: if the azimuth of $AB = Z$, that of AC will equal $Z \pm m$. But in order to determine the direction of a line extending from C, as CD, the azimuth of CA must be known. If the earth's surface were a plane, Z' would equal $180° + Z$; but the spheroidal shape of the earth complicates this as well as all other geodetic problems.

Again referring to figure on page 208, in the triangle APB, by Napier's Analogies,

$$\tan \tfrac{1}{2}dM : \cot \tfrac{1}{2}(x + x') :: \cos \tfrac{1}{2}(\lambda' - \lambda) : \cos \tfrac{1}{2}(\lambda + \lambda'),$$

from which $\cot \tfrac{1}{2}(x + x') = \dfrac{\cos \tfrac{1}{2}(\lambda + \lambda')}{\cos \tfrac{1}{2}(\lambda' - \lambda)} \tan \tfrac{1}{2}dM$;

but $\qquad\qquad\qquad x = 180° - Z,$

therefore $\quad x + x' = 180 - Z + x' = 180° + (x' - Z)$;

$$\cot \tfrac{1}{2}[(180° + (x' - Z)] = - \tan \tfrac{1}{2}(x' - Z),$$

but $(x' - Z) = dZ$, also $\lambda = 90° - L$, and $\lambda' = 90° - L'$,

therefore $\lambda + \lambda' = 180° - L - L' = 180° - (L + L')$;
$$\lambda' - \lambda = 90° - L' - (90° - L) = L - L' = dL;$$

$$\cos \tfrac{1}{2}[(180° - (L + L')] = \sin \tfrac{1}{2}(L + L') = \sin L$$

the formula then reduces to

$$\tan \tfrac{1}{2}dZ = - \tan \tfrac{1}{2}dM \frac{\sin L_m}{\cos \tfrac{1}{2}dL}.$$

Supposing that $\tan \tfrac{1}{2}dZ : \tan \tfrac{1}{2}dM :: dZ : dM$,

$$- dZ = dM \frac{\sin L_m}{\cos \tfrac{1}{2}dL}.$$

This is not exactly correct; the correction can readily be found by adding a term, say x, to the fourth term of the above proportion and solving for the value of x. It will be found that $\tfrac{1}{12}dM^2 \cos^2 L_m \sin L_m \sin^2 1''$ must be added to the above value of dZ. The factor $\dfrac{\cos^2 L_m \sin L_m \sin^2 1''}{12}$ can be tabulated as factor F, a table of which is appended; the expression then becomes

$$- dZ = dM \frac{\sin L_m}{\cos \tfrac{1}{2}dL} + dM^2 F;$$

$$Z' = Z \pm 180° + dZ.$$

The algebraic sign of dZ will depend upon dM. As the azimuth is estimated by common consent from the south around by the west, so long as the initial azimuth is less than 180°, the reverse azimuth $Z' = Z + 180° + dZ$; but if more than 180°, $Z' = Z - 180° + dZ$.

A table of values is given for $\cos \tfrac{1}{2}dL$ for lines of twenty miles and under. The term involving F can be omitted, and the value of dM deduced above substituted in its place, giving $Z' = Z \pm 180° + \dfrac{u'' \sin Z}{\cos L'} \cdot \sin L_m.$ It has also been found sufficiently accurate to omit $\cos \tfrac{1}{2}dL$ and write $- dZ = dM \sin L_m.$

In accurate work the azimuth should be determined at least once in every figure by astronomic observation. This operation is fully described in works on practical astronomy.

L. M. Z. FORM FOR PRIMARY TRIANGULATION.

		°	′	″
Z	Mount Blue to Mount Pleasant............................	26	19	27.01
L	Mount Pleasant and Ragged (R. is to the left of M. P.)........	85	35	25.67
Z	Mount Blue to Ragged (360° − (85° − 35′ etc. − 26° − 19′ . . .).......	300	44	1.34
dZ	....		50	3.71
	....	301	34	5.05
Z′	Ragged to Mount Blue (Z + dZ − 180°)...................	121	34	5.05

(with +)

	°	′	″			°	′	″
L	44	43	40.121	Mount Blue..........................	M	70	20	11.921
dL	−	30	55.978	110740.6M, log 5.0443070.............	dM −		11	27.659
L′	44	12	44.143	Ragged....	M′	69	08	44.262

K	5 0443070	K²	10.08861			h	3.2632
cos Z	9.7084622	sin² Z	9.86854	(dL)²	6.5372	K² sin²	9.9571
B	8.5104895	C	1.39991	D	2.3933	E	6.2069
h	3.2632587		1.35706		8.9305		9.4271
1st term	1833.406	3d term	0.085			(dM)²	10.896²
2d term	22.754	4th term	− 0.267	arg.		F	7.840
dL	1856.160	K	5.0443070	K	− 218		8.736
3d and 4th	− .182	sin Z	9 9342721²	dM	+ 317	dM	3.6322302
− dL	1855.978	A′ cos L′ ar. co.	8.5090158	cos	+ 99	sin L_m cos ½dL ar. co.	9.8454305
L_m	44−28−12.13		0.1446254				0.0000040
		dM	99 3.6322302 − 4787.757			− dZ 2d term	3.4776647² 3003.76 − 05 3003.71

Notes upon the Computation.—The angle Mount Pleasant and Ragged is recorded minus, since the second point is to the right of the first—contrary to the graduation of the instrument. 180° is subtracted, since the general direction is east. In the sixth column, − 218 and 317 correspond to the correction due to the supposition that the arc and sine are equal; the value, 99, is added to dM; dM is negative, since sin Z is minus. In the azimuth-computation, the second term, .05, is the antilogarithm of 8.736; this is negative, therefore .05 is subtracted.

The data here used were taken from the Coast Survey records. There the L, M and Z were computed, using Bessel's constants: the results are, Z^B = 05″.55, Z^C = 5″.05, L^B = 43″.955, L^C = 44″.143, M^B = 43″.578, M^C = 44″.262.

In using the abbreviated formula, the third and fourth terms would be omitted in latitude, but in their place should be inserted $h^2 D$.

In longitude, the correction for the ratio of sine to arc is not inserted. Also, for azimuth-computation cos $\frac{1}{2}dL$, and $(dM)^2F$ are insignificant, and consequently left out. The terms that are disregarded could not affect the result beyond the tenth of a second, in lines less than a hundred miles in length. A very convenient form in use in the U. S. Geological Survey is appended, employing the abbreviated formula already given :

Names of Stations.	Position.	Observed Angles.	Correction by L. S.	Corrections arbitrary.	Spherical Angles.	Spherical Excess	Final Plane Angles.
		° ′ ″	″	″	″	″	° ′ ″
Big Knob.....	Sought,	144 17 55.62		−.4	55.22	−1.83	144 17 53.39
Holston	Right,	13 29 28.86		−.1	28.76	−1.83	13 29 26.93
High Knob...	Left,	22 12 41.69		−.18	41.51	−1.83	22 12 39.68

(In the Position column, spanning the Right and Left rows: "Known side. Triangle, No. 1.")

Computing Letter.	Logarithms of their Sines.	Calculation of the Sides.	Sides in Yards.	Designation.
S.	9.7660909	log RL............ = 4.8391933 a. c. log sin S..... = 0.2339091 log sin R ... . = 9.3678952	4.8780609	Holston—High Knob.
R.		log LS............ = 4.4409976	4.4798652	Big Knob—High Knob.
		log $RL.$ + a. c. log sin S } ... = 5.0731024 log sin L.......... = 9.5775136		
L.		log RS......... ... = 4.6506160	4.6894836	Holston—Big Knob.

The column marked correction by *L. S.* is for the corrections obtained in figure-adjustment. When it is not possible to make this adjustment, the error, after deducting spherical excess, must be distributed arbitrarily. If the angles are approximately equal, one third the error should be applied to each angle; if not equal, the distribution should be proportional to the size of the angles. If one signal should be dim, or uncertain, it may be best to give to the angle between it and the other point the bulk of the error. Occasionally the angle deserving the greatest correction can be determined by examining the individual readings. If they vary considerably, showing a wide range, the inference is that the average is somewhat uncertain, and that the principal source of error in the triangle is at this point. Such evidence as this, and the appearance of the signals from each other should have some weight in distributing the error. The most convenient form of blank for computation is to have three or four sets of the upper slip printed on the left side, and the same number of the lower, on the right side of a book.

Names of Stations.	LATITUDES.	
	$L'= L-u'' (1+\epsilon^2 \cos^2 L) \cos Z - \frac{1}{2} \sin 1'' \sin^2 Z u''^2(1+\epsilon^2 \cos^2 L) \tan L.$	
Holston......	Authority,　　U. S. Geo. Survey.	
	Latitude (L)......$=36\ 27\ 27.41$	
	log K (yds)......$=\ 4.8780609$	$\frac{1}{2}$ sin 1''.......$=\ 4.3845448$
	log $\dfrac{1}{N \sin 1''}$......$=\ 8.4703976$	2 log sin Z....$=\ 9.7058236$
	log u''.............$=\ 3.3484585$	2 log u''......$=\ 6.6969170$
	log $(1 + \epsilon^2 \cos^2 L)$..$=\ 0.0018710$	..............$=\ 0.0018710$
	log cos Z......$(-)=\ 9.8460032$	log tan L.....$=\ 9.8685368$
	log 1st term.......$=\ 3.1963327$	log 2d term...$=\ 0.6576932$
	1st term.......$(+)=\ \ \ \ 1571.57$	
	2d term........$(-)=\ \ \ \ \ \ \ 4.55$	2d term......$=\ \ \ \ 4''.55$
	1567.02	
	δL............$(+)=\ \ \ \ 26\ 07.02$	
	L...............$=36\ 27\ 27.41$	$L+L'$........$=73\ 21\ 01.84$
High Knob...	Latitude (L')......$=36\ 53\ 34.43$	$\dfrac{L+L'}{2}$......$=36\ 40\ 30.92$

$K = 75519.81$ yards.　Triangle, No. 1: Book, 1: Page, 1.

LONGITUDES.	AZIMUTHS.	REMARKS.
$M' = M + \dfrac{u'' \sin Z}{\cos L'}$.	$Z' = Z \pm 180° - (\delta M)\sin\dfrac{L+L'}{2}$.	
Authority, U. S. G. S.	.... U. S. G. S.	
Longitude M .... $= 82\ 04\ 38.17$	Azimuth Z...... $= 134\ 32\ 39.47$	
log sin Z......(+)$= $ 9.8529118	180	
log u''.... ..... $=$ 3.3484585	$Z\,(+)\,180°$...... $= 314\ 32\ 39.47$	
3.2013703		
log cos L'....(+)$= $ 9.9029592	log sin $\dfrac{L+L'}{2}$... $= $ 9.7761771	
log (δM).....(+)$=$ 3.2984111	...........(+)$= $ 3.2984111	
(+)$= $ 1987.98	log δZ......(−)$= $ 3.0745882	
	δZ in seconds... $= $ 1187.38	
δM.........(+)$= $ 33 07.98	δZ.........(−)$= $ 19 47.38	
M.............. $= 82\ 04\ 38.17$	$Z\,(+)\,180°$...... $= 314\ 32\ 39.47$	
M'............. $= 82\ 37\ 46.15$	Azimuth Z'..... $= 314\ 12\ 52.09$	

The latitude blank should occupy the left, and the longitude and azimuth the right side of a book. Two forms should be on each page, the second serving as a check computation, by determining the third point of the triangle from the other end of the base. For example: in triangle ABC, suppose $L. M. Z.$ of A and B is known, C can be determined from A, and also from B. The average of these values is to be taken, to be used in connection with A or B in determining D, etc. ...

CHAPTER VIII.

FIGURE OF THE EARTH.

WITH the geographical positions of the termini of a line and its length known, it is possible to find an equivalent for its length along a meridian or a parallel, thus obtaining a value for a degree in that latitude.

Assuming that the earth's meridian section is an ellipse of small ellipticity, we can develop a formula giving the length of an arc in terms of the terminal latitudes, the semi-axes, and ellipticity. Also the problem almost the converse, by which the values of the axes and ellipticity can be found.

Let L, L', and l represent the terminal and middle latitudes of an arc whose amplitude is λ; a, b, and ε, the semi-major, semi-minor axes of the meridian-section, and the ellipticity; S, the length of the arc; r, the radius vector, and θ, the geocentric latitude.

The equation for the ellipse is

$$\frac{x^2}{a^2} + \frac{y^2}{b^2} = 1 ; \qquad (1)$$

$x = r \cos \theta, y = r \sin \theta$, substituting in (1),

$$\frac{r^2 \cos^2 \theta}{a^2} + \frac{r^2 \sin^2 \theta}{b^2} = 1 ;$$

divide by r^2, $\dfrac{\cos^2 \theta}{a^2} + \dfrac{\sin^2 \theta}{b^2} = \dfrac{1}{r^2}.$ (2)

On page 207 we found

$$\tan \theta = \frac{b^2}{a^2} \tan L, \quad \text{or} \quad \frac{\sin^2 \theta}{\cos^2 \theta} = \frac{b^4 \sin^2 L}{a^4 \cos^2 L},$$

from which

$$\sin^2 \theta = \frac{b^4 \sin^2 L \cos^2 \theta}{a^4 \cos^2 L}.$$

Substituting for $\cos^2 \theta$, $1 - \sin^2 \theta$, and solving, we get

$$\sin^2 \theta = \frac{b^4 \sin^2 L}{a^4 \cos^2 L + b^4 \sin^2 L}.$$

By a similar process we get

$$\cos^2 \theta = \frac{a^4 \cos^2 L}{a^4 \cos^2 L + b^4 \sin^2 L}.$$

Placing these equivalents in (2),

$$\frac{a^2 \cos^2 L + b^2 \sin^2 L}{a^4 \cos^2 L + b^4 \sin^2 L} = \frac{1}{r^2}. \tag{3}$$

In the ellipse, $b^2 = a^2(1 - \varepsilon)^2$ in which ε is the ellipticity; substituting this in (3),

$$\frac{a^2 \cos^2 L + a^2(1 - \varepsilon)^2 \sin^2 L}{a^4 \cos^2 L + a^4(1 - \varepsilon)^4 \sin^2 L} = \frac{1}{r^2}.$$

Dividing out a^2, and writing $1 - \sin^2 L$ for $\cos^2 L$, after reduction, we have

$$r^2(1 - 2\varepsilon \sin^2 L + \varepsilon^2 \sin^2 L)$$
$$= a^2(1 - 4\varepsilon \sin^2 L + 6\varepsilon^2 \sin^2 L - 4\varepsilon^3 \sin^2 L + \varepsilon^4 \sin^2 L);$$

omitting terms involving powers of ε above the second,

15

$$r^2 = a^2(1 - \epsilon \sin^2 L)^2,$$
$$r = a(1 - \epsilon \sin^2 L).$$

The formula for rectifying a polar curve is,

$$\frac{ds}{dL} = \sqrt{r^2 \frac{d\theta^2}{dL^2} + \frac{dr^2}{dL^2}}, \qquad \frac{dr}{dL} = -2a\epsilon \sin L \cos L,$$

$$\frac{d\theta}{dL} = 1 - 2\epsilon + 4\epsilon \sin^2 L.$$

This is obtained by differentiating the equation

$$a^2 \tan \theta = b^2 \tan L, \qquad \text{or} \qquad \tan \theta = (1 - \epsilon)^2 \tan L;$$

$$\frac{dL}{ds} = \sqrt{a^2(1 - \epsilon \sin^2 L)^2 (1 - 2\epsilon + 4\epsilon \sin^2 L)^2 + 4a^2\epsilon^2 \sin^2 L \cos^2 L}$$
$$= a(1 - 2\epsilon + 3\epsilon \sin^2 L);$$

omitting in the above all terms involving ϵ above the second power before extracting the square root.

$$ds = a(1 - 2\epsilon + 3\epsilon \sin^2 L)dL = a(1 - \frac{\epsilon}{2} - \frac{3}{2}\epsilon \cos 2L)dL,$$

placing $\qquad \sin^2 L = \frac{1}{2}(1 - \cos 2L).$

Integrating the above between the limits L and L', we have

$$s = a[(1 - \tfrac{1}{2}\epsilon)(L - L') - \tfrac{3}{4}\epsilon(\sin 2L - \sin 2L')],$$

$b = a(1 - \epsilon)$, from which $\epsilon = \dfrac{a - b}{a}$. Substituting this in the above equation,

$$s = a\left[\left(1 - \frac{a-b}{2a}\right)(L - L') - \frac{3(a-b)}{4a}(\sin 2L - \sin 2L')\right]$$

$$= \left(\frac{a+b}{2}\right)(L - L') - \frac{3(a-b)}{4}(\sin 2L - \sin 2L')$$

$$= \tfrac{1}{2}(a+b)\lambda - \tfrac{3}{8}(a - b)(\sin L \cos L - \sin L' \cos L')\ . \quad (4)$$

$$L - L' = \lambda, \quad \text{and} \quad l = \frac{L+L'}{2}; \quad 2l = L + L';$$

$$\sin \lambda = \sin (L - L') = \sin L \cos L' - \sin L' \cos L;$$
$$\cos 2l = \cos (L + L') = \cos L \cos L' - \sin L \sin L';$$
$$\sin \lambda \cos 2l = \sin L \cos L \cos^2 L' - \sin^2 L . \sin L' \cos L'$$
$$- \sin L' \cos^2 L \cos L' + \sin^2 L' \sin L \cos L.$$

Substituting in this

$$\sin^2 L' = 1 - \cos^2 L', \quad \text{also} \quad \sin^2 L = 1 - \cos^2 L,$$

it reduces to

$$\sin \lambda \cos 2l = \sin L \cos L - \sin L' \cos L',$$

which is the same as the last term in (4); therefore

$$s = \tfrac{1}{2}(a + b)\lambda - \tfrac{3}{8}(a - b)\sin \lambda \cos 2l. \quad (5)$$

This requires a particular ellipsoid from which to obtain the value of a and b, but it gives a means of finding a and b, if all the other terms are known, which is the problem geodesy attempts to solve. Suppose s, λ, l, s', λ', l' be the lengths, amplitudes, and mean latitudes of two arcs, we will have

$$s = \tfrac{1}{2}(a + b)\lambda - \tfrac{3}{4}(a - b)\sin\lambda\cos 2l;$$
$$s' = \tfrac{1}{2}(a + b)\lambda' - \tfrac{3}{4}(a - b)\sin\lambda'\cos 2l';$$

solving for $\dfrac{(a+b)}{2}$, and $\dfrac{(a-b)}{2}$,

$$\frac{a+b}{2} = \frac{s'\sin\lambda\cos 2l - s\sin\lambda'\cos 2l'}{\lambda\sin\lambda'\cos 2l' - \lambda'\sin\lambda\cos 2l};$$

$$\frac{a-b}{2} = \frac{1}{3}\cdot\frac{s'\lambda - s\lambda'}{\lambda'\sin\lambda\cos 2l - \lambda\sin\lambda'\cos 2l'};$$

from which a, b, and ε can be found. s and s' are the distances between parallels, whereas in practice our lines make an angle with the meridian, so that its projection upon the meridian must be found.

To find the effect of errors in the values s and s' upon a and b, we would differentiate the above equations, regarding s and s' only as variables. In the result the denominators would remain; consequently the minimum error would occur when the denominator is a maximum, that is, when $2l' = 0$, and $l = 90°$, or when one arc is at the equator and the other near the pole.

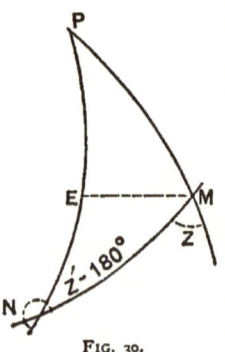

Fig. 30.

Let P be the pole of the spheroid, PM and PN two meridians passing through the points M and N, whose geographic and geocentric latitudes are L, L', θ, and θ'. $PM = 90° - \theta$, and $PN = 90° - \theta'$, from which $NE = \theta - \theta'$, which we will call x; also the line $NM = s$, a known quantity.

In the spherical triangle MPN, by Gauss's formulæ,

$$\sin \tfrac{1}{2}(PN - PM) \cos \tfrac{1}{2}MPN = \sin \tfrac{1}{2}MN \sin \tfrac{1}{2}(PMN - PNM);$$
$$\cos \tfrac{1}{2}(PN - PM) \cos \tfrac{1}{2}MPN = \cos \tfrac{1}{2}MN \sin \tfrac{1}{2}(PMN + PNM).$$

Dividing the first by the second,

$$\tan \tfrac{1}{2}(PN - PM) = \tan \tfrac{1}{2}MN \frac{\sin \tfrac{1}{2}(PMN - PNM)}{\sin \tfrac{1}{2}(PMN + PNM)};$$

$$PMN = 180° - Z, \qquad PNM = Z' - 180°.$$

hence
$$\tfrac{1}{2}(PMN - PNM) = \tfrac{1}{2}(360° - (Z + Z'))$$
$$= 180° - \tfrac{1}{2}(Z + Z'),$$

and
$$\tfrac{1}{2}(PMN + PNM) = \tfrac{1}{2}(Z' - Z).$$

Substituting these values,

$$\tan \frac{x}{2} = \tan \tfrac{1}{2}s \frac{\sin \tfrac{1}{2}(Z + Z')}{\sin \tfrac{1}{2}(Z' - Z)}.$$

Placing $h = \dfrac{\sin \tfrac{1}{2}(Z + Z')}{\sin \tfrac{1}{2}(Z' - Z)}$, we have $\tan \dfrac{x}{2} = h \tan \dfrac{s}{2}$; writing for $\tan \dfrac{x}{2}$ and $\tan \dfrac{s}{2}$ their developments,

$$\frac{x}{2} + \frac{x^3}{24} + \frac{x^5}{240} \cdots = h\left(\frac{s}{2} + \frac{s^3}{24} + \frac{s^5}{240} \cdots\right).$$

Solving this equation for x in terms of s, by approximation, we have for the first value $x = sh$; substituting this for x' and x^{2}, we have, after transposing,

$$\frac{x}{2} = \frac{sh}{2} + \frac{s^{3}h}{24} - \frac{s^{3}h^{3}}{24} + \frac{s^{5}h}{240} - \frac{s^{5}h^{5}}{240} \cdots = \frac{sh}{2} + \frac{sh}{2}\left(\frac{s^{2} - s^{2}h^{2}}{12}\right)$$
$$+ \frac{sh}{2}\left(\frac{s^{4} - s^{4}h^{4}}{120}\right),$$

or $x = sh\left[1 + \frac{s^{2}}{12}(1 - h^{2}) + \frac{s^{4}}{120}(1 - h^{4}) \cdots \right]$

for the second approximation ; and this value of x, substituted in the first equation, gives

$$x = sh\left[1 + \frac{s^{2}}{12}(1 - h^{2}) + \frac{s^{4}}{240}(1 - h^{2})(2 - 3h^{2}) \cdots \right]$$

for the (A) third approximation.

If $h = \dfrac{\sin \frac{1}{2}(Z + Z')}{\sin \frac{1}{2}(Z' - Z)}$, $1 - h^{2} = 1 - \dfrac{\sin^{2} \frac{1}{2}(Z + Z')}{\sin^{2} \frac{1}{2}(Z' - Z)}$

$1 - h^{2} = \dfrac{\sin^{2} \frac{1}{2}(Z' - Z) - \sin^{2} \frac{1}{2}(Z + Z')}{\sin^{2} \frac{1}{2}(Z' - Z)}$

$= \dfrac{\frac{1}{2}(1 - \cos (Z' - Z) - \frac{1}{2}(1 - \cos (Z + Z'))}{\sin^{2} \frac{1}{2}(Z' - Z)}$

$= \dfrac{- \sin Z \sin Z'}{\sin^{2} \frac{1}{2}(Z' - Z)}.$

Regarding the earth's meridian section as an ellipse, we know from the properties of an ellipse that

$$x = a \cos u, \quad \text{and} \quad y = b \sin u,$$

in which u is the eccentric angle, or reduced latitude.
Differentiating the above,

$$- dx = a \sin u du, \quad dy = b \cos u du.$$

If we consider this point, whose co-ordinates we have just written, to be in latitude L, and an element of the elliptic curve to be ds, it will be the hypothenuse of a right triangle, in which

$$- dx = ds \sin L, \quad \text{and} \quad dy = ds \cos L,$$

or $\quad - dx = a \sin u du = ds \sin L, \quad dy = b \cos u du = ds \cos L.$

Dividing,

$$\frac{a}{b} \tan u = \tan L, \quad \text{or} \quad a \tan u = b \tan L, \quad (1)$$

and

$$ds = \frac{a \sin u du}{\sin L}. \quad (2)$$

The value found for x in (A) was for a spherical surface ; to transform to an ellipsoid it will be necessary to pass to a differential triangle on each.   In the figure on page 228, suppose we call PNM a differential triangle on an ellipsoid, in which $EN = dL$, $NM = d\sigma$, and the angle $PNM = \alpha$, then $d\sigma \cos \alpha = dL$.   To convert dL into arc measure, we multiply it by the radius of curvature of the meridian, or

$$ds \cos \alpha = RdL. \qquad (3)$$

Likewise, if we conceive the same triangle to be on a sphere of radius a, then as will be the length of the arc MN, then

$$ad\sigma \cos \alpha = adu, \quad \text{or} \quad d\sigma \cos \alpha = du. \qquad (4)$$

Dividing (4) by (3), $\dfrac{ds}{d\sigma} = \dfrac{RdL}{du}$;

substituting in this $R = \dfrac{a(1 - e^2)}{(1 - e^2 \sin^2 L)^{\frac{3}{2}}}$, $\dfrac{dL}{du} = \dfrac{(1 - e^2)^{\frac{1}{2}}}{1 - e^2 \cos^2 u}$;

also from (1), we find $\sin L = \dfrac{\sin u}{(1 - e^2 \cos^2 u)^{\frac{1}{2}}}$,

$$\frac{ds}{d\sigma} = \frac{a(1 - e^2)}{(1 - e^2 \sin^2 L)^{\frac{3}{2}}} \cdot \frac{(1 - e^2)^{\frac{1}{2}}}{1 - e^2 \cos^2 u}$$

$$= \frac{a(1 - e^2)^{\frac{3}{2}}}{\left[1 - e^2 \dfrac{\sin^2 u}{1 - e^2 \cos^2 u}\right]^{\frac{3}{2}}} \cdot \frac{1}{1 - e^2 \cos^2 u}$$

$$= \frac{a(1 - e^2)^{\frac{3}{2}}}{1 - e^2 \cos^2 u} \cdot \frac{1}{\left[\dfrac{1 - e^2 \cos^2 u - e^2 \sin^2 u}{1 - e^2 \cos^2 u}\right]^{\frac{3}{2}}}$$

$$= \frac{a(1 - e^2)^{\frac{3}{2}}}{1 - e^2 \cos^2 u} \cdot \frac{1}{\left[\dfrac{1 - e^2}{1 - e^2 \cos^2 u}\right]^{\frac{3}{2}}}$$

$$= \frac{a(1 - e^2)^{\frac{3}{2}}}{1 - e^2 \cos^2 u} \cdot \frac{(1 - e^2 \cos^2 u)^{\frac{3}{2}}}{(1 - e^2)^{\frac{3}{2}}} = a \sqrt{1 - e^2 \cos^2 u},$$

or $\dfrac{ds}{d\sigma} = a \sqrt{1 - e^2 \cos^2 u},$ \hfill (5)

which gives the relation between an infinitesimal length on a sphere to a corresponding length on an ellipsoid.

To integrate this, Jordan takes a spherical triangle with sides equal to u, u^1, and σ, and angle opposite $u^1 = \alpha^1$; then

$$\sin u = \sin u^1 \cos \sigma + \cos u^1 \sin \sigma \cos \alpha^1,$$

placing the serial value for $\cos \sigma$ and $\sin \sigma$,

$$\sin u = \sin u^1\left(1 - \frac{\sigma^2}{2} \ldots\right) + (\sigma \ldots) \cos u^1 \cos \alpha^1,$$

omitting all powers of σ above the second.

Squaring this equation,

$$\sin^2 u = \sin^2 u^1(1 - \sigma^2) + \sigma^2 \cos^2 u^1 \cos^2 \alpha^1$$
$$+ 2\sigma \sin u^1 \cos u^1 \cos \alpha^1.$$

For $\sin^2 u$, write $1 - \cos^2 u$, then transpose, change signs, mul tiply by e^2, subtract from 1, and extract the square root; this gives

$$\sqrt{1 - e^2 \cos^2 u} = 1 - \frac{e^2}{2} \cos^2 u' + e^2 \sigma \sin u' \cos u' \cos \alpha'$$

$$+ \frac{e^2}{2} \sigma^2 (\cos^2 u' \cos^2 \alpha' - \sin^2 u'). \quad (6)$$

Placing this in (5), and integrating with respect to $d\sigma$, we find

$$\frac{s}{a} = \sigma \left(1 - \frac{e^2}{2} \cos^2 u'\right) + \frac{e^2 \sigma^2}{2} \sin u' \cos u' \cos \alpha'$$

$$+ \frac{e^2 \sigma^3}{6} (\cos^2 u' \cos^2 \alpha' - \sin^2 u'). \quad (7)$$

This can be written, including e^4,

$$\frac{s}{a} = \sigma \left(1 - \frac{e^2}{2} \cos^2 u'\right)$$

$$\left[1 + \frac{e^2}{2} \sigma \sin u' \cos u' \cos \alpha' + \frac{e^2}{6} \sigma^2 (\cos^2 u' \cos^2 \alpha' - \sin^2 u')\right].$$

If we place $\alpha' = 0$, we have $\sigma = u - u'$, then the last equation becomes, after placing S for s,

$$\frac{S}{a} = (u - u')\left(1 - \frac{e^2}{2} \cos^2 u'\right)$$

$$\left[1 + \frac{e^2}{2}(u - u') \sin u' \cos u' + \frac{e^2}{6}(u - u')^2 (\cos^2 u' - \sin^2 u')\right]. (8)$$

From $\qquad \sin u = \sin u'\left(1 - \dfrac{\sigma^2}{2}\right) + \sigma \cos u' \cos \alpha',$

we get by transposition

$$\sin u - \sin u' = \sigma \cos u' \cos \alpha' - \frac{\sigma^2}{2} \sin u'. \tag{9}$$

But we had

$$u - u' = x, \quad \text{or} \quad u = u' + x; \quad \text{hence} \quad \sin u = \sin (u' + x).$$

Developing this by Taylor's formula,

$$\sin u = \sin u' + x \cos u' - \frac{x^2}{2} \sin u'; \tag{10}$$

or $\qquad \sin u - \sin u' = x \cos u' - \dfrac{x^2}{2} \sin u'$

$$= \sigma \cos u' \cos \alpha' - \frac{\sigma^2}{2} \sin u'. \tag{11}$$

Solving this equation by approximation,

$$x \cos u' = \sigma \cos u' \cos \alpha', \quad \text{or} \quad x = \sigma \cos \alpha'.$$

Substituting this in (11),

$$x \cos u' - \frac{\sigma^2}{2} \cos^2 \alpha' \sin u' = \sigma \cos u' \cos \alpha' - \frac{\sigma^2}{2} \sin u';$$

dividing by cos u',

$$x - \frac{\sigma^2}{2}\cos^2 \alpha' \,.\, \tan u' = \sigma \cos \alpha' - \frac{\sigma^2}{2} \tan u'.$$

$$x = \sigma \cos \alpha' - \frac{\sigma^2}{2} \tan u' + \frac{\sigma^2}{2}\cos^2 \alpha' \tan u'$$

$$= \sigma \cos \alpha' - \frac{\sigma^2}{2} \tan u'(1 - \cos^2 \alpha')$$

$$= \sigma \cos \alpha' - \frac{\sigma^2}{2} \tan u' \sin^2 \alpha' = u - u'; \qquad (12)$$

substituting this in (8),

$$\frac{S}{a} = (u - u')\left(1 - \frac{e^2}{2}\cos^2 u'\right)\left[1 + \frac{e^2}{2}\sigma \sin u' \cos u' \cos \alpha'\right.$$

$$\left. + \frac{e^2\sigma^2}{12}(-\sin^2 u' + 2\cos^2 u' \cos^2 \alpha' + \sin^2 u' \cos^2 \alpha')\right]. \quad (13)$$

Dividing this equation by (7), we have

$$\frac{S}{s} = \frac{u - u'}{\sigma}\left[1 - \frac{e^2\sigma^2}{12}(-3\sin^2 u' + 2\sin^2 u' + \sin^2 u' \cos^2 \alpha')\right]$$

$$= \frac{u - u'}{\sigma}\left[1 - \frac{e^2\sigma^2}{12}(-\sin^2 u' + \sin^2 u'(1 - \sin^2 \alpha'))\right]$$

$$= \frac{u - u'}{\sigma}\left(1 - \frac{e^2\sigma^2}{12}\sin^2 u' \sin^2 \alpha'\right). \qquad (14)$$

If we had taken u' as the unknown side in our spherical triangle, giving

$$\sin u' = \sin u \cos \sigma + \cos u \sin \sigma \cos \alpha,$$

we would have found, by pursuing a course similar to the above

$$\frac{S}{s} = \frac{u - u'}{\sigma}\left(1 - \frac{e^2\sigma^2}{12} \sin^2 u \sin^2 \alpha\right),$$

from which we could obtain

$$\sin^2 u' \sin^2 \alpha' = \sin^2 u \sin^2 \alpha, \quad \text{or} \quad \sin u' \sin \alpha' = \sin u \sin \alpha \,;$$

hence we can involve both the direct and reverse azimuth as well as the terminal latitudes by writing for $\sin^2 u' \sin^2 \alpha'$, $\sin u' \sin \alpha' \sin u \sin \alpha$, so that (14) will become

$$\frac{S}{s} = \frac{u - u'}{\sigma}\left(1 - \frac{e^2\sigma^2}{12} \sin u' \sin \alpha' \sin u \sin \alpha\right). \quad (15)$$

Resuming the former notation, we will put $\alpha = Z$, and $\alpha' = Z' - 180°$; also, remembering that $1 - h^2 = -\dfrac{\sin Z \sin Z'}{\sin^2 \frac{1}{2}(Z' - Z)}$, we can for $-\sin Z \sin Z'$ write $\sin^2 \frac{1}{2}(Z' - Z)(1 - h^2)$, and substitute in (15) the value of $u - u'$ in (A), which gives

$$\frac{S}{s} = h\left(1 - \frac{e^2\sigma^2}{12} \sin u' \sin u \sin Z' \sin Z\right)$$

$$\left[1 - \frac{\sigma^2}{12}(1 - h^2) + \frac{\sigma^4}{240}(1 - h^2)(2 - 3h^2)\right]. \quad (16)$$

This still involves s and σ, so there is needed a relation between them. To attain this we take equation (7), using only two terms,

$$\frac{s}{a} = \sigma\left(1 - \frac{e^2}{2}\cos^2 u'\right) = \sigma\left(1 - \frac{e^2}{2}\cos u \cos u'\right).$$

Squaring this, and omitting terms in e^4,

$$\frac{s^2}{a^2} = \sigma^2(1 - e^2 \cos u \cos u'),$$

or

$$\sigma^2 = \frac{s^2}{a^2 (1 - e^2 \cos u \cos u')}. \tag{17}$$

Writing

$$p^2 = 1 + e^2 \cos u \cos u',$$

(16) becomes

$$S = sh\left[\left(1 - \frac{e^2 s^2 p^2}{12a^2}\sin n' \sin u \sin Z' \sin Z\right)\right.$$

$$\left(1 + \frac{s^2 p^2}{12a^2}\left(\frac{\sin Z \sin Z'}{\sin^2 \frac{1}{2}(Z'-Z)}\right) - \frac{s^4 p^4}{240a^4}\frac{\sin Z \sin Z'}{\sin^2 \frac{1}{2}(Z'-Z)}(2 - 3h^2)\right],$$

in which

$$h = \frac{\sin \frac{1}{2}(Z + Z')}{\sin \frac{1}{2}(Z' - Z)}.$$

This is substantially the same formula as given by Bessel in *Astronomische Nachrichten*, No. 331, pp. 309–10, except Z' is within the polar triangle, which gives

$$h = \frac{\cos \frac{1}{2}(Z + Z')}{\cos \frac{1}{2}(Z - Z')},$$

and
$$1 - h^2 = \frac{\sin Z \sin Z'}{\cos^2 \frac{1}{2}(Z' - Z)},$$

or approximately $\sin Z \sin Z'$.

Then, writing

$$p^2 = 1 + e^2 \cos u \cos u', \qquad \text{and} \qquad q^2 = 1 + e^2 \cos(u + u'),$$

Bessel's formula becomes

$$S = sh\left[1 + \frac{1}{12}\left(\frac{sq}{a}\right)^2 \frac{\sin Z \sin Z'}{\cos^2 \frac{1}{2}(Z - Z')} \right.$$
$$\left. + \frac{1}{240}\left(\frac{sq}{a}\right)^4 \frac{\sin Z \sin Z'}{\cos^2 \frac{1}{2}(Z - Z')}(2 - 3h^2) \right].$$

In both of these formulæ it is to be remembered that $\tan u = \sqrt{1 - e^2} \tan L$, and $\tan u' = \sqrt{1 - e^2} \tan L'$.

Also, if the line deviates but little from the meridian, the first term will be sufficient.

When a long arc has been measured, it has been found best to divide it into several sections, from each of which data can be obtained for finding the axes of the earth, and the ellipticity. When these arcs are small, the method given on page 228 will give fair results. But Clarke's solution is perhaps the best; it is, in the main, as follows:

Let R, x, and y be the radius of curvature of an ellipse, and co-ordinates of the point whose latitude is L, then $\frac{x^2}{a^2} + \frac{y^2}{b^2} = 1$; but we have shown that

$$x = a \cos u, \qquad \tan u = \sqrt{1 - e^2} \tan L,$$

from which

$$x = a \cos L (1 - e^2 \sin^2 L)^{-\frac{1}{2}},$$

also

$$y = b \sin u = a \sin L (1 - \cdot^2)(1 - e^2 \sin^2 L)^{-\frac{1}{2}};$$

$$R = a(1 - e^2)(1 - e^2 \sin^2 L)^{-\frac{1}{2}}.$$

Expanding, and neglecting e^6,

$$x = a[(1 + \tfrac{1}{8}e^2 + \tfrac{3}{64}e^4)\cos L - (\tfrac{1}{8}e^2 + \tfrac{9}{128}e^4)\cos 3L + \tfrac{3}{128}e^4\cos 5L];$$

$$y = a[(1 - \tfrac{5}{8}e^2 - \tfrac{9}{64}e^4)\sin L - (\tfrac{1}{8}e^2 - \tfrac{1}{128}e^4)\sin 3L + \tfrac{3}{128}e^4\sin 5L];$$

$$R = a(1 - e^2)(1 + \tfrac{3}{2}e^2 \sin^2 L + \tfrac{15}{8}e^4 \sin^4 L).$$

Substituting $1 - \cos^2 L$ for $\sin L^2$,

$$R = a[1 - \tfrac{1}{4}e^2 - \tfrac{3}{64}e^4 - (\tfrac{3}{4}e^2 + \tfrac{3}{16}e^4)\cos 2L + \tfrac{15}{64}e^4 \cos 4L].$$

Writing $A = a(1 - \tfrac{1}{4}e^2 - \tfrac{3}{64}e^4)$, $B = -a(\tfrac{3}{8}e^2 + \tfrac{3}{32}e^4)$, $C = \tfrac{15}{128}ae^4$,

we have $\qquad R = A + 2B \cos 2L + 2C \cos 4L,$ \hfill (B)

This is an ellipse if $5B^2 = 6AC$.

Now, if S be the length of an arc of an elliptic meridian, it was shown on page 231 that

$$dS \sin L = a \sin u\, du, \qquad dS = \frac{a \sin u\, du}{\sin L}.$$

From $a \tan u = b \tan L$, we found

$$\frac{du}{dL} = \frac{\sqrt{1 - e^2}}{1 - e^2 \sin^2 L},$$

therefore

$$\frac{ds}{dL} = \frac{a \sin u \sqrt{1 - e^2}}{\sin L(1 - e^2 \sin^2 L)}.$$

But from the preceding relation

$$\sin u = \frac{\sin L \sqrt{1 - e^2}}{\sqrt{1 - e^2 \sin^2 L}}.$$

Substituting this, we have

$$\frac{dS}{dL} = \frac{a(1 - e^2)}{(1 - e^2 \sin^2 L)^{\frac{3}{2}}} = R = A + 2B \cos 2L + 2C \cos 4L :$$

by integration,

$$S = AL + B \sin 2L + \tfrac{1}{2}C \sin 4L + \text{a constant.}$$

If L be the mean latitude of an arc whose amplitude is λ, and the above expression be integrated between the limits $L - \frac{1}{2}\lambda$ and $L + \frac{1}{2}\lambda$, we will obtain

$$S = A\lambda + 2B \cos 2L \sin \lambda + C \cos 4L \sin 2\lambda. \qquad (19)$$

In this A, B, and C are the only unknown quantities, so that if S, L, and λ be free from errors, three equations would be sufficient for determining A, B, or C, and, consequently, a, e, and

16

b.   But every arc is affected with an error, in length as well as middle and terminal latitudes, so that from a number of discordant results we must find the most probable values for A, B, and C by the principles of least squares.

Suppose the terminal latitudes have a small error in each of x_1 and x_1', so that the amplitude would be $\lambda + x_1' - x_1$, and the latitudes $L - \frac{1}{2}\lambda + x_1$, and $L - \frac{1}{2}\lambda + x_1'$.

Placing these corrected values in (19),

$$S = A(\lambda + x_1' - x') + 2B \cos 2L \sin (\lambda + x_1' - x_1)$$
$$+ C \cos 4L \sin 2(\lambda + x_1' - x_1). \quad (20)$$

In expanding this we treat $x_1' - x_1$ as a single term, and being small, $\cos (x_1' - x_1) = 1$, and $\sin (x_1' - x_1) = x_1' - x_1$, so

$$\sin (\lambda + x_1' - x_1) = \sin \lambda + \cos \lambda(x_1' - x_1);$$

$$\sin 2(\lambda + x_1' - x_1) = 2 \sin [\lambda + (x_1' - x_1)] \cos [\lambda + (x_1' - x_1)]$$
$$= 2[\sin \lambda + \cos \lambda(x_1' - x_1)][\cos \lambda - \sin \lambda(x_1' - x_1)]$$
$$= \sin 2\lambda + 2(x_1' - x_1) \cos 2\lambda;$$

substituting these expressions in (20),

$$S = A(\lambda + x_1' - x_1) + 2B \cos 2L[\sin \lambda + \cos \lambda(x_1' - x_1)]$$
$$+ C \cos 4L[\sin 2\lambda + 2(x_1' - x_1) \cos 2\lambda].$$

Solving for $x_1' - x_1$

$$(x_1' - x_1)(A + 2B \cos 2L \cos \lambda \, 2C \cos 4L \cos 2\lambda) = S - A\lambda$$
$$- 2B \cos 2L \sin \lambda - C \cos 4L \sin 2\lambda. \quad (21)$$

If we write $A + 2B \cos \lambda \cos 2L \, 2C \cos 4L \cos 2\lambda = \dfrac{A}{\mu}$, (21) will reduce to

$$x_1' - x_1 = \left(\frac{S}{A} - \lambda\right)\mu - \frac{2B\mu}{A}\sin\lambda\cos 2L$$

$$- \frac{C\mu}{A}\sin 2\lambda\cos 4L. \quad (22)$$

Expressing x_1', x_1, and λ in seconds—we approximate the length of a second of latitude by assuming the average radius of curvature to be 20855500 ft.—we must write

$$v = 20855500 \sin 1''.$$

Then we assume three auxiliary quantities, u, v, and Z, and place

$$\frac{1}{A} = \frac{1}{20855500}\left(1 + \frac{u}{10000}\right),$$

$$-\frac{2B}{A} = \frac{1}{200} + \frac{v}{10000},$$

$$-\frac{C}{A} = \frac{Z}{10000}.$$

Substituting these, (22) becomes

$$\frac{1}{\mu}(x_1' - x_1) = \frac{S}{v} + \frac{Su}{10000v} - \lambda + \frac{\sin\lambda\cos 2L}{200\sin 1''}$$

$$+ \frac{\sin\lambda\cos 2Lv}{10000\sin 1''} + \frac{\sin 2\lambda\cos 4LZ}{10000\sin 1''}. \quad (23)$$

Again we assume

$$m = \left(\frac{S}{v} - \lambda + \frac{\sin\lambda\cos 2L}{200\sin 1''}\right)\mu, \qquad a = \frac{Su}{10000v},$$

$$b = \frac{\sin \lambda \cos 2L\mu}{10000 \sin 1''}, \qquad c = \frac{\sin 2\lambda \cos 4L\mu}{10000 \sin 1''},$$

$$\mu = 1 + \tfrac{1}{800} \cos \lambda \cos 2L.$$

Then (23) can be written

$$x_1' - x_1 = m + au + bv + cZ,$$

or $\qquad\qquad x_1' = x_1 + m + au + bv + cZ.$ $\qquad$ (24)

For each arc or partial arc we will have an equation like (24), which is to be solved by the principles of least squares, by making the sum of the squares of the errors a minimum; then equating the differential coefficients of the symbolic errors with respect to u, v, z, x_1', etc., to zero, there will be as many equations as there are unknown quantities to be solved by algebraic methods. Knowing u, v, and z, we find A, B, and C, which substituted in (B) give R.

To determine the axes and ellipticity, we take the equations on page 240 and find that the coefficient of $\cos L = (A - B)$, of $\cos 3L = \tfrac{1}{8}(B - C)$, and of $\cos 5L = \tfrac{1}{8}C$; also, of $\sin L = A + B$, of $\sin 3L = \tfrac{1}{8}(B + C)$, and of $\sin 5L = \tfrac{1}{8}C$. By making these substitutions, we have

$$x = (A - B) \cos L + \tfrac{1}{8}(B - C) \cos 3L + \tfrac{1}{8}C \cos 5L; \quad (25)$$

$$y = (A + B) \sin L + \tfrac{1}{8}(B + C) \sin 3L + \tfrac{1}{8}C \sin 5L. \quad (26)$$

But on page 231,

$$x = -\int a \sin L \, dL, \qquad \text{and} \qquad y = \int b \cos L \, dL.$$

So (25) and (26) are the values of these integrals, which if integrated between the limits $L = 0$ and $L = 90°$, will give
the semi-axes,

$$a = A - B + \tfrac{1}{3}(B - C) + \tfrac{1}{5}C = A - \tfrac{2}{3}B - \tfrac{2}{15}C ; \quad (27)$$

$$b = A + B - \tfrac{1}{3}(B + C) + \tfrac{1}{5}C = A + \tfrac{2}{3}B - \tfrac{2}{15}C ; \quad (28)$$

$$e^2 = 1 - \frac{b^2}{a^2} = -\frac{8B}{3A}\left(1 + \frac{4B}{3A}\right), \text{ approximately.}$$

If these values be substituted in (25) and (26), we would have

$$x' = \left(A - B - \frac{2}{15}C + \frac{1}{9}\frac{B^2}{A}\right)\cos L$$
$$+ \left(\frac{1}{3}B - \frac{5B^2}{18A}\right)\cos 3L + \frac{B^2}{6A}\cos 5L ; \quad (29)$$

$$y' = \left(A + B - \frac{2}{15}C + \frac{1}{9}\frac{B^2}{A}\right)\sin L$$
$$+ \left(\frac{1}{3}B - \frac{5B^2}{18A}\right)\sin 3L + \frac{B^2}{6A}\sin 5L. \quad (30)$$

(29) and (30) are the values of the co-ordinates of a point in
an *elliptic* curve whose axes are a and b, while (25) and (26)
are the co-ordinates of a point in the actual curve. The difference between the two will be the deviation of the actual
from the elliptic curve at any point.

$$x - x' = \left(C - \frac{5B^2}{6A}\right)\left(\frac{2}{15}\cos L - \frac{1}{3}\cos 3L + \frac{1}{5}\cos 5L\right). \quad (31)$$

$$y - y^{\text{I}} = \left(C - \frac{5B^2}{6A} \right) \left(\frac{2}{15} \sin L + \frac{1}{3} \sin 3L + \frac{1}{5} \sin 5L \right). \quad (32)$$

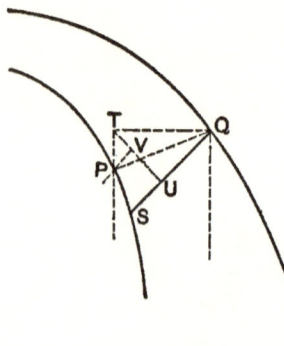

Suppose P be the point on the elliptic curve in latitude L, and Q the point on the actual curve in the same latitude. P and Q will coincide when $C - \dfrac{5B^2}{6A} = 0$, for this will reduce (31) and (32) to $x - x' = 0$, $y - y^{\text{I}} = 0$, and will differ from one another as $C - \dfrac{5B^2}{6A}$ changes from a zero value.

FIG. 31.

If we take PS an infinitesimal distance on the elliptic curve, and QS a corresponding length along the normal, we will have

$$PT = y - y^{\text{I}}, \qquad TQ = x - x^{\text{I}},$$

$$QS = QU + SU = QU + PV$$
$$= (x - x^{\text{I}}) \cos L + (y - y^{\text{I}}) \sin L,$$

or $\qquad dR = (x - x') \cos L + L(y - y') \sin L. \qquad (33)$

$$PS = VU = TU - TV$$
$$= -(x - x^{\text{I}}) \sin L + (y - y^{\text{I}}) \cos L,$$

or $\qquad dS = -(x - x') \sin L + (y - y') \cos L. \qquad (34)$

Substituting in these equations the values of $(x - x')$ and $(y - y')$ from (31) and (32), we find

$$dS = \frac{8}{15}\left(C - \frac{5B^2}{6A}\right) \sin 4L,$$

$$dR = \frac{4}{15}\left(C - \frac{5B^2}{6A}\right) \sin^2 2L.$$

Clarke's values of a and b of 1866 would give

$$dR = (177 \pm 70) \sin^2 2L,$$

showing but a slight deviation of a meridian section from an ellipse.

The Anglo-French arc places the actual curve 3.6 feet under the ellipse in latitude 58°, and 18.9 feet above in latitude 44°; while the Indian arc places it 19.6 feet under, in latitude 14°, and 9.3 feet above, in latitude 26°.

The amplitude of an arc depending upon the latitude determinations of its extremities is subject to an error from local deflection. In some cases, at least a portion of these errors can be corrected by computing the effects of attraction upon a physical hypothesis; but in the main they are best treated as accidental, and the figure of the earth determined by the principle of least squares, in which the sum of the squares of all errors shall be a minimum.

This was suggested by Walbeck in 1819, continued by Schmidt in 1829, and perfected by Bessel in 1837.

Laplace in 1822, published the second volume of *Mécanique Céleste*, in which he discussed the figure of the earth, using seven arcs: the Peruvian, Lacaille's Cape of Good Hope arc, Mason and Dixon's, Boscovich's Italian, Delambre and Mechain's, Maupertuis' Lapland arc, and Liesganig's Austrian arc.

The second is unreliable, from an erroneously assumed correction for local attraction which shortened the arc by 9″ too
much. The third was a measured arc, and not comparable
with a trigonometric one. And no confidence is now placed
in either the fourth or the last.

Bowditch, in his translation of the above-named work, considers only the Peru and France arcs, and adds those of England and India as completed in 1832. His conclusion is:

" It appears that this strictly elliptical form of the meridian
is more conformable to these observations than the irregular
figure obtained by Mr. Airy's calculation."

Sir George Airy published in the *Encyclopædia Metropoli-
tana*, under the heading " Figure of the Earth," in 1830, a discussion of fourteen meridian arcs and four arcs of parallel.
In 1841, Bessel gave to the public the results of his laborious
investigation of ten meridian arcs, having a total amplitude of
50°.5, and embracing thirty-eight latitude stations. The result gave an elliptic meridian, and the elements then published
are still known as those of Bessel's spheroid.

In 1858, in the " Account of the Principal Triangulation of
Great Britain and Ireland," Captain Clarke gives a most elaborate discussion of eight arcs, having a total amplitude of 78°
36′, and embracing sixty-six latitude stations.

Again, in 1880, he revised his previous computations, using
corrected positions from which slightly different results were
obtained.

Mr. Schott discussed the combination of three American
arcs of meridian for determining the figure of the earth considered as a spheroid. He used the Pamlico-Chesapeake, Nantucket, and Peruvian, having a total amplitude of 11° 01′ 12″,
and embracing twenty-three latitudes. The conclusion deduced by Mr. Schott is: " The result from the combination of
the three American arcs is the preference it gives to Clarke's
spheroid over that of Bessel."

TABLE GIVING THE ELLIPTICITY AND LENGTH OF A QUADRANT ON THE SPHEROIDAL HYPOTHESIS.

Date.	Authority.	Ellipticity.	Quadrant in Metres.
1819	Walbeck................	1 : 302.8	10 000 268
1830	Schmidt.................	1 : 297.5	10 000 075
1830	Airy....................	1 : 299.3	10 000 976
1841	Bessel..................	1 : 299.2	10 000 856
1856	Clarke..................	1 : 298.1	10 001 515
1863	Pratt...................	1 : 295.3	10 001 924
1866	Clarke.	1 : 295	10 001 888
1868	Fischer...	1 : 288.5	10 001 714
1872	Listing.................	1 : 289	10 000 218
1877	Schott..................	1 : 305.5	10 002 232
1878	Jordan........	1 : 286.5	10 000 681
1880	Clarke..................	1 : 293.5	10 001 869

Data for the Figure of the Earth.	Bessel, 1841.	Clarke, 1866.	Coast Survey, 1877.	Clarke, 1880.
Equatorial radius, a..	6 377 397.2M	6 378 206.4M	6 378 054.3M	6 378 248.5M
Polar semi-axis, b. ...	6 356 079	6 356 583.8	6 357 175	6 341 895.6M
Compression, $\dfrac{a-b}{a}$..	1 : 299.15	1 : 294.98	1 : 305.48	1 : 293.5
Mean length of a deg.	111 120.6M	111 132.1	111 135.9	111 131.8

The value of the ellipticity as deduced by pendulum-observations in accordance with Clairaut's theorem is 1 : 292.2, being almost the same as that obtained from geodetic measurements.

Clarke's length of the quadrant would give for the metre 39.377786 inches, whereas the legal length is 39.370432 inches, or .0073 inch too short.

LITERATURE OF THE FIGURE OF THE EARTH.

Pratt, A Treatise on Attractions, Laplace's Functions, and the Figure of the Earth. London, 1861.

Roberts, Figure of the Earth. *Van Nostrand's Engineering Magazine*, vol. xxxii., pp. 228–242.

Merriman, Figure of the Earth. New York, 1881.

U. S. Coast Survey Report for 1868, pp. 147-153.

U. S. Coast and Geodetic Survey Report for 1877, pp. 84-95.

Clarke, Geodesy, pp. 302-322. London, 1880.

Laplace, Mécanique Céleste. Bowditch's Translation, vol. ii., pp. 358-485. Boston, 1830.

Ordnance Survey, Account of Principal Triangulation, pp. .733-782. London, 1858.

Bruns, Die Figur der Erde. Berlin, 1878.

Baeyer, Grösse und Figur der Erde. Berlin, 1861.

Jordan, Handbuch der Vermessungskunde, vol. ii., pp. 377-463. Stuttgart, 1878.

FORMULÆ AND FACTORS.

TRIGONOMETRIC EXPRESSIONS.

$\sin^2 a + \cos^2 a = 1$;

$$\sin a = \sqrt{1 - \cos^2 a}$$

$$= \frac{\cos a}{\cot a}$$

$$= \frac{1}{\sqrt{1 + \cot^2 a}}$$

$$= \cos a \tan a$$

$$= 2 \sin \tfrac{1}{2}a \cos \tfrac{1}{2}a$$

$$= \frac{1}{\operatorname{cosec} a}.$$

$$\cos a = \frac{\sin a}{\tan a}$$

$$= \sin a \cot a$$

$$= \sqrt{1 - \sin^2 a}$$

$$= 1 - 2 \sin^2 \tfrac{1}{2}a.$$

$$= \frac{1}{\sec a}.$$

$$\tan a = \frac{\sin a}{\cos a}$$

$$= \frac{1}{\cot a}$$

$$= \frac{\sin a}{\sqrt{1 - \sin^2 a}}$$

$$= \frac{1 - \cos 2a}{\sin 2a}.$$

$$= \sqrt{\frac{1 - \cos 2a}{1 + \cos 2a}}.$$

$$\cot a = \frac{1}{\tan a}.$$

$$\sec a = \frac{1}{\cos a}.$$

$$\operatorname{cosec} a = \frac{1}{\sin a}.$$

$$\operatorname{versin} a = 1 - \cos a = 2 \sin^2 \tfrac{1}{2}a.$$

$$\operatorname{chord} a = 2 \sin \tfrac{1}{2}a.$$

$$\sin (a \pm b) = \sin a \cos b \pm \cos a \sin b;$$

$$\cos (a \pm b) = \cos a \cos b \mp \sin a \sin b.$$

$$\tan (a \pm b) = \frac{\tan a \pm \tan b}{1 \mp \tan a \tan b}.$$

$$\cot (a \pm b) = \frac{\cot a \cot b \mp 1}{\cot b \pm \cot a}.$$

$$\sin 2a = 2 \sin a \cos a.$$

$$\cos 2a = \cos^2 a - \sin^2 a$$
$$= 2 \cos^2 a - 1 = 1 - 2 \sin^2 a.$$

$$2 \cos^2 \tfrac{1}{2}a = 1 + \cos a.$$

$$2 \sin^2 \tfrac{1}{2}a = 1 - \cos a.$$

$$\tan^2 \tfrac{1}{2}a = \frac{1 - \cos a}{1 + \cos a}.$$

$$\sin a \pm \sin b = 2 \sin \tfrac{1}{2}(a \pm b) \cos \tfrac{1}{2}(a \mp b).$$
$$\cos a + \cos b = 2 \cos \tfrac{1}{2}(a + b) \cos \tfrac{1}{2}(a - b).$$
$$\cos a - \cos b = 2 \sin \tfrac{1}{2}(a + b) \sin \tfrac{1}{2}(b - a).$$
$$\sin^2 a - \sin^2 b = \sin (a + b) \sin (a - b).$$
$$\cos^2 a - \sin^2 b = \cos (a + b) \cos (a - b).$$

$$\sin 2x = 2 \sin x \cos x.$$
$$\sin 3x = 3 \sin x - 4 \sin^3 x.$$
$$\sin 4x = (4 \sin x - 8 \sin^3 x) \sqrt{1 - \sin^2 x}.$$
$$\cos 2x = \cos^2 x - \sin^2 x = 2 \cos^2 x - 1.$$
$$\cos 3x = 4 \cos^3 x - 3 \cos x.$$
$$\cos 4x = 8 \cos^4 x - 8 \cos^2 x + 1.$$

$$\tan 2x = \frac{2 \tan x}{1 - \tan^2 x}.$$

$$\tan 3x = \frac{3 \tan x - \tan^3 x}{1 - 3 \tan^2 x}.$$

$$\tan 4x = \frac{4 \tan x - 4 \tan^3 x}{1 - 6 \tan^2 x + \tan^4 x}.$$

TRIGONOMETRIC SERIES.

$$\sin x = x - \frac{x^3}{2 \cdot 3} + \frac{x^5}{2 \cdot 3 \cdot 4 \cdot 5} - \frac{x^7}{2 \dots 7} + \dots$$

$$\cos x = 1 - \frac{x^2}{2} + \frac{x^4}{2 \cdot 3 \cdot 4} - \frac{x^6}{2 \dots 6} + \dots$$

$$\tan x = x + \frac{x^3}{3} + \frac{2x^5}{3 \cdot 5} + \frac{17x^7}{3^2 \cdot 5 \cdot 7} \dots$$

$$\cot x = \frac{1}{x} - \frac{x}{3} - \frac{x^3}{3^2 \cdot 5} - \frac{2x^5}{3^3 \cdot 5 \cdot 7} - \dots$$

$$\sec x = 1 + \frac{x^2}{2} + \frac{5x^4}{2^2 3} + \frac{61x^6}{2^4 \cdot 3^2 \cdot 5} \dots$$

$$\operatorname{cosec} x = \frac{1}{x} + \frac{x}{2 \cdot 3} + \frac{7x^3}{2^2 \cdot 3^2 5} + \frac{31x^5}{2^2 \cdot 3^2 \cdot 5 \cdot 7} + \cdot$$

$$\operatorname{arc} x = \sin x + \frac{\sin^3 x}{2 \cdot 3} + \frac{3 \sin^5 x}{2 \cdot 4 \cdot 5} + \frac{3 \cdot 5 \sin^7 x}{2 \cdot 4 \cdot 6 \cdot 7} \dots$$

$$= \tan x - \tfrac{1}{3} \tan^3 x + \tfrac{1}{5} \tan^5 x \dots$$

For very small angles Maskelyne's series is best.

$$\sin x = x^3 \sqrt{\cos x} + \dots = x\left(1 - \frac{x^2}{6} - \frac{x^4}{72}\right).$$

$$\tan x = x^3 \sqrt{\sec^2 x} + \dots = x\left(1 + \frac{x^2}{3} + \frac{x^4}{9}\right).$$

BINOMIAL, EXPONENTIAL, AND LOGARITHMIC SERIES.

$$(a + b)^n = a^n + na^{n-1}b + \frac{n(n-1)}{2}a^{n-2}b^2 \dots b^n.$$

$$a^x = 1 + \log a \frac{x}{1} + \log^2 a \frac{x^2}{1 \cdot 2} + \log^3 a \frac{x^3}{2 \cdot 3} \dots$$

$$\log (x + 1) = 2M\left(\frac{1}{2x+1} + \frac{1}{3(2x+1)^3} + \frac{1}{5(2x+1)^5} \cdot \ldots\right).$$

$$M = \text{nodulus} = 0.4342945.$$

$$\log M = \qquad\qquad 9.6377843.$$

CONVERSION OF METRES TO FEET.

Metres × 3.280869	= feet, or to log of metres add 0.5159889
" × 1.093623	= yards, " " 0.0388676
" × 0.000621377	= mile, " " 6.7933550—10.

1 toise	= 76.734402 inches = 864 lines.
1 Prussian foot	= 139.13 lines.
1 klafter	= 840.76134 lines.

The toise is that of Peru, which is a standard at 13° R.

CONVERSION TABLES.

METRES INTO YARDS.

1 metre = 1.093623 yards.

Metres.	Yards.	Metres.	Yards.	Metres.	Yards.
100 000	109 362.3	3 000	3 280.87	60	65.617
90 000	98 426.1	2 000	2 187.25	50	54.681
80 000	87 489.8	1 000	1 093.62	40	43.745
70 000	76 553.6	900	984.26	30	32.809
60 000	65 617.4	800	874.90	20	21.872
50 000	54 681.2	700	765.54	10	10.936
40 000	43 744.9	600	656.17	9	9.843
30 000	32 808.7	500	546.81	8	8.749
20 000	21 872.5	400	437.45	7	7.655
10 000	10 936.2	300	328.09	6	6.562
9 000	9 842.61	200	218.72	5	5.468
8 000	8 748.98	100	109.36	4	4.374
7 000	7 655.36	90	98.426	3	3.281
6 000	6 561.74	80	87.490	2	2.187
5 000	5 468.12	70	76.554	1	1.094
4 000	4 374.49				

CONVERSION TABLES—*Continued.*

YARDS INTO METRES.

1 yard = 0.914392 metre.

Yards.	Metres.	Yards.	Metres.	Yards.	Metres.
100 000	91 439.2	3 000	2 743.18	60	54.864
90 000	82 295.3	2 000	1 828.78	50	45.720
80 000	73 151.3	1 000	914.39	40	36.576
70 000	64 007.4	900	822.95	30	27.432
60 000	54 863.5	800	731.51	20	18.288
50 000	45 719.6	700	640.07	10	9.144
40 000	36 575.7	600	548.64	9	8.230
30 000	27 431.8	500	457.20	8	7.315
20 000	18 287.8	400	365.76	7	6.401
10 000	9 143.9	300	274.32	6	5.486
9 000	8 229.53	200	182.88	5	4.572
8 000	7 315.13	100	91.44	4	3.658
7 000	6 400.74	90	82.295	3	2.743
6 000	5 486.35	80	73.151	2	1.829
5 000	4 571.96	70	64.007	1	0.914
4 000	3 657.57				

METRES INTO STATUTE AND NAUTICAL MILES.

1 metre = 0.00062138 statute mile.

1 metre = 0.00053959 nautical mile.

Metres.	Statute Miles.	Nautical Miles.	Metres.	Statute Miles.	Nautical Miles.
100 000	62.138	53.959	900	0.559	0.486
90 000	55.924	48.563	800	0.497	0.432
80 000	49.710	43.167	700	0.435	0.378
70 000	43.496	37.772	600	0.373	0.324
60 000	37.283	32.376	500	0.311	0.270
50 000	31.069	26.980	400	0.249	0.216
40 000	24.855	21.584	300	0.186	0.162
30 000	18.641	16.188	200	0.124	0.108
20 000	12.428	10.792	100	0.062	0.054
10 000	6.214	5.396	90	0.056	0.049
9 000	5.592	4.856	80	0.050	0.043
8 000	4.971	4.317	70	0.043	0.038
7 000	4.350	3.777	60	0.037	0.032
6 000	3.728	3.238	50	0.031	0.027
5 000	3.107	2.698	40	0.025	0.022
4 000	2.486	2.158	30	0.019	0.016
3 000	1.864	1.619	20	0.012	0.011
2 000	1.243	1.079	10	0.006	0.005
1 000	0.621	0 540			

STATUTE AND NAUTICAL MILES INTO METRES.

1 statute mile = 1609.330 metres.
1 nautical mile = 1853.248 metres.

Miles.	Metres in Statute Miles.	Metres in Nautical Miles.	Miles.	Metres in Statute Miles.	Metres in Nautical Miles.
100	160 933.0	185 324.8	.9	1 448.40	1 667.92
90	144 839.7	166 792.3	.8	1 287.46	1 482.60
80	128 746.4	148 259.8	.7	1 126.53	1 297.27
70	112 653.1	129 727.4	.6	965.60	1 111.95
60	96 559.8	111 194.9	.5	804.67	926.62
50	80 466.5	92 662.4	.4	643.73	741.30
40	64 373.2	74 129.9	.3	482.80	555.97
30	48 279.9	55 597.4	.2	321.87	370.65
20	32 186.6	37 065.0	.1	160.93	185.32
10	16 093.3	18 532.5	.09	144.84	166.79
9	14 483.97	16 679.23	.08	128.75	148.26
8	12 874.64	14 825.98	.07	112.65	129.73
7	11 265.31	12 972.74	.06	96.56	111.19
6	9 655.98	11 119.49	.05	80.47	92.66
5	8 046.65	9 266.24	.04	64.37	74.13
4	6 437.32	7 412.99	.03	48.28	55.60
3	4 827.99	5 559.74	.02	32.19	37.06
2	3 218.66	3 706.50	.01	16.09	18.53
1	1 609.33	1 853.25			

Major semi-axis = a, minor semi-axis = b, ellipticity = e

$$= \frac{a - b}{a}.$$

Bessel, $a = 6377397 . 15M$,   log = 7.8046434637 ;
          $b = 6356078 . 96M$,   log = 6.8031892839 ;
          $e = \frac{1}{299}$.

Clarke, $a = 6378206 . 4M$,   log = 6.8046985352 ;
          $b = 6356583 . 8M$,   log = 6.8032237974 ;
          $e = \frac{1}{294}$.

CONSTANTS AND THEIR LOGARITHMS.

	Number.	Log.
Ratio of circum. to diameter, π	3.1415926	0.4971499
2π	6.2831853	0.7981799
π^2	9,8696044	0.9942997
$\sqrt{\pi}$	1.7724538	0.2485749
Number of degrees in circum.,	360	2.5563025
Number of minutes in circum.,	21600	4.3344538
Number of seconds in circum.,	1296000	6.1126050
Degrees in arc equal radius,	57°.295779	1.7581226
Minutes in arc equal radius,	3437 .7467	3.5362739
Seconds in arc equal radius,	206264 .806	5.3144251
Length of arc of 1 degree,	.0174533	8.2418774 — 10
Length of arc of 1 minute,	.0002909	6.4637261 — 10
Length of arc of 1 second,	.00000485	4.6855749 — 10
Naperian base,	2.7182818	0.4342945
sin 1″		4.6855749
½ sin 1″		4.3845449

N is the normal produced to the minor axis. R is the radius of curvature in the meridian. Radius of curvature of the parallel is equal to $N \cos L$.

The following tables are based upon Clarke's spheroid of 1866, and were computed in 1882. Since then similar tables have been published by the Geodetic Survey, with which the appended have been compared.

Lat.	$N = \dfrac{a}{(1 - e^2 \sin^2 L)^{\frac{1}{2}}}$. Log N.	$R = \dfrac{a(1 - e^2)}{(1 - e^2 \sin^2 L)^{\frac{3}{2}}}$. Log R.	Log $(1 + e^2 \cos^2 L)$.
24°00′	6.8049418	6.8024790	0.0024628
10	9450	4884	4566
20	9481	4981	4500
30	9512	5076	4436
40	9545	5174	4371
50	9577	5270	4307
25 00	9612	5370	4242
10	9645	5470	4175
20	9677	5569	4108
30	9711	5667	4044
40	9744	5768	3976
50	9777	5869	3908
26 00	9812	5968	3841
10	9846	6070	3774
20	9880	6173	3706
30	9915	6276	3639
40	9948	6379	3569
50	9981	6482	3499
27 00	6.8050017	6585	3432
10	0051	6688	3363
20	0086	6794	3292
30	0120	6899	3221
40	0156	7006	3150
50	0191	7111	3080
28 00	0227	7216	3011
10	0263	7322	2941
20	0299	7429	2870
30	0334	7537	2797
40	0371	7644	2727
50	0407	7752	2655
29 00	0444	7862	2582
10	0480	7971	2509
20	0517	8081	2436
30	0555	8187	2368
40	0591	8296	2295
50	0628	8408	2220
30 00	0664	8524	2140
10	0700	8636	2064
20	0738	8747	1991
30	0776	8858	1918
40	0813	8972	1841
50	0849	9084	1765
31 00	0891	9198	1693
10	0928	9310	1618
20	0976	9426	1550
30	1014	9540	1474
40	1054	9654	1400
50	1089	9769	1320

Lat.	$N = \dfrac{a}{(1 - e^2 \sin^2 L)^{\frac{1}{2}}}.$ Log N.	$R = \dfrac{a(1 - e^2)}{(1 - e^2 \sin^2 L)^{\frac{3}{2}}}.$ Log R.	Log $(1 + e^2 \cos^2 L)$.
32°00′	6.8051128	6.8029885	0.0021243
10	1166	6.8030002	1164
20	1205	0117	1088
30	1244	0232	1012
40	1283	0349	0934
50	1322	0466	0856
33 00	1351	0583	0768
10	1390	0700	0690
20	1429	0818	0611
30	1469	0937	0532
40	1508	1055	0453
50	1548	1174	0374
34 00	1587	1293	0294
10	1627	1414	0213
20	1667	1532	0135
30	1707	1652	0055
40	1746	1769	0.0019977
50	1785	1889	9896
35 00	1828	2014	9814
10	1868	2134	9734
20	1909	2255	9654
30	1949	2376	9573
40	2989	2499	9490
50	2029	2619	9410
36 00	2070	2743	9327
10	2111	2865	9246
20	2152	2987	9165
30	2192	3110	9082
40	2233	3234	8999
50	2274	3354	8920
37 00	2316	3480	8836
10	2358	3602	8756
20	2398	3727	8671
30	2440	3851	8589
40	2482	3975	8507
50	2523	4098	8425
38 00	2565	4225	8340
10	2607	4350	8257
20	2648	4475	8173
30	2690	4599	8091
40	2732	4726	8006
50	2775	4846	7929
39 00	2815	4977	7838
10	2857	5102	7755
20	2899	5228	7671
30	2941	5355	7586
40	2984	5482	7502
50	3025	5608	7417

Lat.	$N = \dfrac{a}{(1 - e^2 \sin^2 L)^{\frac{1}{2}}}.$ Log N.	$R = \dfrac{a(1 - e^2)}{(1 - e^2 \sin^2 L)^{\frac{3}{2}}}.$ Log R.	Log $(1 + e^2 \cos^2 L)$.
40° 00′	6.8053068	6.8035734	0.0017334
10	3111	5859	7252
20	3154	5987	7167
30	3195	6115	7080
40	3237	6242	6995
50	3280	6367	6913
41 00	3321	6497	6824
10	3365	6625	6740
20	3407	6752	6655
30	3450	6880	6570
40	3592	7008	6484
50	3535	7130	6405
42 00	3577	7263	6294
10	3620	7392	6228
20	3663	7519	6144
30	3706	7649	6057
40	3749	7777	5972
50	3792	7905	5887
43 00	3832	8032	5802
10	3877	8160	5717
20	3919	8288	5631
30	3962	8417	5545
40	4004	8549	5455
50	4047	8680	5367
44 00	4090	8803	5287
10	4134	8930	5204
20	4177	9059	5116
30	4219	9188	5031
40	4262	9317	4945
50	4306	9445	4861
45 00	4347	9575	4772
10	4391	9704	4687
20	4434	9834	4600
30	4477	9961	4516
40	4519	6.8040090	4429
50	4563	0218	4345
46 00	4604	0347	4258
10	4648	0476	4172
20	4690	0605	4085
30	4734	0734	4000
40	4777	0860	3917
50	4820	0989	3831
47 00	4861	1118	3744
10	4905	1247	3658
20	4948	1376	3572
30	4991	1504	3487
40	5033	1631	3402
50	5076	1759	3317

Lat.	$N = \dfrac{a}{(1 - e^2 \sin^2 L)^{\frac{1}{2}}}.$ Log N.	$R = \dfrac{a(1 - e^2)}{(1 - e^2 \sin^2 L)^{\frac{3}{2}}}.$ Log R.	Log $(1 + e^2 \cos^2 L)$.
48°00′	6.8055118	6.8041887	0.0013231
10	5160	2016	3144
20	5202	2144	3058
30	5244	2272	2972
40	5289	2400	2889
50	5333	2528	2805
49 00	5374	2657	2717
10	5417	2784	2633
20	5459	2909	2550
30	5501	3037	2464
40	5545	3163	2382
50	5587	3293	2294
50 00	5629	3418	2211
10	5672	3544	2128
20	5714	3671	2043
30	5756	3798	1958
40	5798	3925	1873
50	5841	4048	1790

THE A, B, C, D, E GEODETIC FACTORS.

From latitude 24° to 48°, inclusive.

$$A = \frac{1}{N \text{ arc } 1''}.$$

$$B = \frac{1}{R \text{ arc } 1''}.$$

$$C = \frac{\tan L}{2NR \text{ arc } 1''}.$$

$$D = \frac{\frac{3}{2}e^2 \sin L \cos L}{(1 - e^2 \sin^2 L)^{\frac{3}{2}}}.$$

$$E = \frac{1 + 3 \tan^2 L}{6N^2}.$$

Referred to Clarke's spheroid of 1866.

Lat.	Log *A*.	Log *B*.	Log *C*.	Log *D*.	Log *E*.
24°00′	8.r094834	8.5119462	1.05456	2.2629	5.8147
05	818	415	625	40	59
10	802	368	794	52	72
15	786	320	962	64	85
20	769	271	1.06130	75	97
25	753	223	297	86	5.8210
30	738	174	464	97	23
35	720	127	631	2.2708	36
40	704	078	797	19	49
45	688	028	962	30	62
50	672	8.5118979	1.07128	40	74
55	659	930	⸱93	51	87
25 00	640	882	457	62	5.8300
05	623	833	621	72	13
10	607	782	785	83	26
15	591	733	948	93	39
20	573	684	1.08111	2.2804	52
25	556	634	274	15	66
30	541	585	435	25	79
35	524	535	597	35	92
40	508	484	759	45	5.8405
45	491	437	920	55	18
50	473	383	1.09080	65	31
55	456	337	241	75	45
26 00	440	283	400	85	58
05	423	232	560	95	71
10	406	181	719	2.2905	85
15	388	130	878	15	98
20	372	078	1.10036	24	5.8512
25	354	027	194	34	25
30	337	8.5117977	352	44	39
35	320	924	509	53	52
40	303	874	666	63	66
45	287	811	854	72	79
50	270	770	979	81	93
55	252	718	1.11135	91	5.8606
27 00	235	667	290	2.3000	20
05	218	616	445	09	34
10	201	564	600	18	47
15	182	511	755	27	61
20	166	458	909	36	75
25	148	405	1.12063	45	89
30	132	353	217	54	5.8702
35	113	310	370	63	16
40	095	248	523	72	30
45	077	195	676	81	44
50	059	141	828	89	58
55	041	089	980	98	69

Lat.	Log A.	Log B.	Log C.	Log D.	Log E.
28°00'	8.5094025	8.5117036	1.13132	2.3107	5.8786
05	006	8.5116983	284	15	99
10	8.5093989	930	435	24	5.8813
15	970	876	586	32	27
20	952	823	737	41	41
25	936	768	887	49	56
30	918	715	1.14037	57	70
35	899	661	187	65	84
40	881	608	336	74	98
45	863	552	485	82	5.8912
50	845	498	634	90	26
55	827	444	783	98	40
29 00	808	390	932	2.3206	55
05	790	335	1.15080	14	69
10	772	281	227	22	83
15	753	226	375	29	98
20	735	171	522	37	5.9012
25	716	116	669	45	26
30	698	061	816	53	41
35	679	007	963	60	55
40	661	8.5115950	1.16109	68	70
45	644	896	255	75	84
50	624	841	401	83	98
55	605	787	546	90	5.9113
30 00	588	728	691	98	27
05	570	672	835	2.3305	42
10	552	616	981	12	57
15	533	561	1.17126	19	71
20	514	505	270	27	86
25	494	449	414	34	5.9201
30	476	394	558	41	15
35	458	337	701	48	30
40	439	280	845	55	45
45	420	225	988	62	60
50	401	168	1.18131	69	74
55	376	112	274	75	89
31 00	361	054	416	83	5.9304
05	339	8.5114998	578	89	19
10	324	942	700	96	34
15	305	884	842	2.3402	49
20	286	826	984	09	64
25	267	769	1.19125	16	78
30	248	712	266	22	93
35	229	655	407	29	5.9408
40	211	598	548	35	23
45	192	539	688	41	39
50	173	483	829	48	54
55	153	424	969	54	69

Lat.	Log *A.*	Log *B.*	Log *C.*	Log *D.*	Log *E.*
32°00′	8.5093134	8.5114367	1.20109	2.3460	5.9484
05	115	309	248	66	99
10	096	251	388	73	5.9514
15	077	193	527	79	29
20	057	135	666	85	44
25	037	077	805	91	60
30	018	020	944	97	75
35	8.5092998	8.5113963	1.21082	2 3503	90
40	979	903	221	09	5.9606
45	960	844	359	14	21
50	940	786	497	20	36
55	921	727	635	26	51
33 00	901	669	772	32	67
05	881	611	910	37	82
10	862	552	1.22047	43	98
15	842	492	184	48	5.9713
20	823	434	321	54	29
25	803	374	458	59	44
30	783	315	594	65	60
35	764	257	730	70	75
40	744	197	867	76	91
45	724	137	1.23003	81	5.9807
50	704	078	139	86	22
55	684	018	274	91	38
34 00	665	8.5112959	409	97	54
05	645	898	545	2.3602	69
10	625	839	680	07	85
15	605	779	815	12	5.9901
20	585	720	950	17	17
25	565	660	1.24085	22	32
30	545	600	220	27	48
35	525	540	353	32	64
40	505	481	489	37	80
45	485	420	623	41	96
50	465	363	757	46	6.0012
55	445	299	891	51	27
35 00	424	238	1.25023	56	44
05	404	178	157	60	60
10	383	118	290	65	76
15	363	058	424	69	92
20	344	8.5111997	557	74	6.0108
25	320	936	690	78	23
30	303	875	823	83	40
35	283	814	955	87	56
40	263	753	1.26088	92	72
45	243	693	220	96	88
50	223	633	353	2.3700	6.0204
55	203	571	485	04	21

Lat.	Log *A*.	Log *B*.	Log *C*.	Log *D*.	Log *E*.
36°00′	8.5092182	8.5111509	1.26617	2.3709	6.0237
05	161	448	749	13	53
10	141	387	881	17	69
15	121	326	1.27013	21	86
20	100	265	145	25	6.0302
25	080	203	276	29	18
30	060	142	407	33	35
35	039	080	539	37	51
40	018	018	670	41	67
45	8.5091998	8.5110957	801	44	84
50	978	895	931	48	6.0400
55	956	834	1.28062	52	17
37 00	936	772	193	56	33
05	915	710	323	60	50
10	894	648	454	63	66
15	874	587	584	66	83
20	854	525	714	70	6.0500
25	833	462	845	74	16
30	812	401	975	77	33
35	791	339	1.29104	81	50
40	771	276	234	84	66
45	750	215	364	87	83
50	729	151	494	91	6.0600
55	708	090	623	94	17
38 00	687	027	753	97	33
05	667	8.5109964	882	2.3800	50
10	646	902	1.30011	03	67
15	625	840	140	07	84
20	604	777	269	09	6.0701
25	583	715	398	13	18
30	562	652	527	16	35
35	541	590	656	18	51
40	521	526	785	22	68
45	499	463	913	24	85
50	479	401	1.31042	27	6.0802
55	458	338	170	30	19
39 00	437	275	299	33	37
05	416	212	427	35	54
10	395	150	555	38	71
15	374	099	683	41	88
20	353	023	811	43	6.0905
25	332	8.5108960	939	46	22
30	311	897	1.32067	48	40
35	290	843	195	51	57
40	269	770	323	53	74
45	248	707	450	56	91
50	227	644	578	58	6.1009
55	206	581	706	61	26

Lat.	Log *A*.	Log *B*.	Log *C*.	Log *D*.	Log *E*.
40°00′	8.5091184	8.5108518	1.32833	2.3863	6.1043
05	163	455	960	65	61
10	142	393	1.33088	67	78
15	125	327	215	69	96
20	099	264	342	72	6.1113
25	079	201	470	74	30
30	057	137	596	76	48
35	036	073	723	78	65
40	015	010	850	80	83
45	8.5090998	8.5107946	977	82	6.1201
50	972	883	1.34104	84	18
55	952	820	231	86	36
41 00	930	755	358	88	54
05	909	691	485	90	71
10	888	628	611	91	89
15	867	574	738	93	6.1307
20	845	500	864	95	24
25	824	437	991	96	42
30	803	373	1.35117	98	60
35	781	308	244	2.3900	78
40	760	244	370	01	96
45	739	181	497	03	6.1413
50	718	117	623	04	31
55	696	053	749	06	49
42 00	675	8.5106989	874	07	67
05	653	925	1.36001	08	85
10	632	861	127	10	6.1503
15	610	797	253	11	21
20	590	733	379	12	39
25	568	668	505	14	57
30	547	604	631	15	75
35	524	541	757	16	94
40	504	476	883	17	6.1612
45	483	413	1.37009	18	30
50	460	348	135	19	48
55	439	284	261	20	66
43 00	419	220	386	21	85
05	396	156	512	22	6.1703
10	376	092	638	23	21
15	354	028	764	24	40
20	333	8.5105963	889	25	58
25	312	899	1.38015	25	76
30	290	835	141	26	95
35	269	771	266	27	6.1813
40	247	706	392	27	32
45	226	642	518	28	50
50	204	578	643	29	69
55	183	513	769	29	87

Lat.	Log A.	Log B.	Log C.	Log D.	Log E.
44°00′	8.5090162	8.5105449	1.38894	2.3930	6.1906
05	140	375	1.39020	30	24
10	118	311	145	31	43
15	097	256	271	31	62
20	076	193	396	32	80
25	054	128	522	32	99
30	033	063	647	32	6.2017
35	011	8.5104999	773	32	36
40	8.5089990	935	998	33	55
45	969	870	1.40024	33	74
50	947	806	149	33	93
55	925	741	275	33	6.2112
45 00	904	677	400	33	31
05	883	612	526	33	50
10	861	548	651	33	69
15	840	484	777	33	88
20	818	419	902	33	6.2207
25	797	356	1.41028	33	26
30	776	291	153	33	45
35	754	226	279	33	64
40	733	162	404	33	83
45	711	098	530	32	6.2302
50	690	034	655	32	21
55	668	8.5103969	781	32	40
46 00	647	905	906	31	60
05	625	841	1.42032	31	79
10	604	776	157	30	98
15	583	712	283	30	6.2417
20	561	648	409	29	37
25	539	584	534	29	56
30	518	518	660	28	76
35	497	457	786	28	95
40	475	392	911	27	6.2514
45	454	326	1.43037	26	34
50	431	262	163	26	53
55	410	199	289	25	73
47 00	390	134	414	24	93
05	368	070	539	23	6.2612
10	347	005	666	22	32
15	326	8.5102941	792	21	52
20	304	876	917	21	71
25	283	813	1.44043	20	91
30	261	749	169	19	6.2711
35	240	685	295	17	30
40	219	621	421	16	50
45	197	557	547	15	70
50	176	493	673	14	90
55	155	428	799	13	6.2810

Lat.	Log *A*.	Log *B*.	Log *C*.	Log *D*.	Log *E*.
48°00′	8.5089133	8.5102364	1.44926	2.3912	6.2830
05	112	301	1.45052	10	50
10	091	236	178	09	70
15	070	172	304	08	90
20	048	108	431	06	6.2910
25	027	045	557	05	30
30	005.	8.5101981	683	03	50
35	8.5088984	917	809	02	70
40	963	853	937	00	91
45	941	789	1.46063	2.3899	6.3011
50	920	725	189	97	31
55	899	662	316	95	51
49 00	878	598	442	94	72

FROM UNITED STATES COAST SURVEY REPORT.

AUXILIARY TABLES FOR CONVERTING ARCS OF THE CLARKE ELLIPSOID INTO ARCS OF THE BESSEL ELLIPSOID.

[All corrections are positive.]

	Corrections to dM.						Arguments L' and dM.						
dM	60'	50'	40'	30'	20'	10'	60"	50"	40"	30"	20"	10"	5"
Lat.													
°	"	"	"	"	"	"	"	"	"	"	"	"	"
23	0.481	0.401	0.320	0.240	0.160	0.080	0.008	0.006	0.005	0.004	0.003	0.001	0.0006
24	.484	.403	.322	.242	.161	.080	.008	.006	.005	.004	.003	.001	.0006
25	.486	.405	.324	.243	.162	.081	.008	.006	.005	.004	.003	.001	.0006
26	.489	.407	.326	.245	.163	.081	.008	.006	.005	.004	.003	.001	.0006
27	.491	.409	.327	.246	.164	.082	.008	.006	.005	.004	.003	.001	.0006
28	.494	.411	.329	.247	.165	.082	.008	.007	.005	.004	.003	.001	.0006
29	.496	.413	.330	.248	.166	.083	.008	.007	.005	.004	.003	.001	.0006
30	.497	.416	.332	.250	.167	.083	.008	.007	.005	.004	.003	.001	.0006
31	.502	.418	.334	.251	.168	.084	.008	.007	.006	.004	.003	.001	.0006
32	.505	.420	.336	.253	.169	.084	.008	.007	.006	.004	.003	.001	.0006
33	.507	.422	.338	.254	.169	.085	.008	.007	.006	.004	.003	.001	.0006
34	.510	.425	.340	.255	.170	.085	.008	.007	.006	.004	.003	.001	.0006
35	.513	.427	.342	.256	.171	.086	.008	.007	.006	.004	.003	.001	.0006
36	.516	.430	.342	.258	.172	.086	.009	.007	.006	.004	.003	.001	.0006
37	.518	.432	.345	.259	.173	.087	.009	.007	.006	.004	.003	.001	.0007
38	.521	.434	.347	.261	.174	.087	.009	.007	.006	.004	.003	.001	.0007
39	.524	.436	.349	.262	.175	.088	.009	.007	.006	.004	.003	.001	.0007
40	.527	.439	.351	.264	.176	.088	.009	.007	.006	.004	.003	.001	.0007
41	.530	.441	.353	.265	.177	.089	.009	.007	.006	.004	.003	.001	.0007
42	.533	.444	.355	.267	.178	.089	.009	.007	.006	.004	.003	.001	.0007
43	.536	.446	.357	.268	.179	.090	.009	.007	.006	.004	.003	.001	.0007
44	.539	.449	.359	.270	.180	.090	.009	.008	.006	.005	.003	.001	.0007
45	0.542	0.451	0.361	0.271	0.181	0.091	0.009	0.008	0.006	0.005	0.003	0.001	0.0007

	Corrections to dL.						Arguments $\dfrac{L+L'}{2}$ and dL.						
dL	60'	50'	40'	30'	20'	10'	60"	50"	40"	30"	20"	10"	5"
Lat.													
°	"	"	"	"	"	"	"	"	"	"	"	"	"
23	0.193	0.160	0.129	0.096	0.064	0.032	0.003	0.003	0.002	0.002	0.001	0.001	0.0003
24	.200	.165	.133	.099	.066	.033	.003	.003	.002	.002	.001	.001	.0003
25	.206	.171	.138	.103	.068	.034	.003	.003	.002	.002	.001	.001	.0003
26	.213	.177	.142	.106	.070	.035	.003	.003	.002	.002	.001	.001	.0003
27	.220	.183	.147	.110	.073	.037	.004	.003	.002	.002	.001	.001	.0003
28	.227	.189	.151	.113	.075	.038	.004	.003	.002	.002	.001	.001	.0003
29	.234	.196	.156	.117	.078	.039	.004	.003	.002	.002	.001	.001	.0003
30	.242	.202	.161	.121	.080	.040	.004	.003	.002	.002	.001	.001	.0003
31	.250	.209	.167	.125	.083	.042	.004	.003	.003	.002	.001	.001	.0004
32	.258	.216	.172	.129	.086	.043	.004	.003	.003	.002	.001	.001	.0004
33	.267	.222	.178	.133	.089	.045	.005	.003	.003	.002	.001	.001	.0004
34	.275	.230	.184	.137	.091	.046	.005	.004	.003	.002	.002	.001	.0004
35	.283	.237	.190	.141	.094	.047	.005	.004	.003	.002	.002	.001	.0004
36	.291	.243	.195	.145	.097	.048	.005	.004	.003	.002	.002	.001	.0004
37	.300	.250	.201	.150	.100	.050	.005	.004	.003	.002	.002	.001	.0004
38	.308	.257	.206	.154	.103	.051	.005	.004	.003	.002	.001	.001	.0004
39	.317	.264	.212	.158	.106	.053	.005	.004	.004	.003	.002	.001	.0004
40	.325	.271	.217	.162	.108	.054	.005	.004	.004	.003	.002	.001	.0005
41	.334	.278	.223	.167	.111	.056	.006	.004	.004	.003	.002	.001	.0005
42	.343	.286	.229	.171	.114	.057	.006	.004	.004	.003	.002	.001	.0005
43	.352	.294	.236	.176	.117	.059	.006	.005	.004	.003	.002	.001	.0005
44	.362	.302	.242	.181	.120	.060	.006	.005	.004	.003	.002	.001	.0005
45	0.372	0.310	0.249	0.186	0.124	0.062	0.006	0.005	0.004	0.003	0.002	0.001	0.0005

TAKEN FROM U. S. COAST AND GEODETIC SURVEY REPORT.

SUBSIDIARY TABLE FOR REFERRING VALUES OF COEFFICIENTS A, B, C, D, E, FROM CLARKE'S TO BESSEL'S ELLIPSOID.

Lat.	To log A add.	To log B add.	To log C add.	From log D subtract.	To log E add.
23°	0.0000582	0.0000233	0.00008	0.0061	0.0001
24	584	241	08	61	1
25	587	249	08	61	1
26	590	258	08	61	1
27	593	266	09	61	1
28	596	274	09	61	1
29	599	283	09	61	1
30	602	293	09	61	1
31	605	302	09	61	1
32	609	312	09	61	1
33	612	321	09	61	1
34	615	331	09	61	1
35	619	342	10	61	1
36	622	352	10	61	1
37	625	362	10	61	1
38	629	372	10	61	1
39	632	383	10	61	1
40	636	393	10	61	1
41	639	404	10	61	1
42	643	415	11	61	1
43	647	425	11	61	1
44	650	436	11	61	1
45	654	447	11	61	1
46	657	458	11	61	1
47	661	468	11	61	1
48	664	479	11	61	1
49	668	490	12	61	1
50	672	501	12	61	1

TABLE OF LOG F.

Lat.	Log F.	Lat.	Log F.	Lat.	Log F.	Lat.	Log F.
23°	7.812	30°	7.866	37°	7.876	44°	7.848
24	23	31	70	38	74	45	40
25	32	32	73	39	72	46	32
26	41	33	75	40	69	47	24
27	49	34	77	41	64	48	14
28	55	35	77	42	60	49	04
29	61	36	77	43	54	50	7.792

18

TABLE OF CORRECTIONS TO LONGITUDE FOR DIFFERENCE IN ARC AND SINE.

Log $K(-)$.	Log difference.	Log $dM(+)$.	Log $K(-)$.	Log difference.	Log $dM(+)$.
3.871	0.0000001	2.380	4.913	0.0000119	3.422
3.970	002	2.479	4.922	124	3.431
4.115	003	2.624	4.932	130	3.441
4.171	004	2.680	4.941	136	3.450
4.221	005	2.730	4.950	142	3.459
4.268	006	2.777	4.959	147	3.468
4.292	007	2.801	4.968	153	3.477
4.309	008	2.818	4.976	160	3.485
4.320	009	2.839	4.985	166	3.494
4.361	010	2.870	4.993	172	3.502
4.383	011	2.892	5.002	179	3.511
4.415	012	2.924	5.010	186	3.519
4.430	013	2.939	5.017	192	3.526
4.445	014	2.954	5.025	199	3.534
4.459	015	2.968	5.033	206	3.542
4.473	016	2.982	5.040	213	3.549
4.487	017	2.996	5.047	221	3.556
4.500	018	3.009	5.054	228	3.563
4.524	020	3.033	5.062	236	3.571
4.548	023	3.057	5.068	243	3.577
4.570	025	3.079	5.075	251	3.584
4.591	027	3.100	5.082	259	3.591
4.612	030	3.121	5.088	267	3.597
4.631	033	3.140	5.095	275	3.604
4.649	036	3.158	5.102	284	3.611
4.667	039	3.176	5.108	292	3.617
4.684	042	3.193	5.114	300	3.623
4.701	045	3.210	5.120	309	3.629
4.716	048	3.225	5.126	318	3.635
4.732	052	3.241	5.132	327	3.641
4.746	056	3.255	5.138	336	3.647
4.761	059	3.270	5.144	345	3.653
4.774	063	3.283	5.150	354	3.659
4.788	067	3.297	5.156	364	3.665
4.801	071	3.310	5.161	373	3.670
4.813	075	3.322	5.167	383	3.676
4.825	080	3.334	5.172	392	3.681
4.834	084	3.343	5.178	402	3.687
4.849	089	3.358	5.183	412	3.692
4.860	094	3.369	5.188	422	3.697
4.871	098	3.380	5.193	433	3.702
4.882	103	3.391	5.199	443	3.708
4.892	108	3.401	5.204	453	3.713
4.903	114	3.412			

INDEX.

	PAGE
ABULFEDA, description of Arabian arc-measurement,	3
Adjusting the azimuth	200
Adjustment, figure.	168
station.	146
when directions have been observed.	180
Airy.	248
Alexandria.	2
Anaximander	1
Angles, method of measuring.	97
Arabian arc-determination.	2
unit of measure	28
Arago.	15
Argelander.	18
Auzout.	29
Axes of the earth, Clarke's and Bessel's values of.	259
Azimuth, affected by adjustment.	200
formula for computing.	218
BAEYER.	20
Barrow, Indian arc-measurement.	13
Base apparatus, first form of.	50
requisites of	50
Bache-Wurdeman.	52
Baumann.	60
Bessel.	58
Borda.	51
Colby.	59, 64
Ibañez.	60
Lapland.	50
Peru.	50
Porro.	59
Repsold.	60
Struve.	59

PAGE

Base-line, probable error of... 74

    reduction to sea-level...................................... 78

Base-measurements.. 49

    aligning... 64

    comparison of results.............................. 61

    computation of results............................. 70

    erection of terminal marks......................... 66

    general precautions........ 69

    inclination... 68

    instructions... 64

    sector error... 68

    selecting site....................................... 64

    record, form of...................................... 66

    references... 79

    transferrence of end to the ground.................. 67

Beccaria, arc measurement.. 10

Bessel.. 247

    base apparatus.. 20

    review of the French arc.............................. 15

Biot... 15

Bonne.. 19

Borda, metallic thermometer.. 14

Borden, survey of Massachusetts.. 23

Boscovich, arc-measurement... 10

Bouguer... 7

Boutelle... 81, 86

Brahé, Tycho.. 29

Briggs... 29

CALDEWOOD, glass base apparatus.. 11

Camus.. 8

Cape of Good Hope arc.. 10

Cassini... 4, 11

    revision of the French arc............................ 9

Celsius.. 8

Centre, reduction to.. 196

Chaldean unit of measure.. 28

Chauvenet.. 160

Circle, entire, first used.. 29

Clairault.. 8

    theory of the figure of the earth..................... 9

PAGE

Clarke, solution for the figure of the earth............................. 248
    reference to the great English theodolite........................ 12
Coast Survey, U. S., organized... 23
          form of base apparatus......................... 52, 61
              heliotrope.................................. 46
              signals.................................... 84
              theodolite............................... 32
Colonna... 90
Commission for European degree-measurements 26
Comparison of base-bars with a standard............................... 71
Condamine, De la... 7
Connection of France and England by triangulation..................... 11
Constants and their logarithms, table of.............................. 260
Correction for inclination... 74
Correlatives, equations of... 159
Cutts.. 86

DAVIDSON.. 47, 102
Delambre... 13
      revision of the Peruvian arc.................................. 8
Des Hays, pendulum-investigations 6
Directions, adjustment of 180
      horizontal, copy of record................................... 101
Dividing-engine first used... 30
Dixon. See Mason.
Doolittle.. 195

ECCENTRIC signal 146
      instrument.. 196
Ellipticity of the earth, table of.................................... 249
Errors, mean of... 146
    probable. See Probable Errors.
Equations, conditional, number of..................................... 179
        side.. 171
        solution of, by logarithms.................................. 194
Eratosthenes.. 1
Everest, Indian arc... 14
Expansion coefficient, determination of............................... 72

FERNEL.. 3
Figure-adjustment... 168
Figure of the earth... 234
      literature of... 249

                                                                    PAGE
French Academy arc-measurements in Lapland and Peru................ 6
Froriep... 1

GASCOIGNE, first to use spider-lines............................... 4
Gauss... 19, 159
Géodésie, École spéciale de....................................... 17
Geodetic factors, tables of...................................... 264
Godin... 7
Greek unit of measure.. 28

HANSTEEN.. 18
Heights determined by barometer.................................. 94
                      triangulation 101
Heliotrope, description of....................................... 45
             first used.. 45
             illustration....................................... 46
             use and adjustments................................ 46
Hilgard.. 41
Hipparchus... 29
Hounslow Heath base 12
Humboldt... 29
Huygens's theory of centrifugal motion........................... 6

INGÉNIEUR Corps, organization of................................. 16
Instruments.. 28
Invention of the vernier... 29
Isle, De l'.. 17
Italian commission organized.................................... 25
Italy, co-operation with Switzerland............................ 17

James, Sir Henry, reference to the great English theodolite...... 11

LACAILLE, revision of Picard's arc............................... 4
          arc-measurement at the Cape of Good Hope.............. 10
Lahire... 4
Lambton, Indian arc.. 14
Laplace.. 13, 247
Lapland arc-measurement.. 8
Latitude, formula for computing................................. 203
          illustration..................................... 220, 222
Least squares, theory of.. 104

PAGE

Legendre.. II, 13
Letronne, review of Posidonius's arc............................ 2
Level, table giving difference between the true and apparent 92
Liesganig, arc-measurement.................................... 10
Littrow... 31
Longitude determined by powder-flashes........................ 19
Longitude, formula for computing 217
        illustrations.................................. 220, 223

MACLEAR, continuance of the Cape of Good Hope arc............... 23
Maraldi.. 4
Mason, Maryland-Pennsylvania boundary-line..................... 10
Maupertuis, Lapland arc....................................... 8
Mayer, repeating-theodolites 12
Mechain... II, 15
Metre, determination of its length.............................. 13
     legal and recent values of............................ 249
Metres to feet, table for converting............................ 257
     miles.. 258
     yards 257
Micrometer first used... 29
     determination of run................................. 35
Miles to metres, table for converting........................... 259
Monnier... 8
Mosman... 97
Mudge... 15
Müffling, Von.. 19
Musschenbroeck.. 19

NAPIER.. 29
Newton, theory of universal gravitation demonstrated by Picard's arc..... 4
Normal equations... 155
Normals, table of... 261
Norwood, measurement of the distance from London to York............ 4
Nuñez... 29

OUTHIER 8

PALANDER 14
Pamlico-Chesapeake arc....................................... 24
Phase, correction for 144

PAGE

Picard's triangulation.. 4
Pole, selection of, in figure-adjustment.............................. 179
Posch, view of Ptolemy's length of a degree 2
Posidonius, arc-measurement......................... 2
Probable error of the arithmetical mean.............................. 124
          of a single determination................. 120
          illustration.. 122
          of a base line. 125
               direction.............. 125
          in the computation of unknown quantities in triangles 127, 133,
                                                        136, 137, 138
Prussia, first geodetic work.... 16
Prussian-Russian connection.. 25
Ptolemy, value of earth's circumference ,............................. 2
Puissant, review of the French arc.... ..:............................ 15
Pythagoras I

QUADRANT of the earth, length of 249

RADIUS of curvature, table of.. 261
Reduction to centre.. 196
Reichenbach.. 26, 31
Repetition of angles, principle first announced...................... 12
                    abandoned.......................... 31
Repsold... 26, 31
Riccioli.. 3
Richer, expedition to Cayenne.. 6
Roemer... 29
Roy... 11, 15
Russian arc, accuracy of... 18
Russia, first geodetic work 17

SAEGMÜLLER, principal of bisection................................... 31
Schott... 24, 179, 248
Schmidt.. 247
Schumacher... 19, 31
Schwerd.,.. 19
Series, binomial 256
        exponential.. 256
        logarithmic... 257

PAGE

Signals, form used on coast-survey...................................... 84
    night cost of.... 82
    method of erection...................................... 87
    size and lengths of timbers...................................... 88
Snellius' triangulation...................................... 3
Spain, first geodetic work 25
Spherical excess, computation of...................................... 168
Speyer base...................................... 19
Spider-lines in telescope, first use of...................................... 4
Stations, description of 95
    permanent markings...................................... 96
    intervisibility of...................................... 90
Station-adjustment 146
Struve...................................... 17
Svanberg...................................... 14
Sweden, coast-triangulation 26
Swedish arc-measurement in Lapland... 14
Switzerland, first geodetic work...................................... 17
Syene 1

TENNER...................................... 17
Thales...................................... 1
Theodolites, adjustment of...................................... 33
    construction of...................................... 32
    errors of eccentricity...................................... 36
    graduation...................................... 39
    illustration...................................... 34
    size of...................................... 32
Toise of Peru... 7
Transferring underground mark to the top of a signal...................................... 96
Triangles, best composition of...................................... 86
Triangulation, calculation of. 143
    conditions to be fulfilled 143
Trigonometric expressions...................................... 253
    series...................................... 256

ULLOA...................................... 7

VARIN, pendulum-investigations 6
Vernerius...................................... 29

PAGE

Vernier, invention of 29
    distance apart.. 37

WALBECK 247
Walker....................................... 22
Waugh 22
Weights, application of, in adjustments.............................. 165

YARDS to metres, table for converting................................ 258
Yollond... 184

ZACH, VON, revision of Beccaria's arc................................. 10
    of the Peruvian arc............................... 8